❧

THIS FAR BY
FAITH

❧

THIS FAR BY
FAITH

How to Put God First
in Everyday Living

LINNIE FRANK AND ANDRIA HALL

GALILEE
DOUBLEDAY
NEW YORK LONDON TORONTO SYDNEY AUCKLAND

A GALILEE BOOK
PUBLISHED BY DOUBLEDAY
a division of Random House, Inc.
1540 Broadway, New York, New York 10036

GALILEE, DOUBLEDAY and the portrayal of a ship with a cross above a book
are trademarks of Doubleday, a division of
Random House, Inc.

Book design by Lisa Sloane

This Far by Faith was first published by Doubleday in October 1998.

Grateful acknowledgment is made to Manna Music, Inc., for permission
to quote from "We've Come This Far By Faith": copyright © 1965,
Renewed 1993 by Manna Music, Inc.,
35255 Brooten Road, Pacific City, OR 97135.
All Rights Reserved. Used by Permission. (ASCAP)

The Library of Congress has cataloged the Doubleday hardcover as follows:
Frank, Linnie.
This far by faith: how to put God first in everyday living /
Linnie Frank and Andria Hall.
p.   cm.
1. Christian life—United States   2. Afro-Americans—Religion.
I. Hall, Andria.   II. Title.
BV4501.2.F7145   1998
248.4—DC21   98-19018
CIP
ISBN 978-0-385-49977-4
Copyright © 1998 by Linnie Frank and Andria Hall
All Rights Reserved
Printed in the United States of America
First Galilee Edition: September 2000

ANDRIA: *This book is for all those who help me believe. To my husband Clayton,
for always being there—no matter what. To my children Amber, Cameron, and
Chase for loving me unceasingly. To my parents W.J. and Mabel, without whom
I would be lost, and to my sister Akosua, for forever giving me insight. In
remembrance of my grandparents: Aurealia and Grant Agabus, Evelyn and Walter
Clarington. And to the Holy Spirit for never leaving me alone.*

LINNIE: *I dedicate this book to my husband Greg, for giving me room to dream.
To my son Gregory, for providing me so much joy. To my daughter Kyra Rachelle,
what a blessing you are. And to my mother Mable, for always pushing me out of
the nest. In memory of Will J. and Rosa Brown, Alphretta Collins,
Archie Dixon, and Berman Frank.*

Acknowledgments

"... IF YOU HAVE FAITH AS SMALL AS A MUSTARD SEED, YOU CAN SAY TO THIS MOUNTAIN, 'MOVE FROM HERE TO THERE' AND IT WILL MOVE. NOTHING WILL BE IMPOSSIBLE TO YOU."

MATTHEW 17:20 (NIV)

ANDRIA: *This journey has been a blessing from the very beginning. I'm so grateful to my Lord and Savior, Jesus Christ, for giving me a chance to bring others into His marvelous light. I am forever thankful to the black church for nurturing me. Thanks to my family for adjusting to my new life: Amber for her marshmallow smile; Cameron for his constant hugs and kisses; Chase for his many interruptions reminding me of what's real; and Clayton—the most secure man I know. It is through his security that I've found my strength to live, and love, and trust. Thank you to my loved ones: my sister Akosua, for her spiritual brilliance; my unending gratitude to my mother Mabel; my father Willie James; my mother-in-law Hazel; all my dear sisters in Christ, especially, Veronica, Mary, Trina, René, Vicki, Carol, Jestacia, and "my new friend Vickie." Thank you, Miss Elvia, for caring for my children as if they were your own. I am grateful to Gregory I and II, for your support and special brand of humor. Thank you, Mable P., for getting that switch when necessary. To all of those who have ever sent up a prayer for me, and I am indebted to Linnie, for matching me every step of the way with love, generosity, honesty, and Christian affection.*

LINNIE: *I'm still not sure why God chose me for this path, but I'm so glad He did. It has been a glorious journey and I'm so thankful for all those* who believed in me, nurtured me, and encouraged me along the way: my husband and son—Greg and Gregory II; my mom, Mable Marie, and dad Carl; my brother, Carlton, and his family, Lynn, Christopher, and Sidney; my beloved goddaughter, Melinda Kristina; Uncle Eugene and Aunt Louise; Uncle Randolph and Aunt LeeOla; Aunt Faye, Pam, and Cassandra; my in-laws, Ammie and Norris and family; my adopted family, Clayton, Amber, Cameron, and Chase; my special friends, Natalie Denise and Bill; Paula and Bob; Delores W.; Shirley, Ayeisha, Stephanie, and Tanya; Joan L.; Clemmie and Mr. Kennedy; Marietta W.; Gladys J.; Chet; Betty; Julie and Wendy and the sisters and brothers of the Circle of Seven; and, last but not least, a special thanks to my traveling partner, Andria Hall.

Both of us would like to warmly thank our agent, Marie Dutton Brown, and our editor, Janet Hill (with assistance from Frances Jones and Mayuri Reddy), for believing in the worthiness of this project, in us, and in His Word.

LIST OF BIBLE ABBREVIATIONS

KJV	The King James Version
NIV	The New International Version
God's Word	The God's Word Bible
NAS	The New American Standard Bible
Amplified	The Amplified Bible
NRSV	The New Revised Standard Version
CEV	The Contemporary English Version
YLT	The Young's Literal Translation Bible
TLB	The Living Bible
RSV	The Revised Standard Version

Note: Ellipses are used in Bible quotes when middle verses or words are left out of scriptures.

Contents

INTRODUCTION   **XIII**

CHAPTER ONE: THE SOUND OF HIS VOICE   **1**

Sweet Hour of Prayer   **7**
The Voice I Hear   **8**
Remember This   **11**
Prayer: Lord, Let Me Listen   **12**

CHAPTER TWO: MY SOUL LOOKS BACK AND WONDERS . . . 13

Let Go and Let God   **18**
The Master's Plan   **22**
Here Am I, Send Me   **24**
Just as I Am   **26**
I Surrender All   **29**
Remember This   **31**
Prayer: Prayer of Surrender   **32**

CHAPTER THREE: GIVE ME THAT OLD-TIME RELIGION   **33**

Take It to the Lord in Prayer   **38**
We Are Family   **40**
Lest We Forget   **42**
I Am on the Battlefield   **45**
Remember This   **48**
Prayer: The Heritage Prayer   **49**

CHAPTER FOUR: FAMILIES—THE TIES THAT BIND   **51**

Grandma's Hands   **54**
Suffer the Children   **56**
Precious Memories   **60**

We Are Our Heavenly Father's Children   **64**

The Family That Prays Together . . .   **67**

Remember This   **70**

Prayer: Prayer for Love   **71**

CHAPTER FIVE: FRIENDSHIPS—REAL AND IMAGINED   **73**

A Friend in Need Is a Friend in Deed   **76**

Betrayal   **80**

What a Friend We Have in Jesus   **86**

Remember This   **88**

Prayer: Friendship Prayer   **89**

CHAPTER SIX: LOVE—ALWAYS AND FOREVER   **91**

Looking for Love   **94**

What's Love Got to Do with It?   **97**

The Spirit Within   **101**

What You Won't Do for Love   **104**

Stand by Me   **107**

Remember This   **109**

Prayer: A Prayer for Romantic Fulfillment   **110**

CHAPTER SEVEN: MARRIAGE—FOR BETTER OR WORSE   **111**

A Noble Marriage   **114**

Keeping the Home Fires Burning   **119**

Infidelity   **122**

May the Circle Be Unbroken   **125**

A Parent's Advice   **128**

Remember This   **131**

Prayer: The Matrimonial Prayer   **132**

CHAPTER EIGHT: CHILDREN AND PARENTHOOD   **135**

Faith of Our Fathers   **138**

Teach the Children 141

Spare the Rod 143

It Takes a Sanctuary 147

Save the Children 150

Remember This 151

Prayer: A Parent's Prayer 153

CHAPTER NINE: A HOUSE IS NOT A HOME 155

Is This as Good as It Gets? 158

How to Make Your Home a Retreat 160

A Shelter in the Time of Storm 164

Home Cooking 166

Home Is Where the Lord Is 171

Remember This 174

Prayer: Prayer for the Home 175

CHAPTER TEN: JOBS, CAREERS, AND CALLINGS 177

The American Dream 179

Door Closers 182

Soul Survivor 185

Answer the Call 190

This Little Light of Mine 194

Remember This 195

Prayer: Prayer for Guidance at Work 196

CHAPTER ELEVEN: CROSSING RAGING WATERS 199

His Eye Is on the Sparrow 200

When Darkness Comes 204

Forgiveness 206

Where Peaceful Waters Flow 209

Amazing Grace 213

He'll Make a Way 217

Remember This   220
Prayer: Prayer for Safe Crossing   221

CHAPTER TWELVE: A PLACE WHERE MY SOUL
CAN FIND REST   223
Rock of Ages   225
All Church Folk Ain't Religious   228
Preachers of the Word   231
A Prayer for Your Servant   235
Close to Thee   236
A New Day   241
Remember This   245
Prayer: Prayer for a New Day   246

SCRIPTURAL REFERENCES   249

THIS FAR BY
FAITH

We've come this far by faith,

Leaning on the Lord,

Trusting in His Holy Word,

He's never failed us yet.

Oh, we can't turn [around];

We've come this far by faith.

❧

—*Albert A. Goodson*

Introduction

"NOW FAITH IS THE SUBSTANCE OF THINGS HOPED FOR,
THE EVIDENCE OF THINGS NOT SEEN."

HEBREWS 11:1 (KJV)

Words to live by. Think about them for a moment. Faith? It is the essence of that inner knowing that propels us forward, without the tangible evidence to substantiate that life will go on. Generations of black folks sing, "I've got a feeling everything's gonna be all right .   " In faith, we go on   and in time, find that it is indeed all right.

It was "all right" straight from the start for us—Linnie Frank and Andria Hall. We met in Albany, New York, in 1979 where we both had come to begin our professional careers—Linnie as a computer programmer, Andria as a broadcast journalist. A young African-American career woman was a rarity in Albany in those days, and Linnie, from Los Angeles, and Andria, from Brooklyn, felt alone both culturally and socially. We were ecstatic to meet each other and quickly shared all the necessary information—from where to get our hair done, to where the black folks hung out.

We became fast friends and spent most weekday lunches sitting in a park discussing what we wanted in the years ahead—what type of man we would marry, how many children we would have, and how far we would advance in our careers. Most of all we wondered where the Lord was leading us. With our friendship we found common ground that would sustain us in Albany and in the years to come. This common ground was our shared belief that through faith in God all things were possible.

We shared only a few months together in Albany before life sent us on separate paths. But during those few months, over many home-cooked meals and conversations in the park pondering what life had in store for us, we formed the foundation of what has become a lasting friendship.

Ours became not a bosom buddy, "talk on the phone every day" friendship, but rather the type that could be compared to the warmth and familiarity of a favorite old song, or a cherished photograph. We all know what it's like, meeting that special friend you connect with right from the start.

From the beginning, we were determined to have it all—or at least try. The naïveté of our youth made us believe that the road would be straight and smooth. Real life taught us differently. And, although we often went many months without talking, when we would connect, we'd spend hours discussing what was going on in our lives. Relationships, jobs, children, friends, family. We discussed what went right and what went wrong, and we marveled that much of the advice we had gotten from our folks *was* right. And at the end of each conversation we always thanked God for bringing us so far.

This Far by Faith: How to Put God First in Everyday Living is a compilation of many of the conversations we have had over the years regarding God's intervention in our lives. We talk about lessons learned, tears cried, moments shared. *This Far by Faith* is a written monument to the family members who spent so much time assuring that not only would we be formally educated but that we'd have common sense as well. Or, as the old folks would say, we'd have street learning as well as book learning.

But, mostly, they taught us the importance of knowing God and we discuss Him throughout this book. We express God's richness using colloquialisms, common sense, and good old-fashioned advice. Advice on everything from raising kids and maintaining friendships, to staying grounded, to keeping your mate happy, to making yourself happy, to understanding the true meaning of friendship, to understanding there's a perfect path the Lord has placed us upon. And yes, even with all of that, we have to have faith. We have to make faith our constant companion—taking it everywhere we go, including it in everything we do. This is the lesson Linnie and Andria have learned. This is what we wish to pass on to you.

In penning this book, the true gift for us is in the giving. So, we offer you, our readers, the commonality of our heritage, the common sense from our elders, and the common ground we must strive to share in order to lift each other up and allow our spirits and our souls to soar free. But, most of all, *we give you our faith!*

Faith is the greatest gift we can give ourselves and one another. Faith is the acknowledgment that no matter what, our trust in the Lord and in ourselves will prevail. When you get right down to it, faith is the one thing those who came before us have always had to hold on to. We too continue to hold to God's unchanging hand.

Faithfully Yours,
LINNIE AND ANDRIA

CHAPTER ONE

The Sound of His Voice

"THE VOICE OF THE LORD IS OVER THE WATERS; THE
GOD OF GLORY THUNDERS, THE LORD THUNDERS OVER
THE MIGHTY WATERS. THE VOICE OF THE LORD IS
POWERFUL; THE VOICE OF THE LORD IS MAJESTIC. THE
VOICE OF THE LORD BREAKS THE CEDARS . . . THE VOICE
OF THE LORD STRIKES WITH FLASHES OF LIGHTNING.
THE VOICE OF THE LORD SHAKES THE DESERT . . . THE
VOICE OF THE LORD TWISTS THE OAKS AND STRIPS THE
FORESTS BARE. AND IN HIS TEMPLE ALL CRY, 'GLORY!' "

PSALMS 29:3–9 (NIV)

Many people wonder what God sounds like when He speaks to us. Does He speak with a whisper or a shout? Does He speak while we are awake or while we are sleeping? Is His voice the sound of rolling thunder or of a falling leaf? And how do we know if it's really Him we are hearing, or just our own ego?

Some people say we don't hear God, but feel Him—as a warm summer breeze when we are doing something good, or as a sudden cold chill when we are doing wrong. Others say they converse with God on a regular basis—He dictates to them what they need to know and what they need to do. They simply follow His command.

Maybe the voice you hear depends on your definition of God. Perhaps if you view God as an omnipotent power, external to yourself, you expect to hear His booming voice at every turn. You wait for the earth to move or for bricks to fall on your head to know that He is indeed talking to *you*.

Or, if you look for God within yourself, you may pursue peaceful, meditative moments to feel His presence and guidance. You seek sunrises, sunsets, and solitude to commune with your God.

We are here to tell you that God does speak! He speaks in all the ways mentioned above and many more. He speaks through others and He speaks directly. If you are not hearing God, it is not because He isn't speaking, it is because you are not listening. Know that God is speaking to you continuously and constantly—you've just got to learn how to listen.

We know there are animals that can hear a range of sounds that we as humans cannot. It works the same way with those who are in tune with God. When others can't or won't, they hear Him. They see Him. They feel Him. *They listen!*

LINNIE: *The fact that Andria and I came together to write a book is nothing short of miraculous. A true gift from God! Although we've been friends for many years, we never spent a lot of time together in the same location. Our paths would cross for a few months and then we would go our separate ways. Our friendship, though solid, was distant. We caught up on things over long phone calls and occasional visits. Whenever we were in proximity to each other we would make a special effort to get together.*

Such was the case in Philadelphia in 1995 when I was attending the annual convention of the Black Data Processing Associates. I knew the National Association of Black Journalists was also meeting in Philadelphia, so I called Andria to see if she would be attending. She wasn't, but we used the time on the phone to catch up on things—husbands, kids, jobs, life in general.

At the time, one of my clients was a church in Los Angeles and I told Andria I was considering writing a screenplay or a novel about a black church. Andria, being a preacher's kid, also understood the inner workings of the black church and the richness of African-American church life. She said she also had lots of stories to tell and had considered writing a book someday.

Now, this is where God stepped in, pushed us forward, and showed us what we needed to do! And thank God we had sense enough to listen! Right then and there we decided to write a book together about the black church. We figured we could do it because we had both grown up in the church and witnessed the good and the bad. From our unique perspective we could tell the story in a way that would be honest, but still preserve the integrity of the church.

At the time we were both very busy, with family, careers, and everything else we "superwomen" try to accomplish. Not to mention that we lived on opposite coasts, I on the West and Andria on the East. To write a book together would be a monumental task, but, we knew immediately this idea was bigger than the both of us and that "When God Talks, You Better Listen."

While we were on the phone we each pulled out our appointment books and arranged to get together to begin our writing project. We knew it would require lots of juggling and explaining to those closest to us, after all we had kids, husbands, and jobs, but we knew we had to do it. We decided to meet in Cambria, California, for a week the following month.

During our week in Cambria we began to construct a novel about three powerful black preachers. We also experienced a number of spiritual revelations that let us know we were on the right path. We continued the writing process over the next few months, using on-line internet services to send text back and forth, and we met whenever we could.

During this time I became pregnant and was excited by the prospect of a second child. Unfortunately, it was not to be and I miscarried in early May of 1996. A few days after the miscarriage, deep into my grief and feeling of emptiness, God spoke to me. I often wonder why He picked *that time, but I guess it was because I needed Him so desperately to ease the pain I was feeling. The sound of His voice was familiar, not unlike my own, but the words and thoughts were not mine. In a nonverbal voice, loud and clear, God told me that Andria and I had to put away the novel we had been working on for the past nine months and start working on another book—a nonfiction book called* This Far by Faith.

I quickly ran and got my journal and started writing. God told me we needed to write about the things we had learned and experienced over the years. Common-sense things, spiritual things, everyday wisdom about life and love. But, most of all, we had to write about the importance of faith in Him.

He told me that This Far by Faith *would be more than a book—it would be a company, not the least of which would be a production company. I had no idea what a production company was, but I kept writing it as He gave it to me. Some of the things sounded far-fetched as I reread them, but, I remembered that with God all things are possible.*

I wasn't sure what Andria's reaction would be when I told her of my "revelation." After all, we had invested a lot of time and energy in the novel by that point. I called her at the news station where she worked: "Andria," I said, "We've got to put down the book we've been working on, and write another one called This Far by Faith. *God just told me this."*

ANDRIA: *And I said . . . okay on the spot. No hesitation. No adjustment period. No questions asked. I submitted right then and there to His will. Remember, there are times when God speaks to us, but not necessarily through us. Linnie and I trust each other's spiritual sincerity enough now that if one or the other of us says, He speaks . . . then we listen and follow suit. But not blindly. I would have known if His message was for her alone to follow. There would have been discomfort somewhere deep inside me. There would have been doubt. But there was none of that. Just a deep, innocent enthusiasm about what God had just offered to both of us. A chance for us to get closer* to Him. A chance to move others toward Him. An opportunity to help build His kingdom.

Clarity in Christ is the goal. Seeking His perfect will and accepting it when revealed is nothing short of a major challenge. Seeing the Divine at work in all things was a milestone for me in my own spiritual walk. And although Linnie and I often wonder why He is using us both in this incredible way, we acknowledge with gratitude that He is indeed using us. He is using us all.

How do we know when it is God who is talking? Flow. There is no initial resistance on our part, just an outpouring that comes from a natural wellspring within. For me, I listen with my heart. Literally! I close myself up . . . quiet myself down (which is hard for me to do) and simply f-e-e-l Him. If it's God talking, the message is comfortable, natural, and unforced. If it's my ego, my will, my way, then it's always a struggle. Always a thought I preface with, "Okay—let me figure this out." With God there is nothing to figure out, just something to hold on to. A promise that He will lead you and guide you, and work out all the details along the way.

God's voice is perfect. His plan is always complete. Neither Linnie nor I would be complete without the other. A complement of spirit, talent, humility, and drive. We both can hear the Sound of His Voice, but trust me, we don't always get it right. There are plenty of times when we allow our own voice to get in the way, and it's often as loud as a shrieking boom box on a New York City bus. You can't hear the silence for the noise. But more and more we are learning to discern how He speaks.

It was definitely the voice of God that gave me a message to start a prayer group back in the summer of 1996. Remember: God speaks to us, and sometimes He does it through other people. I was in the midst of a career crisis at the time. I was stressed, and professionally unfulfilled. Literally, under attack from some very dark forces within the workplace. I needed to talk to someone with insight. A spiritually wise woman I had gone to see told me, "Spirit says you need to start a prayer group. It will help you heal." So what did I do? I tucked that advice deep into my heart, and continued to struggle with my professional problems. It seemed no matter what I did, my situation was still the same. Finally, when I ceased trying to battle it out on my own, I remembered: "Prayer changes things." I needed change. I remembered what she had said.

Once I got past the fear of truly committing myself to God, I decided to start that prayer group and asked six women who were nearest and dearest to me to join. And, as the old folks used to say, "You take one step, and He'll take two." Four of my girlfriends and two of our mothers decided to pray on the phone on the first Sunday of every month. The following six days, on our own, we would announce ourselves before the throne, and speak our sisters' names in silent meditation, giving our prayer needs to Him.

After praying for a couple of months, and getting answers, it became apparent to me that if that one prayer group, where we came to God earnestly and in agreement, was a vessel for making miracles, helping us to heal, bringing prosperity, and increasing our faith, then it was certainly a part of something bigger than myself.

Day by day, moment by moment, this particular experience of prayer became more and more profound. Although she wasn't a member, Linnie had known about my group. I of course had shared this with her. I was keeping her abreast of how this fellowship was changing my life. When it became crystal clear just how important coming together in this way was, we opened our eyes and saw that God wanted prayer to be an integral part of both our lives, and a cornerstone of our company.

That little prayer group is now called: The Circle of Seven. And there are many Circles all over the country. Men and women coming together in prayer and purpose. Women and men all striving to hear the Sound of God's Voice.

SWEET HOUR OF PRAYER

"CONFESS YOUR FAULTS ONE TO ANOTHER, AND PRAY ONE FOR
ANOTHER, THAT YE MAY BE HEALED. THE EFFECTUAL FERVENT
PRAYER OF A RIGHTEOUS MAN AVAILETH MUCH."

JAMES 5:16 (KJV)

Prayer is our way of establishing a dialogue with the Lord. When we come to God in prayer, we go within. When we come to God with others, we increase our prayer potential and open ourselves up to receive all the wonderful blessings He has in store for us, both individually and collectively.

It is analogous to growing a single flower versus growing many flowers. The single flower receives proper nourishment, basks in the sunlight, and grows upward toward heaven reflecting God's splendor. But many flowers growing together can do all of this and much more. They can change a desolate hillside into a mountain of glory, or turn a bunch of weeds into a magnificent garden. This is the beauty of joint prayer. We grow and thrive together. We nourish each other just as He nourishes each of us. Together we radiate in God's love.

LINNIE: *When Andria told me about the impact her prayer group was having on her life I was intrigued, yet cautious. I knew that prayer groups and prayer organizations were gaining in popularity around the country, but, for me, prayer was such an intimate, personal experience. My one-on-one dialogue with the Lord. But then I realized, if I believed in the power of my own requests to the Lord how could I not believe in the greater power of joint prayer. I remembered scripture in* Matthew 18:19 (God's Word):

"IF TWO OF YOU AGREE ON ANYTHING HERE ON EARTH,
MY FATHER IN HEAVEN WILL ACCEPT IT . . "

I was ready to try group prayer. But the Lord had more in mind than just Andria and me being in prayer groups. He showed us that prayer should be at the center of any organization we hoped to build. When God blessed us with the idea to form the Circle of Seven prayer organization, we knew He had given us something special. We knew it was powerful. He showed us we had to spread the word about the power of prayer by getting people involved in intimate prayer circles, where they would come together in joint prayer once a month.

Incorporating the divinity of the number seven (seven is considered divine because of the number of times and the way it is used in the Bible) and the completeness of the circle, the Circle of Seven was born. By early 1997 we had developed goals and objectives for the organization and a format for its quarterly publication — The Mustard Seed. There are recommended activities, all designed to lead to personal and spiritual fulfillment, but the only mandatory activity for each circle is joint prayer, which happens the first week of every month.

We started our first Southern California circle, of which I am a member, in March of 1997. When we initially came together for monthly prayer I was concerned that we would talk and pray only in generalities. Fortunately this was not the case. Although some of us had only recently met, we each felt comfortable discussing our personal prayer needs. I think being on the phone helps facilitate this. On the phone we are free to express our thoughts without watching for others' outward reactions. It was a powerful experience. No pretenses, just seven people having a sincere conversation with the Lord. Now, I anxiously await prayer time with my circle and the new circles I sometimes help initiate each month. Sharing my prayer needs with others has helped me to further incorporate prayer into my daily life.

THE VOICE I HEAR

"I HAVE MUCH MORE TO SAY TO YOU, MORE THAN YOU CAN NOW BEAR. BUT WHEN HE, THE SPIRIT OF TRUTH, COMES, HE WILL GUIDE

YOU INTO ALL TRUTH. HE WILL NOT SPEAK ON HIS OWN; HE
WILL SPEAK ONLY WHAT HE HEARS, AND HE WILL TELL YOU
WHAT IS YET TO COME."

JOHN 16:12–14 (NIV)

When we set aside time for fervent prayer, we are in the presence of the Spirit which increases our faith. This then makes room in our lives for divine intervention—His response to us. The challenge for each of us on an everyday basis is to continually open ourselves up to that awesome power. We must communicate daily with God.

The best time to start our daily conversation with Him is at the beginning of the day. Most of us start our day off like this:

Up at the crack of dawn,
the coffeemaker's on.
Start the shower or the bath,
better get out of our path.
Flick on the radio or TV,
what's happening that affects me?
Get dressed in a hurry,
already anticipating today's worries.
Grab a bite to eat,
Okay ready!—Let's hit the street.

It's as if when we take our first conscious breath in the morning, life sounds an opening bell, and someone else has decided that we're already behind the eight ball. We don't make time, in fact, we rarely take the time to feed our spirits in the same way we feed our minds and bodies. But aren't we more spirit than anything else? Shouldn't we cultivate the purest form of energy we have access to—the energy of Spirit?

We should start each day in prayer. Just as we call God by many names: Lord, Father, Jehovah, Jesus, Holy Spirit, Almighty, prayers can be said in numerous ways. A prayer can be a whisper. It can be a shout. A prayer can be a sigh of thanksgiving, or a drop-to-the-floor—cry all night—talk with God—till you have an answer—scream and moan—laugh out loud—prayer. It is not just one thing, it's an acknowledgment of helplessness in the presence of God—our only source of life, strength, help, and hope. Prayer is what contains us. Prayer is what sustains us. Prayer is where we stand naked before the throne, at His mercy, together alone, in His bosom is where we rest. Prayer gets us close, it gets us into a position where we can boast of His love and grace. Prayer is the only place where we can go and take our all to the Lord.

We all have a relationship with God. Some relationships are good, some are not. Some are rocky. Some are solid. Some are pleasing. Others are not even admitted because we're so afraid someone else might think we're "over the edge." Too much on a "religious trip." Well, what's wrong with that? The road that leads to spiritual awareness and personal fulfillment is a blessed journey that starts with one step. It commences with one conversation. It begins by having a dialogue with God.

You want to know what God sounds like? You want to have a conversation for yourself? Then go inside yourself—seek to know Him better. Search your heart to understand when God is talking, and when He's not, and read on. Maybe He's told us something you need to know about how He speaks. We pray the words written on these pages will be able to help you, and are a Godsend in your life.

Here it is, Lord. Here is the book You told us to write. We thank You for the words and the message. We thank You for speaking so loudly and clearly to us. Sometimes with a soft voice, sometimes with a brick!

THE SOUND OF HIS VOICE

REMEMBER THIS

✲ **GOD DOES SPEAK!** Don't assume that He doesn't. Understand that if you are looking for direction and not finding it, you are probably not silencing yourself long enough to listen. Spend quiet time every day. Listen with your heart. Listen even in despair. Many times it's in our darkest moments that we hear God most clearly. He may come to you in a dream, or through an inner knowing. But it is never God who stops speaking. It is we who fail to be still long enough to hear Him.

✲ **SOMETIMES GOD SPEAKS TO US THROUGH OTHERS.** Listen closely for any and all signs that God is talking to you. Never discount the fact that He may send a messenger. He uses all of us to help build up His kingdom.

✲ **INCORPORATE PRAYER INTO YOUR DAILY LIFE.** Prayer is a conversation. Prayer is a "thank you, God." Prayer is a whisper acknowledging that "Yes, He is Lord." Don't underestimate the power of prayer to change things. In fact, use it as a tool to access your own power—your own purpose. Pray for yourself. Pray for others. Pray together.

THE SOUND OF HIS VOICE

PRAY FOR THIS:
LORD, LET ME LISTEN

If you truly want to learn to listen for Divine direction, it starts with a prayer. Carve out time to be quiet, and ask God to open up your ears and your heart to His voice. Be prepared to honor His will when He speaks.

❦

LORD, LET ME LISTEN

Lord, let me hear Your voice.
Let the rustle of the wind remind me of Your
presence in my life.
Let the stillness of the night inspire me to wait on You.
Let the raging waters stir me to take action on Your behalf.
Let the morning sunshine restore my faith in You.
Lord, I open my heart to Your voice. I silence the
distractions of a noisy world.
I keep You at the forefront of my thoughts and my actions.
I wait in prayerful meditation for Your wisdom and guidance.
I trust You will be there. As I search for answers to the
questions of life,
Lord, let me know when it is Your voice I am hearing.
Let Your response to me come through loud and clear,
without static or false interpretation.
I am ready to follow Your command.
I am ready to hear Your voice.
Lord, let me listen.
Thank you. Amen.

CHAPTER TWO

My Soul Looks Back and Wonders . . .

"GIVE THANKS TO THE LORD, CALL ON HIS NAME;
MAKE KNOWN AMONG THE NATIONS WHAT HE HAS
DONE. SING TO HIM, SING PRAISE TO HIM; TELL OF ALL
HIS WONDERFUL ACTS. GLORY IN HIS HOLY NAME; LET
THE HEARTS OF THOSE WHO SEEK THE LORD REJOICE.
LOOK TO THE LORD AND HIS STRENGTH; SEEK HIS FACE
ALWAYS. REMEMBER THE WONDERS HE HAS DONE, HIS
MIRACLES, AND THE JUDGMENTS HE PRONOUNCED."

PSALMS 105:1–5 (NIV)

When we think about where we are, versus where we could have been, or where we should have been, it sometimes sends a shiver up our spine. And when we wonder exactly what it was that set us straight and put us on the right path, we come to only one conclusion—it wasn't us or anything we did! It was God's grace and mercy.

Left to our own devices we would still be holding on to our less than perfect past. Our fear of what lies ahead keeps us holding on to broken promises and shattered dreams. Some of us spend our whole lives afraid to move ahead because we don't know what awaits us. This is where *faith* comes in! Faith that God will lead us to where it is He wants us to be. Once we understand that God only wants what's best for us, then we realize that regardless of the circumstances, He is leading us to our good. We can leave fear behind and pursue life with vigor and confidence.

When we look back on past situations, we are reminded of how God blessed us—whether we were aware of it at the time or not. We remember moments when we didn't have a dime and yet, we always had a place to eat and sleep. We recall situations that we thought we would never get out of and yet, we did. We think of all the daggers that were thrown our way—some we saw, some we didn't—and, although some were able to pierce us, none were able to stop us. We are reminded that He took care of the big things as well as the small.

ANDRIA: *The thing I have come to know about God's way of blessing us is what the church ladies have said for generations, "He may not come when you want Him, but He's right on time." Understanding and accepting the essence of the spiritual law of divine timing has given me peace of mind. Even when I had no prospects for knowing the details of how a particular challenge would be resolved, I still had peace. Peace, because I remain confident in His promise that He will never leave me alone.*

A true turning point for me in my faith happened when I was twenty-seven years old. I had just taken a job as a news anchor and reporter in New Orleans, Louisiana. I went there knowing that I was taking a step back, in order to take two steps forward. It was a risk I needed to gamble on in order to propel my career as a journalist. I had been there for only two months when through "celestial serendipity" I was given the opportunity to go to work on a great local news magazine program in Boston called: "Chronicle." I went there one weekend, had an interview, and was offered the job. Of course, there was the "small detail" of the two-year contract I had just signed with the New Orleans television station, but the Boston job would double my salary and move me into a top-ten market. There would be greater exposure, travel, a chance to be closer to my family and do really great television. Who would hold me back from such a wonderful blessing?

I went and had a talk with my boss. I told him of the Boston offer, how excited I was, and what a rare opportunity had been placed before me. I apologized and asked if he would let me out of my contract. I was expecting him to say: "Oh, Andria, I understand. You know I only want the best for you. Go, my child, go North with my blessings." Why I expected him to respond in such a way, I'll never know. What he said instead was, "No!" The station after all had paid for my moving expenses down to Louisiana. They had put me up in a hotel for a month while I found an apartment. They had already invested in hiring me. It was business!

Well, there I was, stuck. The news director was not going to let me out of my contract. Then, it got worse. I received a call from the Program Director in Boston rescinding the offer, citing a phone call from the New Orleans station threatening to sue them for tampering with my contract. What was I to do? I couldn't imagine that I would have to pass on such a marvelous job offer. I couldn't fathom working for the next two years at a station that wanted to stymie my professional growth. I had to make a decision. The Boston station told me if I somehow found myself unemployed and the job were still available, it was mine, but they couldn't guarantee it, and could no longer actively pursue the hire. The New Orleans station now knew I was no longer committed in the way I had been two months before when I came on board. My enthusiasm was marred by their desire to keep me from bettering my personal and professional circumstance. I was going to have to leave. I was going to have to take a chance with no promises on the other side of that risk.

So often, when I'm in the dark, clueless of where I'm going or what I should do, I simply open the Bible and let the pages turn where they may. That night, I let the Spirit lead me to this scripture in Luke 12:27–28 (NIV):

"CONSIDER HOW THE LILIES GROW. THEY DO NOT LABOR OR SPIN. YET I TELL YOU, NOT EVEN SOLOMON IN ALL HIS SPLENDOR WAS DRESSED LIKE ONE OF THESE. IF THAT IS HOW GOD CLOTHES THE GRASS OF THE FIELD, WHICH IS HERE TODAY, AND TOMORROW IS THROWN INTO THE FIRE, HOW MUCH MORE WILL HE CLOTHE YOU?"

There it was in black and white. I knew then, God would provide. While just moments earlier, I was worried sick about how I would make ends meet, after reading the scripture I stopped worrying and instead stepped out on faith. The next day I let the TV station in New Orleans know I would be leaving. For the first time in my career, I would be without a paycheck and without a professional platform. I stood firm on the promises of God and moved forward not knowing the specific outcome of all I had hoped for. But then, Hebrews 11:1 (KJV) reminds us that

"FAITH IS THE SUBSTANCE OF THINGS HOPED FOR; THE EVIDENCE OF THINGS NOT SEEN."

I hoped I could still land that job in Boston, yet I had no proof it would be available to me once I closed the door on a sure thing; the job I was leaving.

Well, walking by faith and not by sight paid off. I got the job in Beantown and worked there for nearly ten years. This was clearly Divine intervention placing me on a road I was meant to travel. It was a time when I was most professionally satisfied. It was a path that led me to marriage and having children. My faith was rewarded because I believed what God said instead of what my circumstances dictated. I trusted in His word. I will always stand on His promises.

Have you ever been faced with making a choice where there seemed to be no real win in sight? That is the time to choose God. Have you ever been scrapping to make ends meet in a particular month and out of *nowhere a check comes to you in the mail?* Praise God. *Have you ever been faced with what seem to be insurmountable challenges: the company you work for is downsizing; your apartment building is going co-op in two months and you have no idea where you might move to.* Seek God and have faith. *Or, maybe your challenge is this: You've been staring down the throat of a monster: an unspeakable fear; a physical challenge; a spiritual void. That is the time to* surrender *and let God step in. He is the Rock that bolsters us. He is our Bridge that allows us to cross safely over troubled waters. He is the Doctor who brings us a healing. God can be our everything if we trust Him to be.*

When I face challenges now, I remember the song the old folks would sing. Tears in their eyes. Head and hands up to the sky. I now know the meaning of the spiritual: "My soul looks back and wonders how I got oh-oh-ver." Notice the song says, my soul *looks back. It doesn't say my mind looks back or my doubting self looks back. It says,* my soul. *That's the place we need to find if we want to tap into God's great power and put it to work in our lives. You see, He truly is the same today as He was yesterday, and He will be the same tomorrow. Finding Him means we must live in a constant state of praise and thanksgiving. Finding Him compels us to go deep within and look for Him. Finding Him requires trust and prayers of faith even in the midst of a threatening storm.*

We need to thank God for being God. For loving us, when we don't have any love for ourselves or the sense to know what is in our own best interest. We need to thank God for keeping us surefooted when at times it is certainly easier to give up and stay with what appears to be the safe and obvious course. Thank Him for holding us up when we can no longer bear up on our own. Know this: He will show Himself if we seek Him.

God does reveal Himself. And just like the disciples who failed to recognize the resurrected Jesus after leaving Jerusalem on their way to Emmaus, we too sometimes fail to see His beautiful face. They didn't recognize the son of God, because they thought His being brought back to life was too good to be true. But God is good, and there is always hope. That's what faith is about.

We are as a society slowly drowning in our own sea of impossibilities. To break free and save ourselves we must do so through faith, prayer, and perseverance, no matter what the challenge. We may be looking for a financial windfall or searching for a healing or be busy trying to *think* our way through the tribulations of life. But we can't forget to hold on to hope and drop to our knees.

And, while we're waiting for the Lord, let's remember to listen not with our heads but with our hearts, always giving Him the glory. If we do, we'll be amazed at how God does indeed work out the details of life's problems. And if you're impatient, take a moment for your soul to look back. You will have clear evidence that you are a survivor. How else would you have managed without God?

LET GO AND LET GOD

"ROLL YOUR WORKS UPON THE LORD—COMMIT AND TRUST THEM WHOLLY TO HIM. (HE WILL CAUSE YOUR THOUGHTS TO BECOME AGREEABLE TO HIS WILL), AND SO SHALL YOUR PLANS BE ESTABLISHED AND SUCCEED."

PROVERBS 16:3 (AMPLIFIED BIBLE)

It's hard to relinquish our lives to the Lord, even for those of us who have consciously witnessed God's blessings time and time again. Although we know what God can do, we know our own resources are limited and His are vast, yet we find it nearly impossible to surrender our will to His. We hang on for dear life to our perceived control, only turning to Him when we've run out of options.

Many times we try to force the situations in our lives by working hard to bring about our misguided version of what the outcome should be. We say to ourselves—"This is the path I should be on, this is the job/career I should have, this is the relationship I should be in, this is the city I should live in, these are the friends I should spend time with." But deep down inside, we know that something is not quite right.

There may be outward signs. The high-powered job may make us do things against our morals or values. Or maybe we're making lots of money, but are bored to death and feel unmotivated by what we're doing. Or that "perfect" mate may constantly belittle us, making us feel bad.

Maybe there are no outward signs, just an overwhelming feeling of dread that won't go away. This is a signal! Do not ignore this feeling. It means it's time for a shift—time to shake things up a bit.

Sometimes the Lord has to knock us to our knees before we will make a needed change in our lives. We have to get fired or "down-sized" before we exit a job that was wrong for us anyway. We have to wait until our spouse leaves or divorces us before we accept the reality of a bad relationship.

But when we truly let go and say, "Okay, Lord, have it Your way," then miracles start to happen. Maybe not right away, but they will happen if we let go! The first step is to pray for those things He wants us to have. Ask in prayer that the right people and the right situations come into our lives.

When we *Let Go and Let God*, the obvious sometimes becomes a less likely possibility, and the not-so-obvious starts to feel right with our souls. The person we thought we'd never be interested in turns out to be our ideal mate. The hobby we've been pursuing for fun becomes our life's calling. The friend whom we only talked to every now and then is the one who sticks by us during hard times.

Letting go and letting God is not easy, but it is the best way to simplify your life. Plainly put: It's a decision. We can have faith and surrender—*Let Go and Let God*—or we can struggle and wonder why life is so hard.

LINNIE: *I know I have been blessed! I also know it's not because of anything that I've done. I can't say that my actions have caused all the blessings in my life. What I do have is faith and a strong belief in a power greater than myself—God—who looks after me and protects me and puts me on the right path if only I listen—and obey. Sometimes it takes me a while to listen, and even longer to obey, but when I do—wondrous things happen!*

I've heard the phrase "Let Go and Let God" many times, but for those of us with a strong will, this can be the hardest thing in the world to do. When faced with a problem, we start working on a solution; when faced with an obstacle, we start looking for a way around it. We think, well, the Lord has blessed me with intelligence, talents, and resources so I can take it from here. We can't. At least not by ourselves. Sometimes not at all.

There was a period in my life—from 1983 to 1986, when I put God on the shelf. Not purposefully, it's just that I figured he had given me everything I needed to succeed in life so I didn't have to bother Him anymore. After all, I had managed to build a life for myself on the East Coast, three thousand miles away from home and family. I was in control of my destiny.

I envisioned how I wanted my life to be in the years ahead and went about trying to make it happen. Problem was I forgot to get God's opinion on what I was doing. Forgot to pray and ask for His guidance. Didn't wait for Him to tell me what I needed to do.

So in my quest to be "Ms. Thang," I filled my life with the people, possessions, and activities I thought would bring me joy. But, surprisingly, no matter what I did I couldn't seem to shake a feeling of emptiness. It seemed that nothing I thought I wanted could make me happy or content. I had friends, a career, a full social life and community activities I participated in, but nothing brought me fulfillment.

Eventually, a feeling of dread overcame me and would not go away. I would wake up with it and go to bed with it. Something was wrong and

I couldn't put my finger on it. I tried to ignore it, but that didn't work either. I felt guilty complaining because other people had what I felt were much more serious concerns and problems. I wasn't even sure what to pray for. But I remembered learning in church that sometimes all we have to say is "Precious Lord Take My Hand" and have faith that God will deliver us. So this is what I did, I asked God to help me. Over and over I asked for enlightenment, surrendering a little bit of my will with each request. I spent a lot of time on my knees.

Slowly the answers started to come. I saw that I was traveling down a pitch-black path searching for light. I saw that my will had led me too far down this wrong path. God showed me that I had to turn around and walk back toward the right path—the way He wanted me to go. By spring of 1987 I knew I had to take action.

This was very hard to do. It meant making major changes in my life, without knowing what lay ahead. I put it off as long as possible, thinking if I just tried harder I could will myself into feeling better. It didn't happen. I surrendered! I admitted to myself that I really didn't know what I wanted in life, and I had more to lose by holding on than by letting go. I surrendered to Him!

Within a few weeks, in May of 1987, I quit my job, put my stuff in storage, said good-bye to friends, and returned home to California. I knew I needed to spend some time thinking about what God wanted me to do. I spent the next few months praying and reflecting, getting back in touch with God. I devoured books on spirituality and psychology. I read scripture and wrote incessantly in my journal. I thought about the meaning of life as I walked through museums, parks, and flower gardens. I went to church every Sunday and participated in the service. I went to the beaches of Southern California and sat for hours watching the ebb and flow of the waves.

Slowly but surely my strength returned and even though I didn't know what was coming, I knew that God and I would face it together. I had planned on returning to the East Coast that fall. I didn't. God had

other plans for me. By summer's end I had a new job and had met my fu-
ture husband. God surrounded me with light and put me on the path
that brought me the happiness and fulfillment I had been searching for.

I wish I could say that the road was entirely smooth from that point
on, but it hasn't always been so. There have been bumps in the road that
have caused me to stumble. And, every now and then I've missed a turn
and had to retrace my steps. But I can say this—He's never failed me yet!
Never, even in the toughest of times, have I felt alone. God always
makes His presence known to me even when I'm not necessarily looking
for it. And, thankfully, God always leads me, albeit sometimes kicking
and screaming, back to the right path.

THE MASTER'S PLAN

"IN HIM WE WERE ALSO CHOSEN, HAVING BEEN PREDESTINED
ACCORDING TO THE PLAN OF HIM WHO WORKS OUT EVERYTHING IN
CONFORMITY WITH THE PURPOSE OF HIS WILL."

EPHESIANS 1:11 (NIV)

So many of us question God's divine inspiration in our lives. We
wonder: Is it God, or is it something else? Is it free will? Is it luck? Is
it fate? What is it that determines our path in life? If we examine the
fabric of our lives, we can see a pattern, and yet we still wonder how
much of it was preplanned by the Master.

We like to think we have control of our destiny, yet when we look
closely, we see all of the times when He interceded on our behalf. We
see the *coincidences*—when someone we are thinking about, whom we
haven't spoken to in years, calls us out of the blue or we meet a
stranger who turned out not to be a stranger at all, but someone intimately connected to our family or friends. We see the divine timing—
how a slowdown on the freeway keeps us from being involved in an
accident or how being at the right place at the right time brings unexpected good fortune.

We see the signs. They are all around us if only we pay attention. To walk by faith means we have to examine the things that happen to us. We have to look past the obvious and find meaning in the subtleties of the situation. What seems bad on the surface may really be a blessing in disguise or maybe even a lesson. We just have to move past our limited perspective and into the realm of His divine desire. Or, as popular songstress Patti LaBelle says in her well-received book *Don't Block the Blessings.*

God shows us what it is *He* wants us to do—*His* will. Our own will, while laced with good intentions, can only get us so far. But *God's will* leads us to our good. *God's will* is what we should seek. That is why we pray as in *Matthew 6:10 (KJV):*

". . THY WILL BE DONE ON EARTH AS IT IS IN HEAVEN."

Try this as a faith exercise:

- **Closely examine the things that happen in your life within a two-week period**—the people you meet, places you go, things you learn, the coincidences, and the divinely timed events. Live two weeks where you are in tune with what is happening around you. Follow the signs. Go with the flow.
- **If you think about someone you haven't talked to in a while, contact that person.** He or she may need to hear from you. Also, carefully look at the people who come into your life during this period. Imagine what their purpose is; why you crossed paths.
- **If a particular subject comes up that you are interested in,** pay attention to how many times it reveals itself. Learn more about it. Research it—it may be a hobby or a career in waiting.
- **Try to live with no regrets and no complaints over things which are beyond your control,** such as traffic and other people's schedules. Realize there may be a higher reason for a missed appointment or a late arrival.

• If there is something you know you shouldn't be doing, stop doing it for two weeks. Enjoy the lack of guilt, and soar in the freedom
of small triumphs. Surrender to His will for two weeks. It may
change the way you live. It may last a lifetime.

HERE AM I, SEND ME

"THOSE WHO ARE FAR AWAY WILL COME AND HELP TO BUILD THE
TEMPLE OF THE LORD, AND YOU WILL KNOW THAT THE LORD
ALMIGHTY HAS SENT ME TO YOU. THIS WILL HAPPEN IF YOU
DILIGENTLY OBEY THE LORD YOUR GOD."

ZECHARIAH 6:15 (NIV)

Never is God more illuminating than when He allows us to cross
paths with people who will help us grow closer to Him. If we are in
tune, we will realize that God has a purpose for everyone *He* sends our
way. Just as the Lord sent Ruth to Naomi and Jonathan to David, He
will send whom we need, when we need them.

Our goal then is to determine who is God sent and who is not.
Those who are God sent will help us to grow spiritually. Those who
are not will try to stand in the way of our spiritual growth.

We never know where we might meet a God-sent person. We
may meet him or her "accidentally," or the person may be on the
boundary of our lives for many years before we invite the individual
in. He or she may be right next door or come from far away. But have
faith that God will bring the person to us.

ANDRIA: *When we stop to think about how God has placed certain
people in our lives, we start to open up doors of possibilities. The
miracle in all this is He places them in our lives at just the right time
for His divine purpose. Whether we choose to acknowledge it or not,
our lives will bear out this truth.*

Linnie and I came together for only a few short months in Albany,

New York. Looking back, we see now that without divine intervention we never would have met. It never had to be that way. In fact, it's pretty amazing either of us ended up in Albany at all. At the time, we both had other job opportunities to choose from. But we chose Albany. Or is it that He knew all along just what to do?

Linnie and I have been friends since our time in Albany. We met each other through my sister Akosua, who worked with Linnie. I remember Linnie's introduction into my life so distinctly. My sister came home one day and said, "Hon. There's this girl named Linnie. She's going to come by the house for dinner. I really think you two would be much better friends than we are. You guys are just alike." She was right!

So since then, way back in 1979, ours has been a friendship I could count on. Even long after we had both left the "budding metropolis" of Albany (how did we survive that place?) we stayed in touch. We visited each other. We wrote letters, shared tears and fears and laughter and above all else, God. We now know that our friendship was given to us by God. He chose us even back then to be vessels of light. He decided back then the two of us had something special to offer the world. The light He sparked in each of us from a "chance" friendship is a light we must now shine on the world together.

You will know when you have met a God-sent person because you will relate to him or her differently than others. You will not want to envy or compete with that person. You will feel rested and relaxed around that individual—you will be more yourself. Your bond with him or her will not be superficial, it will be spiritual.

LINNIE: *Andria was the first friend I could share my spirituality with. You see, I had other friends, but we never really talked about prayer and faith and the kinds of things Andria and I talked about. I felt back then, my other friends would have thought I was corny or straight-laced if I started talking about God to them. We all went to church,* *but we sure didn't have a personal relationship with God and we sure didn't talk about God. All we talked about were boyfriends and making money. But with Andria I could openly embrace spirituality and I loved her for it.*

The time in Albany was so significant for me because it was there I finally did establish my personal relationship with God and my religion. And it became not my mother's God, or my grandmother's God, but my God! I believe it was my friendship with Andria that helped bring about an awakening in me that made that revelation possible—and for that I am grateful.

JUST AS I AM

"CAST NOT AWAY, THEREFORE, YOUR CONFIDENCE WHICH HATH GREAT RECOMPENSE OF REWARD. FOR YE HAVE NEED OF PATIENCE THAT, AFTER YE HAVE DONE THE WILL OF GOD, YE MIGHT RECEIVE THE PROMISE."

HEBREWS 10:35–36 (KJV)

One of God's greatest gifts to us is His total and complete acceptance of us—just as we are. We are not all-powerful. *He* is. We are not the miracle worker. *He* is. We did not form the mountains and paint the sky with stars as *He* did. We are mere mortals—flawed and imperfect, moving through life struggling to provide all that we, and those we care for, need.

But in His sight, we are a circle . . . complete, perfect, and divine, for we were made in His likeness. We are all children of the Most High. This is a reason to rejoice for it gives us the foundation for fully accepting ourselves too.

It's only when we take a long, hard look at what we perceive as faults that we begin to buy into the labels. Society wants to put us in a little box. Too often we give others an identifiable tag which stamps us as limited. As is stated in *Matthew 12:37 (KJV)*:

"FOR BY THY WORDS THOU SHALT BE JUSTIFIED, AND BY THY WORDS
THOU SHALT BE CONDEMNED."

It is out of our own mouths that we, at times, seal our own fate.
*"I'm an introvert. I'm overweight. I'm too short, too tall, not smart enough,
not good enough."* But what we need to see instead is that we are all a
work in progress. The Universe never tries to tell us who we are. It
accepts any good thing we have to offer. Think of the world as an open
stage waiting for us to show it whom we may become.

If only we could accept this truth about ourselves. There would
be no excuses put forth saying we are this way or that—because of the
way we were raised, or the tough breaks we suffered along the path of
living. We wouldn't constantly be trying to make up for a part of us
that got lost somewhere between our perfection at birth and our deficiencies now. No, we would make no apologies, but instead rejoice as
we strive to simply—be better.

We should celebrate the good things in life—God's blessings, instead of focusing on the bad. Pat yourself on the back every now and
then and give God the glory. Scripture tells us in *Philippians 4:8 (God's
Word)*:

". . . KEEP YOUR THOUGHTS ON WHATEVER IS RIGHT OR DESERVES
PRAISE: THINGS THAT ARE TRUE, HONORABLE, FAIR, PURE,
ACCEPTABLE OR COMMENDABLE. . ."

Find reasons to praise Him right now!

- **Celebrate your strengths instead of your shortcomings.** Maybe
that mate treated you like worn shoes for a long time, but somehow
you found a way to leave; maybe you didn't have the best of up-
bringings, but you managed to raise a child you could be proud of;
or, maybe nobody thought you had it in you to succeed—but, you
showed them anyway!
- **Highlight your accomplishments instead of your failures.**

Maybe it took you more than twenty years, but you kept at it and finally got your diploma; maybe you sometimes got passed over, but you finally got the promotion you deserved; or, maybe you can't get around the way you used to, but you can still get to where you need to be, when you need to be there.

• **Count your blessings instead of your challenges.** Maybe you don't have a lot of money, and you're not quite sure how you're going to pay your bills—but you're healthy and your family is healthy and you know He'll make a way somehow. Maybe, try as you might, you can't seem to find that special someone to share your life with, but you have managed to build a rich and rewarding life for yourself. Or, maybe, even if you starve yourself, you'll never be the size you were twenty years ago, but you look marvelous for the age you are now!

• **Don't judge yourself by other people's standards.** There will always be someone better-looking, smarter, wealthier, healthier, etc. Likewise, there will be those who see you as possessing attributes they wish they had. The point is not to compare ourselves to others. Scripture tells us in *Proverbs 14:30 (NIV)*:

> "A HEART AT PEACE GIVES LIFE TO THE BODY,
> BUT ENVY ROTS THE BONES."

• **Enjoy what you have today.** Don't spend your life always grasping for more. Tomorrow isn't promised, but today is alive with possibilities. Life may not be picture perfect, but it is still good to be alive! Whenever we feel less than, remember the words in *Deuteronomy 18:13 (KJV)*:

> "THY SHALT BE PERFECT WITH THE LORD THY GOD."
> IT IS OUR LIFE IN HIM THAT MAKES US WHOLE.

I SURRENDER ALL

"NEVER WORRY ABOUT ANYTHING. BUT IN EVERY SITUATION LET GOD KNOW WHAT YOU NEED IN PRAYERS AND REQUESTS WHILE GIVING THANKS. THEN GOD'S PEACE, WHICH GOES BEYOND ANYTHING WE CAN IMAGINE, WILL GUARD YOUR THOUGHTS AND EMOTIONS THROUGH CHRIST JESUS."

PHILIPPIANS 4:6–7 (GOD'S WORD)

When we move ourselves and our expectations of how things are supposed to be out of the way, we lay the foundation for God's blessings. Spiritual surrender is paramount if we are to experience the limitless blessings He has in store for us. The Universe will lead us toward our good if we just let it. But take it from experts, too often we get in the way of our own good. Be careful. Self-imposed will can take us just where *we* want to be. But God's will always leads us to where He wants us to be.

Here's the deal—we can either let life unfold on its own—for it will—or decide to actively participate through prayer and faith in God's plan for us. Here is the blueprint for a concept we call *Divinely Inspired Living*. It is the *Faith Formula*. Surrender (Let Go and Let God) + Belief (know that God will lead you to your good) + Patience (wait on the Lord) = Faith.

What we submit to you is that each series of events in life is *divinely inspired*, despite whatever *your* desires might be at the time. Life is about lessons, learned the hard way or otherwise. When you make the decision to move toward *divinely inspired living* the road traveled is more peaceful.

Don't forget: The Lord helps those who help themselves, or as you've heard time and time again, if you take one step, He'll take two. That means waking up each day with the intent to let Him order your steps. If you stay open to the *Faith Formula* of *Divinely Inspired Living*, that, in and of itself is spiritual progress. Then watch what happens. And, if the path He has chosen for you at the time seems tough, thank Him anyway, right then and there. For even through the tough times, Divine order prevails, we persevere and we grow.

You have to trust the Lord in all areas of your life: relationships, careers, finances, friendships, all of it! The apostle *James* said it best in *chapter 4 verse 7 (NIV):*

> "SUBMIT YOURSELVES, THEN TO GOD
> COME NEAR TO GOD AND HE WILL COME NEAR TO YOU."

You must make it second nature to put Him first in all things. You must learn to surrender yourself to Him.

MY SOUL LOOKS BACK AND WONDERS

REMEMBER THIS

- **GET IN TUNE WITH THE MASTER'S PLAN.** This means not yielding to our own understanding, but trusting in Him. Each day we ask God to order our steps, and then, through will or ego, fail to get in tune with His plan. Life is like a puzzle with a thousand pieces. By looking at each individual piece we can't see the big picture. But God can. Let God's master plan work for you.

- **PUT THE PAST BEHIND YOU.** Stop holding on to broken dreams and promises. Throw away old pictures, records, and letters that only cause you heartache and remind you of bad times. Don't try to relive the past. Let Go and Let God, He will lead you toward your good if only you let Him.

- **CELEBRATE YOUR BLESSINGS.** Try counting them out loud one by one. Praise the Lord for your accomplishments, your triumphs over failure, and your perseverance. If for no other reason, praise Him for life itself, being thankful for who you are, just as you are.

Remember the Faith Formula: To attain our good we must let go, trust and wait on the Lord.

Surrender + Belief + Patience = Faith

MY SOUL LOOKS BACK
AND WONDERS

PRAY FOR THIS:
SURRENDER

To start on your spiritual journey, a path which will enrich your life, the first step is to surrender your will to God. Until you take this first step you cannot receive the grace that awaits you.

❧

PRAYER OF SURRENDER

Lord, I thank You for giving me the ability to choose.
And right now, I choose You. I want always to choose You.
I recognize the need to put You first in all things,
and yet, I am still learning how to do this.
You have shown me that nothing is too small,
nothing too insignificant for You to guide in my life.
Teach me to trust as I take baby steps toward Your light.
Show me what is wrong, and what is right.
Gently unclothe my will, instead dressing me in
Your Divine garments.
I want to wear Your will like a fine wool suit
that is right for all seasons and all occasions.
I am cloaked in Your mercy. I am protected by Your grace.
I am one with You. I pray to surrender and let
Your will be done.
Today and every day in every way. I trust You.
Thank You. Amen.

CHAPTER THREE

Give Me That Old-Time Religion

"BUT TAKE CARE AND WATCH YOURSELVES CLOSELY, SO AS NEITHER TO FORGET THE THINGS THAT YOUR EYES HAVE SEEN NOR TO LET THEM SLIP FROM YOUR MIND ALL THE DAYS OF YOUR LIFE; MAKE THEM KNOWN TO YOUR CHILDREN AND YOUR CHILDREN'S CHILDREN . . ."

DEUTERONOMY 4:9 (NRSV)

So many African Americans thought we had "arrived" during the seventies. We felt we had finally been delivered from the bondage of segregation. No longer would there be barriers telling us where we could live, go to school, or work. We were no longer confined to the inner cities. The suburbs beckoned. America's colleges actively sought black students. Corporate America left its doors slightly ajar, and those of us who benefited from a college education were able to slip through and don suits and briefcases.

And so in large numbers, we did what few of those who came before us had been able to do. We enrolled in predominantly white universities, accepted corporate positions, moved to the suburbs, and some of us even joined country clubs. Where sisters once held high their Angela Davis Afro's—as we entered corporate America—a straightening comb replaced our red, black, and green Afro picks. For so many of us, the church, the family, and the community, all cornerstones for our parents and grandparents, took a backseat to happy hours, networking socials, health clubs, and Caribbean vacations.

Our world, to us, began to look very different from the world in which our parents and grandparents had grown up. Of course, we would later find out that things weren't really as different as we thought, and in many ways things had become worse. We thought we had won the war, when in reality we had only won a battle.

What we forgot was, even in the midst of troubled times, there were still lots of certainties for African Americans during the civil rights era and before. Sure we had differences depending on what part of the country we lived in, and our religion, but, generally speaking, for most African Americans, life revolved around family, church, and community.

Everyday life, and how we spent our free time, was similar in most aspects. Especially our weekends. Friday night meant sitting down with the family for a fish fry. Friends and neighbors would come over for a game of dominoes or bid whist (black people's bridge). On Saturday, we kept our much needed hair appointments at barber and beauty shops. And on Sunday? Well on the Sabbath we spent most of the day in church.

The foundation of the community was the church. Maybe you grew up Baptist or Methodist or perhaps Pentecostal. No matter what your denomination, the church still represented a home away from home, where we were at ease, safe, and always welcome.

The church was and still is in many ways our "talking drum." It is here where we learned of both the good news and bad news emanating from our communities. You see the New York Times back then wasn't writing stories about the things that were most important to us. Some would argue, it still doesn't today.

What is the talking drum? Probably the oldest form of communication. One person tells another, who tells another, who tells another. We kept the lines of communication open so we could support one another and the causes we shared as a people.

Most of our social and political activities were centered at the church—literally. Church basements became our ballrooms, our theaters, and our meeting sites. Every evening there was some church activity to keep us occupied—a missionary meeting, Bible study, choir rehearsal. The church was also there for us in time of need. We'd pass around the plate when the situation warranted—a relative needed burying and there were no funds, a family had too many mouths to feed, someone's child was in trouble and needed a lawyer, or someone else was going away to college. In good times and bad, the church was our extended family.

ANDRIA: *I was with that extended family nearly every Sunday of my life. I know all about that old-time religion. You see church was literally my second home. I'm what you call a P.K. A preacher's kid. My family moved up from North Carolina when I was four. My dad had been called to pastor a large church in Brooklyn, New York—Bethel Baptist. It's amazing to me to think how much my life has been influenced by that time.*

The black Baptist church is truly a microcosm. A little world reflective of black society. What would I be like now, were it not for the church? There is a deep feeling of familiarity when I revisit my childhood. An upbringing millions of us share. The stirring sounds of psalms coming down from atop the choir loft. The smells of fried chicken and collard greens wafting from the sanctuary vents and through the pews. How do you begin to do justice to the gift growing up in the church has given so many of us? You begin first by thanking God.

I guess I took it all for granted back then. After all, life was what it was. I didn't know anything else. Now, however, I realize just how stabilizing a force church was for me. Sometimes my mind is flooded by lessons learned there. First and foremost I learned a lesson of generosity.

My sister, Akosua, and I were expected to go to college. And we did. But not without the help of many prayers and Mrs. Cornell's money.

Mrs. Isabella Cornell was a longtime member and trustee of Bethel Baptist. She was devoted to the church and to my family. She worked on Sundays at Bethel, and part time at our house during the week. It was Mrs. Cornell who taught me how to iron a shirt. You start with the collar, then the sleeves, the sides and then the back. Mrs. Cornell also taught me how to count one-dollar bills . . . fast! (That's pretty much all you saw back then in the wicker offering baskets as they passed by.) And Mrs. Cornell with her stern face and deep croaking voice was one of many who helped to make me who I am. She loaned my father the money to send my sister and me to college. No state assistance necessary. She never even pressured him to pay her back, but he did, and then some.

Back then, in the days of that old-time religion, your life was about praising the Lord, but it was also about family and community. It was the village of the black church that raised me. And thank God it did. Now I understand what the song is all about: "Give me that old-time religion, give me that old-time religion, give me that old-time religion, it's good enough for me."

All of us had a Mrs. Cornell back then. Someone either in the school, in the neighborhood, or at church who cared enough to take the time to teach us a lesson, sing us a song, or pray a prayer.

Church for many of us was the highlight of our week. For the adults it was a day to exhale the problems of the world and inhale the full glory of God. The week before had been long and hard and full of social challenges in an ever-changing world. For the children it was a time to dress up and run free. But mostly when Sunday came, it was a time to release our worries and express our joy.

At church, you didn't have to worry about what to say and how to say it. Everyone there knew exactly the meaning of an amen, a praise be to God, and a hallelujah! You didn't have to worry about your kids. You dropped them off at Sunday school, and some fine sister or brother would care for your children as if they were his or her own. The hugs and kisses were as plentiful as the discipline.

Back then, we didn't worry about a child's individual rights; we just worried about what *was* right and tried our best to keep our kids out of trouble. Back then, on a Sunday morning we pushed our worries to Monday. For on the Sabbath, for at least one day out of the week, we were worry-free and happy just to be with each other and with God.

There were three things that we as a people understood years ago: the power of prayer, the importance of family, and the need for community. Today, those things seem to have escaped us. These essential ingredients can be restored in our lives once again. We just have to make them important enough to focus on, step by step, day by day.

Our ancestors sustained their families through faith. Let's find ways to introduce the practices of yesterday to the families of today.

- **Make faith a fundamental part of your daily family life.** If your family begins to understand that you do have a relationship with a living God, they will follow by example. Whenever you intend to spend quiet time in prayer, let your loved ones know you're in conference. Tell them you've got to spend fifteen minutes, a half hour, however much undisturbed time you need, in His presence. Whenever you can, include them in your prayer rituals.
- **Let your family members see you studying the Word.** The Bible is the number-one bestseller of all time. Get excited about the parables and poetry found throughout its pages. When teaching your children, or dealing with family issues, use these as examples to get your point across.
- **As a family, always lift one another up.** Whether in times of triumph or tragedy, exalt one another in prayer and deed. Go out of

your way to show your love. Take the time to talk. Foster conversation without distractions. Get back to touching one another. A gentle stroke on the hand, a reassuring hug, a loving glance can at times say more about your solidarity as a family than anything else.

• **Time is tight for all of us, but get as involved as you can with one another.** Get the neighborhood kids together for a good cause or have a block party and ask for community cleanup donations. One family can have an annual summer backyard barbecue, another the yearly winter holiday dessert and coffee gathering. Learn to appreciate where you live, and make an effort to be an asset to the community. Knowing your neighbors doesn't have to be an intrusion, it can be the embodiment of the extended family.

TAKE IT TO THE LORD IN PRAYER

"EVENING, AND MORNING, AND AT NOON, WILL I PRAY, AND CRY ALOUD, AND HE SHALL HEAR MY VOICE."

PSALMS 55:17 (KJV)

From the simple prayer, to the most elegant, talking to God is a part of our heritage. From the slaves' prayers for freedom, to the civil rights prayers for equality, we are a praying people. We woke up praying and we went to bed praying. We started every meal praying. Whether it was at the family dinner table or the corner diner. We were taught to pray and give thanks before putting one bite of food in our mouths. In the evening we didn't think about it, it was second nature to fall to our knees, no matter how tired we were and at the very least recite the quickest and most memorable of prayers:

"Now I lay me down to sleep,
I pray the Lord my soul to keep.
If I should die before I wake.
I pray the Lord my soul to take."

The challenge nowadays is to give to our children that which we inherited from our ancestors—a personal sense that God is always there—listening with forgiveness and ready to bless us. How many of us make the effort to prepare our children spiritually? It's hard. There's hardly time to sit down together as a family and break bread. There's hardly patience enough to take the time to read to our kids at night. There's hardly energy enough to fall to our knees ourselves, let alone insisting that our little ones do the same. But until we get back to making prayer a priority in our lives and in the lives of our children, we will never know the power of prayer.

Just as in the past, prayer needs to be an integral part of our lives if we are to pass hope to the coming generations. Life presents us with unlimited opportunities to pray and ask for God's blessings. Most of us know to pray during times of crisis or turmoil, but daily activities can also benefit from a prayer or two. And, remember, a prayer can be as plain as a "Thank you, Lord" or as simple as this one word: "Help." There are always opportunities to pray:

- Pray when you get up in the morning, asking God to bless the coming day.
- Pray when you send your children off to school, asking God to look after them and protect them.
- Pray when you get into a car, bus, subway, or airplane and ask for traveling mercies.
- Pray when you enter your place of employment for a safe and productive workday.
- Pray before you eat breakfast, lunch, or dinner, thanking God for the meal.
- Pray when you go to bed at night, thanking God for letting you see another day.

WE ARE FAMILY

"AND HE ANSWERED THEM, SAYING, WHO IS MY MOTHER, OR MY
BRETHREN? AND HE LOOKED ROUND ABOUT ON THEM WHICH SAT
ABOUT HIM, AND SAID, BEHOLD MY MOTHER AND MY BRETHREN!
FOR WHOSOEVER SHALL DO THE WILL OF GOD, THE SAME IS MY
BROTHER, AND MY SISTER, AND MOTHER."

MARK 3:33–35 (KJV)

Can you remember a time when we claimed not just our closest
of friends as family, but those who were just trying to make it the way
our families were too? Sometimes years would pass before we found
out that Aunt Bea or Cousin Henry really wasn't related to us at all.
Even if our parents had people on the periphery of their lives, we addressed them as either ma'am or sir, aunt or uncle. If you were a child,
no adult was ever called by his/her first name.

We were proud to name our children after our relatives and
friends. Naming a child after someone was bestowing a great honor
upon that person and they knew it. People took care of their name-
sakes as if they were their own.

If some cousin of a friend was coming up North from down South
and needed a place to stay just until she could get on her feet, usually
there was room in somebody's basement. That's just the way it was.
As if through some sort of ancestral osmosis, we all became part of the
same tribe. The support we gave reached far beyond our own homes
and into the homes and hearts of so many others.

Our lives revolved around our families and communities. Maybe
because we weren't really welcome anywhere else. If we worked outside of the neighborhoods where we lived, at the end of a long day, we
took solace in coming back home. The blocks and streets where we
lived were truly our comfort zone.

We sat on front porches or stoops chatting with neighbors and watching the goings-on on our street. We kept an eye on the children whether they were ours or not and they addressed the elders with respect. We'd see them when they came home from school and we knew when it was time for them to go in at night. We didn't worry about drive-by shootings or the crack dealer on the corner.

Back then, we almost exclusively spent our money in our own communities, since our dollars, like us, were not welcomed elsewhere. Of course, this didn't stop others from coming into our communities, setting up shops, and charging outrageous prices because we were limited as to where we could buy.

But for the most part we supported our black businesses. The barber and beauty shops, the restaurants, the nightclubs, and, of course, the black funeral homes. We congregated at black establishments and enjoyed the camaraderie of hanging out with each other. And our communities were stronger for it.

Today we buy designer labels and shop at exclusive stores that are more interested in our money than us. We see the boarded-up businesses of yesterday throughout our communities on our way to suburban malls. We don't encourage our young people to learn a skill or become entrepreneurs, instead of working for someone else. We take all of our resources, financial and otherwise, out of the community, and don't bring anything back.

Family is more than those we share a bloodline with, and community is more than a geographical area. We need to have a sense of community wherever we might live. Even if you don't still live in the neighborhoods our families established long ago, you can do your part to regain the pride we felt back then.

- **Take back the community.** Develop a sense of ownership for our neighborhoods. Work with the people who live in the neighborhood today regardless of their race, creed, or color. We all want the same things for our families and communities. Make sure the people who live there have the same access to resources and services as others. Volunteer, tutor, mentor, donate, or if nothing else contact elected officials. Let them know communal concerns.

- **Help clean up the community.** If there are older relatives or friends who live nearby, help them with the upkeep of their houses and the block. Help them to rid their neighborhood of crime. Plant trees and gardens. Support libraries and cultural programs.
- **Support the businesses in the community.** Target several businesses a year and make a special effort to support them. Each year add one or two more establishments. Encourage friends and neighbors to do the same.
- **Don't forget the basics.** Let's greet each other warmly when we pass on the street, no matter where we are. If we see someone in trouble, let's do what we can to help. And, never forget—*always* respect the elders.

LEST WE FORGET

"I WILL REMEMBER THE DEEDS OF THE LORD; YES, I WILL REMEMBER YOUR MIRACLES OF LONG AGO."

PSALMS 77:11 (NIV)

We cannot glorify or rewrite the past. Nor should we. Although there was strength in our communities and families, we can't pretend all things were wonderful in the pre-civil rights era. We can't forget the indignities and injustices we suffered as a people.

It's good to reflect and marvel at the endurance of our existence. When He turned a desperate circumstance into a distinct victory. While an uphill struggle, with God's help, was made easier. Always we should thank Him for moving us from the seemingly impossible to the very imaginable reality many blacks are now living. Success does indeed run in our race. But there is a difficult chapter in *our* American history, many of us seem to have forgotten.

Let's remember what our ancestors faced. Let's openly honor them for their courage and suffering. There was a time of great strength within our communities and families, and while this brave reality is to be remembered, we can't forget the indignities and injustices we suffered as a people.

Discrimination and poverty were our constant companions. We were forced to live on the "other" side of the tracks. Our children received used textbooks that never depicted *our* history—*our* accomplishments. We were jailed or killed for trying to exercise our rights. Not just the rights of America's Constitution, but our God-given rights as human beings.

You see, our quest for civil rights was based on God's teachings of equality—not man's. We knew we had to fight every step of the way for that which was due us. But the road was made easier knowing that, while every bit of gained territory was a struggle, it moved us forward. The Lord was still in charge. We had faith that He would not bring us that far to leave us. And through it all, many of our mothers and fathers, while sour from the struggle, still offered their children words of encouragement and constant reminders of God's love. Yes, many of us had *Ephesians 6:4 (God's Word)* families:

"FATHERS, DON'T MAKE YOUR CHILDREN BITTER ABOUT LIFE.
INSTEAD, BRING THEM UP IN CHRISTIAN DISCIPLINE AND
INSTRUCTION."

LINNIE: *Sometimes it's inconceivable to me when I think about how only a few decades ago African Americans couldn't get a room at the major hotel chains, or shop in big department stores. And if we were allowed in to spend our money, we certainly couldn't try on garments. We couldn't swim in public pools and unless we were performing, we could only go to the "colored" section of tourist towns like Las Vegas. We were relegated to the back doors in the few places outside of our own communities where we were allowed to enter. People act like this hap-*

pened three hundred years ago, but it's only been what? Thirty-five, forty years?

I can remember as a child how my parents would get really excited about a black person on television! There would be a major commotion in the house with everyone scrambling to get near the TV. Neighbors and family members would call each other to make sure everyone was watching. You see we just weren't seen in the media in those days. It was as if we didn't exist beyond our own communities.

But the thing that I most remember today about that period in our history is, despite the discrimination and segregation we faced in those years, my family never instilled in me a sense of despair. My parents, like most parents of the time, held high expectations for their children. I grew up thinking that I could do or be anything that I wanted. I was raised not to accept the limitations society would try to impose on me.

I don't remember my mother sitting around bemoaning the fact that she couldn't try on a dress in a department store. I don't remember my dad complaining about the lack of advancement opportunities at his job. And yet I know my family members faced these and other adversities. But, thank God, they didn't pass on this feeling of lack and limitation to their children. If anything, they seemed determined that we strive for a better life than they themselves had.

You know why? First, because they had pride as a people and as a family. They knew from whence they came and the odds they had overcome just to survive. But most important, they had their faith in God. Faith that the world would be better for their children.

It was their faith that got them up every morning to go to jobs where they could neither grow nor advance. It was their faith that sent them to the polls to vote despite those who didn't want them there. It was their faith that made them march and protest, putting their lives at risk. It was their faith that told them to pass hope to their children instead of despair.

We seem to have lost some of that faith today. Maybe that's why sometimes our future doesn't seem quite as bright as our ancestors imagined. But those of us who have it so much better than our parents and grandparents did need to grab hold of the faith of our ancestors and pass it on.

That's what I try to do, especially when I cross paths with someone who is depressed or discouraged. I refuse to lose hope that poverty and racism can be resolved. I refuse to be limited by the stereotypes that still exist. I refuse to let them tell me what black people can't do. I tell my son that he can be President of the United States one day if he wants to be, and I believe it. But more important, he believes it!

I AM ON THE BATTLEFIELD

"OH GOD, THOU ART MY GOD; EARLY WILL I SEEK THEE: MY SOUL THIRSTETH FOR THEE, MY FLESH LONGETH FOR THEE IN A DRY AND THIRSTY LAND, WHERE NO WATER IS."

PSALMS 63:1 (KJV)

Our parents, our grandparents, our great-grandparents, and further back—fought for *us!* They shed blood, sweat, and tears for *our* future, not theirs. They knew they would not see significant change in *their* day—but they fought so *we* would have opportunities and a chance to succeed. They fought with God on their side.

Today, as in years past, we must put on the armor of our Lord as we confront injustice. From the 1970s until today, we know as we relaxed, as we let go of our religion and beliefs, our communities fell prey to society's ills: drugs, crime, hopelessness, and defeat. It's not just our poor communities, but our rich ones too.

Whether or not we want to admit it, we are all on the battlefield—the mother struggling to work and provide adequate day care for her children; the executive trying to find his place in a corporation that does not understand or appreciate his culture; the athlete trying—despite the temptations—to become a role model for those who will follow. The battlefield is life itself. Sometimes the enemy is in re-treat, sometimes he is coming straight at us with full force. But you can't fight him without God, and your first line of defense has got to be The Word.

> "HE ONLY IS MY ROCK AND MY SALVATION: HE IS MY DEFENSE;
> I SHALL NOT BE MOVED."
>
> PSALMS 62:6 (KJV)

If you find yourself in situations where you know your only help is God; seek Him. Call upon Him. It might be one in which you feel physically threatened, like our ancestors who fought for our civil rights. It might be one where your reputation and livelihood are un-der attack on the job. It might be one where you've been diagnosed with a health problem. Here is scripture you can stand upon during such trying times:

> ".. GET THEE BEHIND ME SATAN.."
>
> MATTHEW 16:23 (KJV)

> "WEAPONS MADE TO ATTACK YOU WON'T BE SUCCESSFUL, WORDS
> SPOKEN AGAINST YOU WON'T HURT YOU AT ALL"
>
> ISAIAH 54:17 (CEV)

> ".. WITH HIS STRIPES WE ARE HEALED"
>
> ISAIAH 53:5 (KJV)

Here are a couple of activities to try when you are in the midst of battle:

- Visualize a force field around you. A field that emanates from your heart, where Spirit resides and extends outward, beyond your body, protecting you and surrounding you with God's power.
- Place your enemy—real or perceived—in God's hand. Imagine your enemy surrounded by light. Slowly release all anger and fear. Know that God will take care of it.

When you are challenged on the battlefield you need to know you've got the best linebacker in all the heavens defending you. If you begin to see God as an active agent—a celestial warrior willing to fight your battles for you, you will look at conflict in a totally different way. When you begin to feel overwhelmed by the strife in your life, you can also think back to the struggles endured by our courageous loved ones of not so long ago. Maybe the might of their fight is strong enough to help us endure.

Let's continue our quest for equality. Let's not turn back the clock. Let's not allow our people to be hidden, defined by negativity or limited to mediocrity. Let's keep open those doors that should be open and not permit them to be slammed shut in our face. Let's honor and commit once again to prayer, family, and community. As we embrace the values of the past, let's not forget the battles that were fought and why we must continue fighting them today and every day on the battlefield of life. We will pay homage to those souls who have sacrificed for us by honoring our words, deeds, and actions toward others.

GIVE ME THAT OLD-TIME RELIGION

REMEMBER THIS

- While we do not want to glorify the past, we must get back to some of the priorities of yesterday: the family, the community, and the church. We must make prayer an essential part of our life. We should rebuild and preserve the integrity of neighborhoods our ancestors built. We must make our churches the center of our community, holding our meetings, our social affairs, and our performances in our church auditoriums and social halls.

- A critical aspect to surviving the challenges, which will then lead to our personal growth, is to draw on the strength of those who have come before us. We must honor those who came before us and uphold the institutions and communities that they built. Scripture tells us in *Proverbs 22:28 (God's Word)*

  "DO NOT MOVE AN ANCIENT BOUNDARY MARKER THAT YOUR ANCESTORS SET IN PLACE."

- Let's not pass our despair about the conditions of the world to our children. Fill them with hope and constantly tell them with God all things are possible. Have high expectations for our future generations. Don't let them settle for mediocrity or giving anything less than their best.

- Know that there will be "battlefield" situations in your life. While in these situations, envision yourself cloaked by the Holy Spirit. Let Spirit go before you in word, deed, or action. Use "the Word" as actual armor in crisis. Say it aloud—tell Satan to get thee behind!

GIVE ME THAT OLD-TIME RELIGION

PRAY FOR THIS:

LET ME HONOR MY PAST

Our past is nothing to be ashamed of. It represents our struggles, but most important, our strength. Just as the sun symbolizes the possibility for a brighter day, so too does our past paint a portrait of hope for a better tomorrow.

THE HERITAGE PRAYER

Dear Lord, I thank You and I praise You for those
who have come before me.
Thank You for their presence, thank You for their lessons,
and thank You for their endurance.
Lord, help me to always remember their sacrifices.
Help me to know, as they did, that Your love encompasses
all bondage and all trials.
Allow me to continue their magnanimous fight for freedom,
dignity, and justice.
Envelop me with their faith.
And, Lord, help me to stay on the path that they,
and You, have so graciously laid
before me.
Thank You for placing the baton in my hand.
Help me to run with it.
Amen.

CHAPTER FOUR

Families—The Ties That Bind

"REMEMBER THAT IT IS NOT YOU THAT SUPPORT THE
ROOT, BUT THE ROOT THAT SUPPORTS YOU."

ROMANS 11:18 (AMPLIFIED)

For many of us, our family histories are languishing on the vines. Our branches have strayed too far from their roots to receive any sustenance. Migration and this age of opportunity have taken many of us away from the familiarity of home and hearth. We continue to search for our good, stretch to reach our goals, and pray to fulfill our God-given potential. But as the winds of change and possibilities continue to blow, they also continue to scatter many of us across the country.

For those who have ventured North, West, and East in this great land, we have in the process left behind family members and the closeness we so deeply long for. We consider ourselves lucky if we see our parents or grandparents once a year. And, if we passed a first cousin on the street, we probably wouldn't be able to identify him or her. We have overlooked the importance of family ties.

Do you know the names of your maternal and paternal grandmothers? Do you know where your grandfather was born and what he did for a living? Do you know the origin of your family name? Do you know the location of land your ancestors once owned? Maybe these things were told to us, we just never took the time to listen.

We lose so much when we don't know our families. We lose the love, wisdom, and faith passed down through the ages. It is our faith that ultimately sustains us through the hard times. Where do we get that faith? From family. We're not born knowing God. We have to be shown the way to Him. Nor do we instinctively understand His promises and love for us. That's something we must be given. This gift usually comes from our parents, grandparents, aunts, uncles, and other relatives. Left to our own devices, we might eventually stumble onto God. But it is our families who bless us by introducing us to Him at an early age. They teach us the importance of having a relationship with God.

It is vital that our children see their loved ones living a spirit-filled life, and that they see their own eyes in the faces of their ancestors. We all need that sense of continuance. We know that as a people so much of our history was lost or never told to us. As we fled our Southern origins, many of us abandoned not only the pain of a restricted society but the details of the lives we led there.

Have we really made an effort to learn about our ancestors? The opportunity to do so is vanishing as our older relatives pass on. Let's not devalue our history. Let's find a way to reattach to our roots.

Every time we pass up a chance to talk, *really talk* to an aunt, an uncle, a mother, or a father, we miss out on an opportunity to learn more about ourselves and where we came from. If we don't understand where we came from or who we are, we can't possibly measure the extent of our personal potential. We need to cling to the root once again, with an attitude of gratitude and appreciation. That appreciation means giving value to *our* life's experiences, *our* traditions, *our* spiritual selves, *our* struggles, *our* faith, and *our* families. Once we start unearthing the personal journeys of our relatives, we will see the richness, the significance of their struggles. We will then be less likely to detach ourselves from the very experiences that support who we are today. Time is passing. Let's not miss an opportunity to learn from whence we've come.

- **Revive the ancestral art of the oral tradition.** Call an older relative. Take him/her out for lunch. Have your relatives over for coffee. Ask them to recall memories of growing up. What was their childhood like? Who were their role models in the family? What real life experiences kept them holding on to God?
- **Have a "Family Worship Day."** Invite members of your family to join you for joint worship at the church of your choice. Some churches have special devotional days for events such as these, but any Sunday morning service will do. Pick a Sunday and send out the invites. And, while you're at it, why not make a day out of it? Do as scripture says in *Deuteronomy 12:7 (NIV):*

"THERE, IN THE PRESENCE OF THE LORD YOUR GOD, YOU AND YOUR FAMILIES SHALL EAT AND SHALL REJOICE IN EVERYTHING YOU HAVE PUT YOUR HAND TO, BECAUSE THE LORD YOUR GOD HAS BLESSED YOU."

- **Ask your mother or father to dig up old photos.** Really look at the faces of your relatives. Do you see yourself in any of the pictures? Look to see whose eyes you have. Look beyond and within. Ask your parents what they know about the relatives in the photos. Whose spirit do you share?
- **Document! Document! Document!** Get a tape recorder or a camcorder, and begin chronicling your family's history. Ask questions and then listen to the old familiar stories that have been told for years. Write them down as well. Let the elders take you as far back as they can—remembering the names, birth dates, and places where the seeds of family life were sown. Make a commitment to do a little digging. You'll be amazed at the treasures you will find.

GRANDMA'S HANDS

"SHE OPENS HER MOUTH WITH SKILLFUL AND GODLY WISDOM,
AND IN HER TONGUE IS THE LAW OF KINDNESS—GIVING
COUNSEL AND INSTRUCTION."

PROVERBS 31:26 (AMPLIFIED)

For many African Americans, circumstances dictated that they be raised entirely or in part by their grandparents. Maybe their parents moved North for better opportunities, leaving them with their grandparents until they could get settled and on their feet. Or, maybe their parents were unable, for whatever reason, to raise them. Time and time again, without hesitation, it was their grandparents who stepped in to shower them with the stability, support, and the wisdom they needed.

Today, many of us don't have time for our grandparents or older relatives. They move too slow . . . they don't talk "proper" . . . they don't understand today's world. These are some of the reasons we avoid them. We don't really care to hear what they have to say because we don't think it's relevant to us. But the Word tells us:

"LIKEWISE, YE YOUNGER, SUBMIT YOURSELVES UNTO THE ELDER.
YEA, ALL OF YOU BE SUBJECT ONE TO ANOTHER, AND BE CLOTHED
WITH HUMILITY: FOR GOD RESISTETH THE PROUD,
AND GIVETH GRACE TO THE HUMBLE."

1 PETER 5:5 (KJV)

So those of us blessed with living grandparents need to make them a vital part of our lives. We need to get to know them, and let them know us. Those whose grandparents have passed on should make an effort to learn about their lives and should *always* cherish and honor their memory.

ANDRIA: *I consider myself one of the fortunate few because I have deep and fond memories of each of my grandparents. Evelyn and Walter Clarington and Grant Agabus and Aurealia. But my father's parents were most active in my life.*

When we were quite young, my mother and father would head for work and drop me and my sister off at our grandparents' house. That's when we lived in North Carolina. Back then, it was Grandmommie and Granddaddy who told us stories, wiped our noses, kissed our tears and our hurts away.

When I was four, we moved to Brooklyn, where my father was called to preach. Eventually, the pressure of sharing a husband with a congregation and a community was too much for my mother. Grandmommie came up to help, just for a few months, of course. She never went back. My grandfather followed a few years later.

Mother Hall, as all the good church ladies called her, taught me kindness and humility. She taught me passion and patience. She taught me tolerance and tenacity. (My husband is most grateful, because she also taught me how to cook!) My grandmother was old-fashioned for sure, but in the absolute best sense of the word. I can honestly say I never heard her raise her voice. What she tried to do was raise me right.

Her passing was especially hard. At ninety-one she was in excellent health, both mind and body. She had a tragic fall, lingered for a week, and moved on to join her husband and what she lived for . . Heaven.

She and my grandfather taught me so much about life and about respect. I address anyone with gray hair or no hair, as ma'am or sir. I don't talk back to elders. I look everyone in the eye, and I pray every day.

When we were preparing to lay my grandmother to rest, my cousins, sister, and I all stood around her at the wake, hand in hand, each of us telling the others just what Grandmommie meant to us. When we were all done, through the flood of tears and memories, my cousin Charles summed it up best. He said, "The thing Grandmommie gave each of us— in her sweet, quiet, unassuming way—is she gave us the Lord."

So now, when darkness surrounds me, light somehow still fills my soul. When challenges are put before me and I am still able to count the many blessings in my life, I thank God for Aurealia Jane Smith Hall, and am reminded why God invented grandparents. I look at my own children, and am so grateful they know their grandparents just as I did. I only hope that one day when they're all grown up, I will be blessed to give their children such a wonderful and marvelous gift. The gift of love. The gift of faith. The gift of God.

SUFFER THE CHILDREN

"IF ANYONE DOES NOT PROVIDE FOR HIS RELATIVES, AND ESPECIALLY FOR HIS IMMEDIATE FAMILY, HE HAS DENIED THE FAITH AND IS WORSE THAN AN UNBELIEVER."

1 TIMOTHY 5:8 (NIV)

Sometimes the people we call family are not related to us at all—they just assume the role. They nurture us and take care of us not because they have to, or are paid to, but because they want to. There are a lot of people out there raising other folks' children. And thank God for them.

God places these caregivers where they need to be because there are times when a parent may not assume responsibility for a child. Neither morally nor financially. We pray for all children who are not blessed with loving, supportive parents. We also pray for those parents who do not recognize God's gift of having been given children.

Maybe you are trying to raise a child alone. Or maybe you had a parent who wasn't there. Know that God is there for the motherless and the fatherless. Scripture says in *Psalms 68:5 (KJV)*:

"A FATHER OF THE FATHERLESS . . . IS GOD IN HIS HOLY HABITATION."

Forgiving those who abandon us as children can happen only with God by our side. There are the bad memories. The wondering about what could have been. Hugs missed and tears wept.

We have the capacity to forgive, however, only when we understand how God forgives. How do we begin? Maybe by remembering that whether we like it or not, they are our parents. If they had not lived, we would not have been born. Maybe the only gift they were able to give was the gift of life. So forgive them we do, and we praise God for filling any voids left behind.

LINNIE: *My "real" father, and by that I mean my biological father, left my mother and me when I was four months old. Berman and my mom had been married around three years when I was born and I was their only child. I didn't see Berman much when I was growing up and don't remember him doing anything for me or showing an interest in my life. No cards, no gifts—I doubt if he even remembered my birth date.*

But through God's grace I never really felt his absence in my life. My uncles stepped forth and provided me with the attention I didn't get from him, and my mother married a wonderful man when I was ten and he became my dad. Carl Perkins never treated me as a "stepchild." He accepted me as his own from day one.

I was reunited with my father when I was in my late twenties. I hadn't seen him in more than eighteen years. I looked him up mostly out of curiosity. I wasn't searching for a father, I just wanted to learn more about this man I had heard so much about. I also wanted to explore his side of my family tree.

He was surprised, yet happy that I called. I think he wondered what it was I wanted from him, and I wasn't quite sure myself. We spent the next few years getting to know each other and trying to define our relationship. It was awkward for both of us because he wanted to assume the role of father—as though nothing had happened. And, to his credit, he did try to make up for all the prior years. Yet, to me, he was always a stranger that I happened to be related to.

Berman died a few years ago, and while we did manage to have a cordial relationship, I never became the doting daughter he wanted. Too many years had passed. I felt his guilt every time he looked at me—but I couldn't erase it. I thought he would find comfort in knowing that I had a happy childhood, but, of course, this made him feel worse at times.

When I think of my father, I think of all the people who are carrying around the same kind of guilt he carried for years. They know they have a child out there . . . somewhere . . and they figure maybe someday they'll work things out—but someday never comes. And then, when it's all over, when their end comes, they think about what was really important in life—not the material possessions, or the independence, or even the good times. No—it is their children they think about. Their legacy.

I try not to judge Berman, I remember what Jesus said:

" 'Do not judge, lest you be judged.' "

MATTHEW 7:1 (NAS)

I'm just thankful for my mom and my stepfather and my other relatives who were always there for me. Forgiveness was harder though—after all he had abandoned me—but I managed to do it by looking at things from his point of view. I realized that at the time I was born, he felt trapped in a marriage he wanted out of. And while many men would have stepped up and done the right thing, he decided to run from his responsibilities. The sad part was that no matter how hard he ran he was never able to escape it. It haunted him until his death.

Berman's final request of me was that I speak at his funeral. I was surprised and not quite sure what to say. I knew I couldn't lie and pretend things were different than they were, but also, because he wanted *this, I felt I should give him some kind of honor. And, yes, I had forgiven him. I realized that when it was all said and done, he was still my father, and if he had not existed, I would not exist.*

So at Berman's funeral, I talked honestly about our relationship and then I recited the following poem I wrote about him.

It's called "In Remembrance."

To Berman Frank,
In remembrance of a father, it took a long time for me to know,
I wasn't there to be your daughter,
You weren't there to watch me grow;
For all the years we spent apart, it sometimes made me sad,
That although you were my father, I could never call you Dad;
But I rejoice today for the years we spent,
catching up and moving on,
We accepted that so much had passed, and could not be undone;
And I've finally come to realize, although it's taken me a while,
That you'll always be my father, and I'll always be your child;
Now it's time for me to say good-bye,
and to mourn all that will not be;
And to say I'm so thankful, . . . so very grateful,
for your blood that runs through me.
Linnie Frank, August 1995

We have to thank God for the life He has given us and the family He has given us too—whatever the problems may be. We should bless them and release them into God's care. But most important, we must forgive them, not just for their sake, but for our sake as well.

Forgiveness doesn't necessarily mean that you keep the person close to you, but you do continue to pray for them. Find a way to get over that which is lacking or painful. Look to add closure. Find a way to move on with your life. Try this exercise.

- Quietly, and sincerely find a peaceful place to pray. Visualize or take with you a picture of the relative you need to release to God. Maybe you want to light a candle or play some relaxing instrumental music. Meditate on the heart connection you have with the person. Find the love. Feel it. Now, let go of the anger, the frustration, the hurt. Repeat this affirmation:

"Lord, I surrender this life to you. I honor the things my loved one has done, and forgive the things that were left undone. Fix it, Lord. Please heal my pain, and my loved one. Thank you. Thy will be done."

PRECIOUS MEMORIES

"TO EVERYTHING . . . A SEASON AND A TIME TO EVERY DELIGHT
UNDER THE HEAVENS . . . A TIME TO LAUGH . . . A TIME TO
EMBRACE . . . A TIME TO LOVE."

ECCLESIASTES 3:1, 4, 5, 8 (YLT)

Some of our most profound memories are from the times we spent with our families: sitting around the table for a holiday meal, weddings, graduations, family picnics, and reunions. These all add to the essence of who we are. Some of us have a family home or a piece of land we can lay claim to. There is no better feeling than pulling up in the driveway or sitting on the stoop or front porch of the house we grew up in. We all have the need to feel we belong somewhere, to somebody.

Many families have family reunions and get-togethers on a regular basis. This is an excellent way to learn about the branches of your family tree. Sometimes it's hard to get the younger folk interested in family gatherings, but include them anyway. Let your children know their aunts and uncles and cousins. They don't have to be best friends, but they should be able to recognize each other as being from the same "tribe." Have family gatherings in which all the generations can mingle.

LINNIE: *I've only attended a few family reunions, but I have fond memories of them all. Two in particular stand out:*

The first took place at our house on a summer day years ago. All of my mother's siblings, most from out-of-town, were gathered in one place for the first time in a long time. Cousins and in-laws from far and near, some I had never even heard of, were at our house. We all sat around eating barbecue, playing cards, and having fun. I was around seventeen—old enough to appreciate the specialness of the day.

As with all gatherings at our house, the music was going continuously—45s, LPs, and eight-track tapes (this was the early seventies!). Aretha, Stevie, the Temps, and, of course, Marvin—we played and danced to it all. Later that evening things slowed down a bit and everyone was sitting in twos and threes with their favorite relatives, talking and reminiscing.

I decided to go to my room and get the long version of a song that was popular at the time—"I'll Take You There" by the Staple Singers. I put it on the record player and suddenly everybody came to life. Soon everyone from eight to eighty was up dancing and popping their fingers. Young danced with old, brothers danced with sisters, and some just danced by themselves. We even did a soul train line. I think some folks who hadn't danced in years got up and danced that day. It was truly a "Kodak" moment.

Whenever I hear that song (and it seems as if I'm hearing it more frequently now) I think back to that summer day. That was the last time all of my mom's brothers and sisters were to be together—death and illness claimed many of them too quickly. But the memories of that day live on with me forever.

The second reunion I remember fondly took place in Lafayette, Louisiana, in 1986. It was a reunion of my father's family and I was ap-

prehensive about going because both he and his family had been es-
tranged from me for many years. It was my first time meeting most of his
siblings—my aunts and uncles. My brother Carlton accompanied me on
the trip. It was neither his father nor his family, but, he didn't want me to
feel like an outcast. Needless to say, my concerns were unwarranted,
and both Carlton and I were treated like long-lost family members returning to the fold.

What I most remember is visiting small towns outside of Lafayette,
like Opalousas and Morrow, where family members have lived for years.
Among the cornfields of Morrow were dirt roads that led to acres of
land and homes—some old, some new—that belonged to family members. But a cherished moment was seeing the "family" church—the
Little Rock Missionary Baptist Church where my ancestors had worshiped. As I stood there, I could imagine generations of family members
worshiping and praising the Lord. In my mind, I could hear the hymns
and see the hands clapping as they had years ago. Outside of the
church was the family cemetery. It was there I saw the graves of my paternal grandparents, Elvina and Cleveland Frank. This was another one
of those Kodak moments for me. I felt the completeness of it all—the
unbroken circle. Even though this was a family that I had not known—
I felt a sense of belonging. I knew that the Lord led me there. I felt the
smiles from heaven.

One way to keep that feeling of closeness is to have something
tangible to hold on to. We prize our family heirlooms. Back in the
day, those things that belonged to our older relatives were simply a
decorative part of their personality. When we were younger, Sista's
silk scarves were tired and outdated. Now that Sista's gone, those
same silk scarves are so precious to us, we've been known to fight
among ourselves when it's time to give her things away.

Whether it's Papa's old Stetson, or Momma's pearls, we want to
hold on to a small piece of those who have gone before us, so we can

hold on to ourselves. These precious memories are what keep us strong as a family. They keep us centered on our lineage. They remind us of who we are. We pass down these pieces of personal history as if we're passing around bits of gold.

When you think about it . the reflections we see in our loved ones are like a looking glass deep inside God's gene pool. It is an amazing creation from such a wondrous Sculptor. For one thing, it shows that He has a sense of humor.

ANDRIA: *It literally tickles me when my mom, my sister, and I all get dressed in the same room to go out. Nowadays, it's hard for us to get together. My sister lives two and a half hours north of me. My mother lives twenty-five minutes south. So when an occasion arises to bring us all together in the same place, we're grateful. My mom is five ten, my sister is five six, and I'm five seven. We're all different sizes too, but we all have the same body. Isn't that funny how God saw fit to give all three of us the same rounded behinds . . . the same apple cheeks . . . and the same slim fingers.*

There are actually moments when I glimpse my reflection in a store window as I'm walking by, and it is my mother I see mirrored back. Not me. I shake my head and can muster up only enough articulation to say, "Oomph! oomph! oomph!" But God knows what those sounds mean. They mean, "Thank you, Lord, for the precision of your blessings, for if You are powerful enough, and patient enough, to duplicate my mother's likeness in my eyes . . . thank you for those blessings I have yet to see. The ones that are not so obvious.

Sometimes those blessings come disguised as pain. People naturally assume, because I didn't grow up with my mother, that somehow I suffered or had a childhood void of a mother's devotion. But I didn't. Even though my parents were divorced, I grew up blessed, healthy, and happy, and secure in my mother's love for me. And even though circumstances beyond her control prevented her from coming back to us, her expression of love for us was clear. It may not have been in keeping with what society at the time might have considered acceptable, but ultimately the greater love was in being without us. It took incredible strength to make the choices she had to make. My mother has passed that strength on to me.

One of my best relationships is with my mother. So many women either can't talk to their moms, don't get along with their moms, or choose to keep their mothers at arm's length because of the drama and pressure in their relationship. But my mother and I are friends as well as family. My mother and I share a bond and a faith in God that is so strong, nothing, not even the past, can keep us from expressing our love for one another, and for Him.

WE ARE OUR HEAVENLY FATHER'S CHILDREN

"SEE HOW VERY MUCH OUR HEAVENLY FATHER LOVES US, FOR HE ALLOWS US TO BE CALLED HIS CHILDREN—THINK OF IT— AND WE REALLY ARE."

1 JOHN 3:1 (TLB)

We are all God's children, but at one time or another we all get separated from Him. We get lost, and need to find our way back home. But it is at home, that we sometimes find it most challenging to remember God the Father is in charge of us all. Striking a balance between loving our families and letting go of their negative habits is paramount to maintaining our spiritual health, however.

Our bonds with our relatives can be strong. When a family member is experiencing pain, we feel it too. But we can't let it overwhelm us to the point where the whole family suffers. We need to understand deeply the ties that bind, but also be aware that we can't let those ties bind us up in unhealthy relationships, no matter who they're with.

Sometimes a family member may be struggling with an obstacle that he or she alone can't bear. Your father may be an alcoholic, your sister may keep having babies that she can't take care of, your mother may be suffering from depression, or your brother may abuse his wife. These are all real problems that many of today's families face. It has nothing to do with income or social status. All families, if they're honest, know that there is a family member who is struggling with some problem.

Our problem is that, try as we might, we can't help. Even though we may toss and turn at night worrying, or we may cajole and threaten our loved ones trying to get them back on track, nothing seems to work. This is the time to take it to the Lord in prayer. Not only that . . we have to leave it there. The best thing we can do for a family member in trouble is to ask the Holy Spirit to intercede on his/her behalf. And, once we do this, we need to have faith that the Lord does answer prayer, and even our relatives who need help have their own path to roam, their own way to find.

Scriptures such as the following can help to guide you when a relative is in trouble.

Instead of spending sleepless nights worrying, recite these scriptures, along with a prayer for your loved one's well-being:

"LISTEN TO MY CRY FOR HELP, MY KING AND MY GOD, FOR TO YOU
I PRAY. IN THE MORNING, O LORD, YOU HEAR MY VOICE;
IN THE MORNING I LAY MY REQUESTS BEFORE YOU
AND WAIT IN EXPECTATION."

PSALMS 5:2–3 (NIV)

- Tell your troubled loved one he/she can find refuge in God's strength. Share with them the following scriptures:

"AS FOR GOD, HIS WAY IS PERFECT; THE WORD OF THE LORD IS
FLAWLESS. HE IS A SHIELD FOR ALL WHO TAKE REFUGE IN HIM. FOR
WHO IS GOD BESIDES THE LORD? AND WHO IS THE ROCK EXCEPT
OUR GOD? IT IS GOD WHO ARMS ME WITH STRENGTH
AND MAKES MY WAY PERFECT."

PSALMS 18:30–32 (NIV)

"THE LORD WATCHES OVER YOU—THE LORD IS YOUR SHADE AT
YOUR RIGHT HAND; THE SUN WILL NOT HARM YOU BY DAY, NOR THE
MOON BY NIGHT. THE LORD WILL KEEP YOU FROM ALL HARM—HE
WILL WATCH OVER YOUR LIFE; THE LORD WILL WATCH OVER YOUR
COMING AND GOING BOTH NOW AND FOREVERMORE."

PSALMS 121:5–8 (NIV)

While we always want to uphold one another, it's up to each of
us to decide how much support we can give a loved one without losing ourselves in the process. If it comes down to your mental and
emotional health, our advice is to take the spiritual high road. Offer
your relatives unconditional love with conditional exposure to your
life, and pray for them. You can't let anyone—friend, foe, or family,
pull you down. God wants us to lift each other up.

If it means loosening ties with toxic loved ones, then by all means
do so. The key point is "loosening" not "severing." You should always keep your loved ones in your heart and in your prayers. But you
don't have to make their afflictions your own.

Many of us carry mental baggage from our upbringing. Especially
if our childhoods were less than perfect. The popular thing to say
nowadays is that we came from a "dysfunctional" family. We say this
when we need reasons to explain our current weaknesses and our in-
ability to cope with life. We look to our past for answers or excuses.

None of our families are perfect, we are after all human. But we must remember that first and foremost we are children of God—and God is not dysfunctional! He created us whole and without equal. This means that whatever the problem our parents have—alcoholism, drugs, physical or mental abusiveness—we do not have to take those problems as our own and carry them forward. We can be stronger than this. Although our parents gave birth to us, God made us. And God doesn't make mistakes.

THE FAMILY THAT PRAYS TOGETHER . . .

"... CHOOSE YOU THIS DAY WHOM YOU WILL SERVE ... AS FOR ME AND MY HOUSEHOLD, WE WILL SERVE THE LORD."

JOSHUA 24:15 (KJV)

There are many distractions today that keep us from enjoying family life as we once did. Everyday living has become so hectic that we seldom have time to sit down together for a family meal. Some families see each other only at weddings and funerals. And these days, on Sunday mornings, we seldom see whole families going to church together—some family members stay home, some go to different churches, and some simply never go to church at all.

We keep ourselves and our kids so busy with the activities of the world that we don't have time for the Lord. God becomes an entry for our calendars or datebooks and try as we might we just can't seem to *squeeze* Him in—"Let's see—maybe I can fit God in two weeks from Friday around three? Whoops—no, can do, I've got a hair appointment."

Many of us call on God as a last resort. We turn to God only when our families are stressed or are being torn apart. But what we should do instead is put God at the forefront of our families. We should *choose Him first!*—ask for His guidance on how to handle family situations. And once we have chosen Him, our families will have a foundation. A foundation that can't be obtained any other way—not by money, birthright, status, or education. When we pray together we strengthen our family. It is then we reap the blessings only the Lord can give.

ANDRIA: *I lived my entire life in the church when I was young. And like many of us who have children now, I used to carry a lot of guilt about not equipping my children with the same spiritual armor that was given to me as a child. Of course, when you're growing up you don't see it that way. As an adolescent, all you know is, you're stuck in church, and the senior choir is singing "Take Me to the Water" again!*

Now as an adult, this is the foundation that holds me up. Those old, tired songs are the ones that flood my spirit when I need an infusion of the power of the Holy Ghost.

I've moved so much in my career as a journalist, that I haven't really had just one church home since I left my dad's church and went off to college—over the years, I've worshiped at so many different places! You know, try this church, try that one, don't go this month, go next month. But finally, I took it to the Lord in prayer. I even asked my prayer partners in my Circle of Seven to stand in agreement with me. I needed to find a church home. God does answer prayer! I found a church within a week of sending my request up to Heaven. As soon as I went inside, my spirit felt at home. My kids like it, and even my husband. Now, I'm not saying that I'll be able to get them to go with me every Sunday. But I've decided to stop waiting for perfect conditions. I've decided the best example is action. Even though we don't always all go to church together, we make it a priority to honor God, and include Him in our lives.

My children are spiritually centered. We make sure to pray before every meal. They initiate their prayers at night. Prayer is a lifelong foundation you want them to always be able to stand firm upon. You want praying to be second nature to them. My children understand that God is love. That God forgives. I'm also trying to teach them that God is Mommy's constant companion. The challenge is to get them to under-

stand this for themselves, that they have to make time for God in their lives. They have to have a relationship with God on their own. Not one where I'm holding their hands, but one where they invite Him into their hearts.

It's sometimes hard to get children to respect the fact that you need to take time out to pray—to worship—to fellowship with others. The demands of family can very easily become an excuse for not going out to worship on a regular basis. If you can find a church home that has an active children's program, great! But sometimes it's difficult. Here's a suggestion you can implement to get everyone in your household to understand and respect that you have a relationship with God—one that takes time—one that requires cultivation.

- Try to stick with the same prayer time every day. Try to select a time when family demands are on the downswing. Tell the children. Tell your husband. Tell whoever needs to know, so they won't interrupt, that you are closing your door so you and God can have time alone. Have them look at the clock with you. Tell them when you'll be out, and not to disturb you. Tell them you'll do the same for them when it's their private time to pray.
- Reinforce family prayer time. When opportunities arise for you all to stand in agreement, do so. No matter what the problem, let children know they can take anything to the Lord in prayer. Maybe it's an upcoming test at school. Maybe it's bad dreams at night. Maybe it's simply a lost book or toy. Children should be encouraged to ask God for guidance, intervention, comfort, and love.

FAMILIES—THE TIES THAT BIND

REMEMBER THIS

❋ Let's value and document who we are, so we can look to the future with the certainty that our contributions will be recognized and exalted. Learn your heritage. Start with your immediate family and move back one branch at a time. Go to family reunions. Think of them as a tribal treasure hunt. Use computer software and read books on tracing your family tree.

❋ Honor your grandparents and your "tribe." Realize that you have much to learn from them. Know that you represent them in everything you do. If your grandparents are still alive, carve out some regular time in your life to spend with them. If they are not alive, make it a goal each year to learn something new about them to honor their memory.

❋ Do not carry the burdens of your family. Place them in God's hands. Remember that sometimes loving means letting go in prayer.

❋ Place God at the top of your family's priority list. Until we call forth our innate spirituality, honor that and take pride in that, we can't effectively pass this on to our children.

FAMILIES—THE TIES THAT BIND

PRAY FOR THIS:

LOVE FOR THE FATHER; LOVE FOR THE FAMILY

Our families are jewels in the Crown of Christ. Sometimes brilliant stones, sometimes diamonds in the rough. Through Spirit, we will let our true selves shine. With one another we will move forward in love.

PRAYER FOR LOVE

When I call on You, Father, I do so with such
reverence and reassurance.
For I know, Lord, You truly are a Father
who watches over me.
I am comforted, for Your love is unmatched.
Your love is forever merciful. Your love is for all time.
Please teach me, God, how to be as tender with others
as You are with me.
Open my heart, so that I might begin to love others in my
family just as You love me.
Jesus said, Love thy neighbor as thyself.
Open my eyes so that I might see my neighbor
as a brother or sister.
The stranger I have yet to meet might just be the person
I have yet to love.
Your majesty is awesome, and forgiving.
Please help me to open my heart wide enough
to allow Your love in,

and my love to come rushing out to others.
Love endures all things.
Help me to find the patience to love.
Thank you. Amen.

CHAPTER FIVE

Friendships—Real and Imagined

"TWO ARE BETTER THAN ONE; BECAUSE THEY HAVE A
GOOD RETURN FOR THEIR WORK. IF ONE FALLS DOWN,
HIS FRIEND CAN HELP HIM UP. BUT, PITY THE MAN WHO
FALLS AND HAS NO ONE TO PICK HIM UP! . . . THOUGH
ONE MAY BE OVERPOWERED, TWO CAN DEFEND
THEMSELVES. A CORD OF THREE STRANDS
IS NOT QUICKLY BROKEN."

ECCLESIASTES 4:9–10, 12 (NIV)

A true friendship is a blessing from God—to be nurtured and treasured as the rare and wonderful gift it is. A true friendship includes God. *He* is the third strand of the cord. To have someone with whom to share your joys and your sorrows, your hopes and your dreams—this is the value of friendship. But the highest rewards of friendship are attained when two people come together to serve God and to do *His* work. When this happens nothing is impossible and great things can be accomplished.

Friends will need each other from time to time. There are things you share with your friend you can't share with your mate, sibling, or parent. Be it a helping hand, some down-to-earth advice, or a needed prayer, our friends know us well enough to know exactly what to do or say.

We may wonder why God places us with the people we call friends. There is often a reason, whether apparent or not. Maybe He joins us in friendship to learn from each other. Or to work on a joint project together. Or maybe He requires that we provide each other with comfort and solace in times of need, just as He does for us.

LINNIE: *After leaving Albany I settled in the Washington, D.C., area. Although I was eventually to return to California, in a lot of ways D.C. still feels like home. Mostly because of the people I met there, the friends I made. Two people in particular stand out—Paula and Denise. Paula and Denise grew up together, but beyond that they are as different as night and day. Paula is feisty and outspoken, while Denise is quiet and pensive.*

Paula was my running buddy in Washington. Each week we couldn't wait until Friday evenings when we would get together and hang out. Paula was my confidante and knew where all my skeletons were hidden. For that reason most of my boyfriends at the time didn't like Paula, but that's okay because they are all gone and she's still around. I love Paula's zest for life, and the fact that she's never been afraid to call a spade a spade.

I met Denise's family before I met her. Her parents, her siblings, and her irrepressible grandmother were to become my family in Washington. It was only natural that Denise and I would become close friends. We are alike in many ways. We both have a deeply rooted desire to solve the problems of the world and those around us. We've spent many hours discussing philosophy, politics, spirituality, and psychology.

Paula and Denise are "real" friends. I thank God for their friendship. I always know that whatever goes down they "have my back" as the kids say. Our friendships have never been about competition or envy. When one of us hurts, the other hurts. We celebrate each other's successes and triumphs. We have laughed together, cried together, and prayed together.

Never was this more true than when Denise's brother and his wife died in a tragic airplane crash, leaving two daughters ages five years and six months. Times like these can make us feel inadequate as friends. You don't know what to say . . . you don't know what to do . . . all you can do is just be there and offer your support.

I remember when I went to see Denise at her family home after she had called to tell me of the accident. I did not want to be there. I did not want to face Denise and her family, and I especially did not want to face those children, but I had no choice. Like the many others who provided solace to her family during this dark time, I had to be there—as her friend, but more important, as a Christian. Scripture guides us on how to provide comfort to friends in the midst of crisis in the story of the downtrodden Job and his three friends:

> "WHEN JOB'S THREE FRIENDS, ELIPHAZ THE TEMANITE, BILDAD THE SHUHITE AND ZOPHAR THE NAAMATHITE, HEARD ABOUT ALL THE TROUBLES THAT HAD COME UPON HIM, THEY SET OUT FROM THEIR HOMES AND MET TOGETHER BY AGREEMENT TO GO AND SYMPATHIZE WITH HIM AND COMFORT HIM.
> WHEN THEY SAW HIM FROM A DISTANCE, THEY COULD HARDLY RECOGNIZE HIM; THEY BEGAN TO WEEP ALOUD, AND THEY TORE THEIR ROBES AND SPRINKLED DUST ON THEIR HEADS.
> THEN THEY SAT ON THE GROUND WITH HIM FOR SEVEN DAYS AND SEVEN NIGHTS. NO ONE SAID A WORD TO HIM, BECAUSE THEY SAW HOW GREAT HIS SUFFERING WAS."

> JOB 2:11–13 (NIV)

In the months and years to come God showed me how He wanted me to help my friend deal with this tragedy. I spent a lot of time with Denise and the children. It was sometimes hilarious as we struggled with combing the oldest daughter's hair or changing the baby's diaper, but we did the best we could. The baby, Melinda, became my god-

daughter. As I watch her today, in her teenage years, I think about how proud her parents would be of her, and how glad I am that she is a part of my life. She's just one more reminder of the many blessings friendship can bring.

Friendship requires time and commitment. A friend is not someone who is simply there for us when it's beneficial. A real friend is there even when it's inconvenient. Real friendship involves compromise and acceptance. Developing the trust that any meaningful relationship requires takes time. We must be patient with our friends, but it is equally important that we be honest with ourselves and others with whom we are blessed to build a friendship.

A FRIEND IN NEED IS A FRIEND IN DEED

"THERE ARE FRIENDS WHO PRETEND TO BE FRIENDS, BUT THERE IS A FRIEND WHO STICKS CLOSER THAN A BROTHER."

PROVERBS: 18:24 (RSV)

There are all types of friends: work friends, church friends, party friends, exercise friends, school friends, club friends, neighbor friends, and some who are not really friends at all. The people in our lives can be put into two categories: the ones who are generally positive and make us feel good about ourselves, and the others—you know the ones: They've always got some snide remark that makes you feel bad, think twice, or stop what you're doing.

You may spend a lot of time with these "fake friends" and get quite close to them, but if you think about it, most of your time is probably spent doing nonproductive things. Here's the million-dollar question: If something real good were to happen to you, what would be your "friends'" reaction? Think about it! These so-called friends are often jealous and envious of you, and the more you accomplish the more they either: 1) try to underrate your accomplishment; 2) try to undermine you; 3) try to take what you've got; or 4) when all else fails they disappear; stop calling—saying that success has spoiled you— you've changed!

We have to watch whom we entangle ourselves with in the name of friendship. We can't underestimate the effect negative people have on our lives. Scripture warns us in *Proverbs* 22:24–25 *(NIV):*

> "DO NOT MAKE FRIENDS WITH A HOT-TEMPERED MAN, DO NOT
> ASSOCIATE WITH ONE EASILY ANGERED, OR YOU MAY LEARN HIS
> WAYS AND GET YOURSELF ENSNARED."

It's important to surround yourself with positive people. It may mean going from ten fake friends to one good friend, but you're better off, and better for it! You know, it's your friends who will always bring you back to center. And always remember, it's a two-way street. Our parents would say: "To have a friend, you've got to be a friend."

If you are fortunate to have good friends . . count your blessings. Thank God for the storehouse of blessings that are your friends. And, if you're not sure, remember this:

- A *real friend* will tell you when you're doing wrong because a friend has your best interest at heart. You should count on your friends to tell you what's right too. But if you're trying to lose weight, go back to school, buy a house, get a job, end a bad relationship, take a trip, get a mate, whatever, and your best bud has nothing good to say— think about it! Does this person really want you to succeed, or does he/she simply want to keep you right where you are because this is where that individual feels comfortable having you? Those are usually people who, in order to feel good about themselves, need to think badly about you.
- A *real friend* is there when you need him/her even though you may only see the person from time to time. You can go a month or maybe even a year without talking, but when you finally connect,

you simply pick up right where you left off. That's not a "sometimie friend." That's a secure relationship with someone with whom you share strong ties, even if there is little common ground between you at that particular time. You've moved, or gotten married, one of you has kids, the other not, or maybe that career track is just moving too fast, and you haven't had the time to catch up—but still, the friendship remains. And when you're in trouble the person is there for you, even if it means dropping everything and flying halfway around the world . . . a friend will.

• A *real friend* accepts you the way you are. They don't care about your job title or the car you drive or your social status. They love you for who you are—your spirit—your essence. You don't have to dress alike or talk alike or try to duplicate each other. A friend respects your individuality. You don't have to compete with a friend. You each understand that God has wondrous journeys in store for you both. You each seek God's blessings in your own unique way, and seek to bless others.

ANDRIA: *My friends are the perennial flowers of my life. They keep my heart in bloom. My friends are those whom I admire, care for with great intent, and protect at all cost. My true friendships have weathered the storms of getting that degree, going on to establish a career, moving through that to get married and have children, and then being reborn into my calling and to Christ. My friends are women who would give me their last dime, stop everything, ask no questions and deliver—no matter what.*

We all met in college. Veronica, Mary, Pauline, and Carol were there from the beginning when I came into womanhood. They've been there for me when I haven't been there for myself. What's wonderful about our relationship is that each of us is different from the other. And it's those very differences that we've learned to respect, appreciate, and under-

stand. Each of our distinct personalities helps to make up the whole of who we are as individuals.

Pauline has moved away, and while we're still close, it's Mary, Veronica, Carol, and me who sit around talking and expressing our gratitude for the blessing of the friendship. We also reminisce about what we've been through. How we've never once given up on the relationship. All of us have been there for one another, through the mountainous highs, and the deepest lows. Or as Mary is fond of saying: "Friends are those who suffer with you." We've each come to the understanding that the only reason we've stayed this close for so long is that we continue to make the others a priority, that and patience.

We tolerate each other's strengths and each other's weaknesses. Which is not easy among four black women with strong personalities. It means overlooking individual idiosyncrasies. Mary can be really argumentative. She is, after all, an extremely effective lawyer, but when you're having trouble at home you don't necessarily want everything cross-examined. Veronica chooses her words carefully, never wanting to offend, which is beautiful. But sometimes it takes her a while to finally get to the point of what she's saying. She weighs every possibility with extreme care. At times, if you're in a hurry, it can be a bit frustrating. Carol is extremely talented and a cautious optimist, which means she tends to play it safe and doesn't always make her light shine. She has never stepped too far outside her comfort zone. And while she has gotten better, she has also been the type of person who limits herself. This means you can't want more for her than she's ready to pursue for herself. As for me, I'm under some sort of delusion that I can do everything well, but sometimes I fall short of the mark because I've overextended myself. My life has built in distractions: three kids, a husband, and an incessantly ringing telephone. It's got to be annoying for all of my friends when I'm trying to have a conversation with them and I allow others to set my agenda. But through it all, we continue to love and honor our relationships with one another.

Unlike family, it is much easier to give up on a friend. But if you have been blessed from above with people in your life with whom you share a heart connection, you realize you are Divinely bound and forever connected.

Sometimes, it's hard work keeping the lines of honest communication open. But we make the effort because we value the other, hardly ever taking what we share for granted, and never losing our sense of humor.

Yeah, it may at times be a little bit of a pain dealing with Mary's contentious ways, but it is also quite laughable, because Mary's going to make her point even over the smallest issues. And when Mary and I are ready to move on something spontaneously, we chuckle at Veronica and how she has to weigh even the most remote and inconsequential possibilities. Carol may try to stay where it's comfortable, but she's finding her wings. She's even learned to drive. And each one of them has tolerated me, laughing to my face at how it is I seem to thrive when I'm juggling fourteen things in my life at the same time. The best part is that none of us would ever want it any different.

We've truly learned that to have a friend, you have to be a friend. We take nothing personally, and yet everything between us is personal. Now that God has us walking our spiritual path together through prayer with the Circle of Seven, it is even more beautiful to know that through it all, and only with Him, we have survived the pitfalls that destroy some friendships and our love grows ever deeper. When we pray with one another and for one another, it is always from the heart. These women have stuck by me closer than any brother or sister. They are my sisters, and will forever have my trust, admiration, and love.

BETRAYAL

"FOR IT WAS NOT AN ENEMY THAT REPROACHED ME; THEN I COULD
HAVE BORNE IT. NEITHER WAS IT HE THAT HATED ME THAT DID
MAGNIFY HIMSELF AGAINST ME; THEN I WOULD HAVE HID MYSELF

FROM HIM: BUT IT WAS THOU, A MAN MY EQUAL, MY GUIDE,
AND MINE ACQUAINTANCE. WE TOOK SWEET COUNSEL TOGETHER,
AND WALKED UNTO THE HOUSE OF GOD IN COMPANY."

PSALMS 55:12–14 (KJV)

It's a sad fact: the more you get in life, and the more you allow the Lord in your life, the more jealousy and envy you will face. Nine times out of ten it will come from where you least expect it—right in your own backyard. The stronger you get in faith, and trying to do the Lord's work, the stronger the evils are that come after you. So strong they sometimes possess those closest to you. These are the folk who, if they are against you, can stop you dead in your tracks if you let them.

Sometimes you will have the feeling that someone is working against you, be it at work, at home, or even at the very place that we go to find solace—the church. You know it's happening, but you just can't put your finger on who it is. Here's some advice. Get to a quiet place and ask the Lord to reveal that person to you. Then relax in faith and know it will be revealed. Remember the saying "What's done in the dark will come to the light." It will. Just have faith. More than likely the person will show his or her hand. Or all the signs that have been right under your nose will become clear, when before you were too blind to see them. Or, maybe it will be the person you least sus-pect—maybe it will be the very person you've been confiding in. Maybe it's your "friend."

LINNIE: *I've had experiences where someone I thought was my friend turned out to be anything but. One woman in particular stands out. Let's call her Miss High Heels because no matter where she's going or what she's doing, she must wear a suit and four-inch heels. The woman could be walking the boardwalk at Venice Beach, and she would still have on stilettos!*

First of all, I let my guard down with her too soon. I know to keep my guard up when new people try to force themselves into my life. My mama always said, "Beware of people who come on too strong before they get to know you." But there were two things that made me accept this woman's professed friendship sooner than I should have. One: She seemed to be a good, churchgoing woman, centered in faith, and, second: She's old enough to be my mother and I gave her undue respect because of that. You know why? Because I grew up knowing that I should respect my elders. This has not been hard for me given the strong older sisters I have encountered on my journey. I have a number of friends who are many years older than I, and have generally found them to be supportive and mentoring. I call them "sage" women: Sisters I can learn from. But not this sister.

Oh, at first she was friendly enough. Always willing to lend a hand or an ear. We would spend hours on the phone chatting about everything under the sun. We seemed to have similar opinions and to agree on everything. (This should have been my first sign that something was wrong.) She had lots of "helpful" suggestions for my job and I came to respect her opinions. What I didn't realize was that Miss High Heels had her own agenda.

You see, I was thinking Miss High Heels was my newfound sage, when in reality, she was getting close to me in an effort to get close to a man I was working with at the time. She didn't seem to care that he flirted shamelessly with anything in a skirt and was only interested in her for what she could do to further his ambitions. And, since she was a retired grandmother, with plenty of time to devote to meeting his every whim, she became a regular fixture at our office. She did everything for him but lick his boots clean—and she probably would've done that if he had asked.

Looking back, I'm sure she befriended me at first just to make sure I wasn't competing with her for this man's affections. And, once she was secure about that, she continued the friendship so that she could keep tabs on him. She was using me to get information about him. It wasn't long before I noticed that she always eventually steered our conversations to him and what he was doing. I soon realized that she was totally obsessed with him, but I figured it wasn't my business. I thought our friendship went beyond whatever she was experiencing at the time.

Wrong! Eventually she showed me what was really behind that phony little smile of hers. Showed me enough to make me wake up and realize she was not my friend and never had been. Soon everything became clear to me. Miss High Heels resented my youth and my abilities, but most of all she was envious of the job I was doing—especially since it put me in proximity to her heartthrob! At first she tried to convince me to quit my job. When that didn't work she started a campaign to discredit me, even going as far as spreading false allegations about me. The same energy that she had put into befriending me, she now used to try to destroy my credibility!

And what did I do in return? Well, I must admit that my first thoughts about what to do with Miss High Heels weren't very Christian. But, after much prayer and reflection, I realized this too was something I should learn from. First of all, I needed to learn to listen more to my radar, intuition, or whatever you want to call it. (Some folks call it God Talking.) The signs were there—I just chose to ignore them. I knew something was wrong when this woman became my "best friend" within a matter of weeks.

But the main lesson for me, the one that was the hardest to accept, was that I had somehow contributed to this woman's psychosis. Many times we give people the very weapons they use to destroy us. You see, even after I knew she was over the edge with this man, I still continued to be her conduit of information. Maybe if I hadn't been so busy gossiping with her about him I would have recognized her desperation sooner and gotten out of the way.

So after I thought about it, I realized that it was best for me to just let it go. And that's what I did. You know we can't worry about what people are saying about us, we can only make sure we are living right. It does surprise me that people will tell what the old folks call a "baldface" lie about another person, but there are sick folk out there. And sometimes they worm their way into our lives—pretending to be our friends.

There will always be instances where friends will betray us. The scriptures tell us this. And, as we live, we learn to stop calling everybody a friend. That is an honor few earn, and even fewer keep. We learn the difference between an acquaintance and a friend. But we also learn to surround all who approach us—whether friend or foe—in prayer. And we trust God to show us the difference.

ANDRIA: *After I left Albany, I lived in a number of cities. In so many of these towns, there was little going on socially for a single black woman. I was young, naive, and usually bored. It would take forever to find a friend, but finally it would happen. In one city where I worked I got pretty close to this brown-skinned, bright, smiling sister, whose name I will change to protect the not so innocent. Let's call her "Miss Switch." 'Cause she was real good at switching those hips, back and forth. She knew how to work 'em . . . for what she wanted to get.*

Unlike me, Miss Switch was married with two beautiful children, and at the time, one of the most sophisticated women I had ever met. I was what? Twenty-two, and she was about ten years older . . . a model and a mom! I actually looked up to this woman. I laugh about it now, but back then I didn't see her evil ways.

Anyway . . . Miss Switch was always on the go. A photo shoot one day, a show across town the next. But me, well, after I was done with work I was free, so I would do things like cook her sweet potato pies and bring them over, even baby-sit for free. It was always my pleasure, after all, those were the kinds of things friends did for one another.

One night, Miss Switch and her second husband invited me and my man over to their house for dinner. We had a great time, went back to my apartment, and didn't think more about it. Weeks later, I noticed whenever I would mention to my fiancé that we should get together with Miss Switch and her husband he would always say no. I noticed my man would do almost anything he could to get out of getting together with them. So I finally sat him down to see what was going on.

The night that we were at their house for dinner, while I was in the living room laughing, looking at pictures, and having a glass of wine, Miss Switch said she needed help in the kitchen. She called my fiancé in, and once alone, "my friend" revealed herself and her intentions toward him with no room for misinterpretation. Let's just say while I was in the other room she boldly propositioned him in a way that was less than Christian.

Fortunately for me, I had a man who, even if he had temporarily lost his senses for a split second, knew I would drop him like a hot potato if he ever took that kind of bait. And he is smart enough to know bait when he sees it! (I also know him well enough to know he looked!)

This experience taught me three things. One: It's important to make sure friendships are balanced. Miss Switch was a woman who, for the most part, I did anything for, and she offered very little in return. (She did give me a lipstick once, I think.) Two: It may not be a good idea to talk too much about how great your man is with another woman, she might want to find out just how good for herself. Three: Now, a bit more spiritually mature (and I still have a ways to go, I realize), for people like that, all you can really do is stay away from them, and pray for them.

Today, I am more conscious of my own spiritual radar, ever attempting to hone it, refine it, and listen to that still small voice within. Now, when I meet new people, I am able to see their intentions a little more quickly than I once did, and make choices about where I want them in my life, if at all. I pray for them, and ask the Lord to bless the relationship.

Some people put romantic relationships over friendships, family, and even before themselves. We all know of women who would cancel plans with a female friend if a man asked them out. And how about those brother friends whom you see hide nor hair of when there's a woman in their lives? But as soon as they are alone . . . they start calling again, asking you where you've been?

The priority of a friendship must be on par with the other relationships in your life. Too many of us work at the relationship with our mate, but never can figure out why our platonic friendships are fleeting and superficial. The answer is, both take hard work, time, and forgiveness. But the benefits are worth the effort and the rewards are many.

WHAT A FRIEND WE HAVE IN JESUS

". . . SO THAT CHRIST MAY DWELL IN YOUR HEARTS THROUGH FAITH.
AND I PRAY THAT YOU, BEING ROOTED AND ESTABLISHED IN LOVE,
MAY HAVE POWER, TOGETHER WITH ALL THE SAINTS, TO GRASP HOW
WIDE AND LONG AND HIGH AND DEEP IS THE LOVE OF CHRIST, AND
TO KNOW THIS LOVE THAT SURPASSES KNOWLEDGE—THAT YOU MAY
BE FILLED TO THE MEASURE OF ALL THE FULLNESS OF GOD."

EPHESIANS 3:17–19 (NIV)

Only the Lord can give us the unconditional friendship we seek from others. He is there for us whenever and whatever, without judgment and condemnation. When there is no one else, God will be there for us. Only He knows all our thoughts, wishes, needs, and desires. Our friends are mere mortals and can't be expected to know everything there is to know about us.

Yes, there will be times when friends disappoint, and do things to us we never thought they would. In any relationship where our heart is a factor, we're vulnerable. After all, when we give someone permission to love us, we also give them the power to hurt us. If a real friend disappoints, we should face it, own up to our part in it, heal the wounds, and move on. After all, scripture tells us in *Proverbs 27:6 (NIV)*:

"WOUNDS FROM A FRIEND CAN BE TRUSTED, BUT AN ENEMY MULTIPLIES KISSES."

Real friendship is about trust, support, and forgiveness. We recognize in one another our strengths and our weaknesses. Therefore, we know we must love each other enough to allow the other to be human. Being human means being imperfect. But thank God for His perfection and His example of unconditional love.

If you're not sure about a friendship, pray about it. Ask the Lord to show you what's really in your friend's heart—but be ready. Remember the saying, "Be careful what you pray for, you just might get it." Too often we want the truth, but aren't prepared to deal with the difficulties that come with it. So if you ask the Lord to give you something, when He does deliver, don't complain if it's not exactly what you expected. Because He may show you that the person who *you* think of as a friend, really isn't—and you have to accept this! That's why when we pray, we always start by thanking Him, and asking: "Lord, let Thy will, not my will, be done." For *His* way is the best way.

If the Lord has blessed us with a true friend, we should be thankful. We need to understand that real friends are to be cherished and protected. When you find someone you can endure all of life's challenges with, hold on to that person at all cost. The friendship will not always be easy, but it will be worth it. Friendship, like love, will always find a way.

FRIENDSHIPS—REAL AND IMAGINED

REMEMBER THIS

- Trust God to put the right people in your life at the right time. There is already a divine plan designed for His purposes. Be prepared to offer solace and comfort to your friends in their times of need. Pray that they will do the same for you.
- Actively work on your spiritual radar. Try meditative exercises where you pay attention to your first intuition, the first thought that comes to mind. Use this inner Divine directional to measure the purity of a real friendship.
- Only God can give us unconditional friendship. Take your relationships, whether old or new, to the Lord in prayer, ask that He lead you, guide you, and bless your common path.

FRIENDSHIPS—REAL AND IMAGINED

PRAY FOR THIS:
BLESSED FRIENDSHIP

True friendships are a blessing from above. These divine relationships are not just for our companionship, our benefit, or to fill a void. Real friends have been offered to one another for a much higher purpose. Scripture tells us:

"FOR IT IS GOD WHICH WORKETH IN YOU BOTH TO WILL AND TO DO OF HIS GOOD PLEASURE."

PHILIPPIANS 2:13 (KJV)

❧

FRIENDSHIP PRAYER

Dear Lord, You have blessed me so very much with hearts and souls like mine. Those You have brought into my life have been a gift. I pray that I might be a blessing to them too. I may not have all the friends I want, but I thank You for the ones I do have. I pray that You might continue to reveal to me the true meaning of friendship. Let my heart, words, and deeds reflect Your light. Protect us, God, from the darkest of human emotions. Keep jealousy, envy, and impatience at bay. Teach me, Dear Father, how to love as Jesus did . . Without judging, without malice   without reservation. I know that with Your help, I will draw those into my life who support and love me, and I will be offered by You as a gift to those souls waiting for my love as well. Thank you. Amen.

⚜

CHAPTER SIX

Love—Always and Forever

**"ABOVE ALL, CLOTHE YOURSELVES WITH LOVE, WHICH
BINDS EVERYTHING TOGETHER IN PERFECT HARMONY."**

COLOSSIANS 3:14 (NRSV)

Since Adam and Eve, the relationship between women and men has been characterized by both mutual love and mutual frustration. We all want loving relationships. We want someone who will stick with us through thick and thin; we want someone who will love us as we are, and perhaps most of all, we want someone to snuggle with on cold, rainy nights. But in our quest to find the right mate we sometimes get sidetracked into relationships that are not good for us.

For many of us, our relationship with the opposite sex becomes the driving force of our lives. We look for guidelines and rules on how to get a mate, how to keep a mate, or what to do when a mate leaves. But the truth of the matter is, you only need *rules* if you're playing games. Mature adult relationships require honesty and respect, not lies and emotional tricks.

Often we spend more time concentrating on our love lives than on ourselves. But healthy relationships require that we find peace within before looking to others for comfort. For even in the closest of relationships, we are still separate people. The old folks used to say,

"You come into this world by yourself, and you're gonna leave this world alone too." It's important never to depend more on someone else than you do on yourself or God.

Most of us start out looking for love. Some of us are just looking for a good time. But none of us can deny the need for some kind of intimacy with a romantic partner. Many of us remain alone, claiming we're holding out for that perfect relationship, but what is it that we really want? We want a soul mate who can read our minds before our thoughts are ever spoken. We want a "real man," you know, one who can be a provider and protector, but . . . he's got to be in touch with his "sensitive side." We all want a remarkable lover who knows what to do, and how to do it—a person with no flaws who overlooks all of ours. Yes, for the most part we all want the same type of mate: perfect! But since there are no perfect people . . . guess what? There are no perfect relationships. We need to give up on perfection, and instead ask God to give us a mate who's real and right for us.

Regardless of our age, we may hold immature or unrealistic expectations of what a partnership should be, and until we grow up and accept the realities and responsibilities of adult relationships, we aren't ready to move forward. It's only when we're truly ready that God will bring about a union sanctioned from above. A union that can withstand the test of time.

LINNIE: *I honestly can't say what I was looking for in a romantic partner in the years before I was married. I remember that by early adulthood I thought all relationships were supposed to be heavy on the melodrama. This probably came from my teenage years of watching "All My Children" and the exploits of Erica Kane. The "Dallas" and "Dynasty" years didn't change this train of thought either (I once canceled a date on Friday night so I could see an episode of "Dallas"—can you believe that?).*

Anyway, the men in my life during those years didn't seem to have any problem adding to the drama. Although, for the most part, I was blessed because the majority of the guys I dated were pretty decent. No one ever hit me, stole from me, or did any of the horrible things that have happened to other women.

What I most remember during those years is not taking anything too seriously, especially things like monogamy and commitment. But there were a few things I wouldn't do: 1) I would never date a man who had dated a friend of mine; 2) I would never date a man who was a friend of someone else I had dated (well, at least not a close friend); and 3) I would never pick up men at bars or have one-night stands. That was pretty much it.

I can't say I ever actively got out there and looked for a man, they just seemed to always appear. They normally stayed a year or two until we had gone as far as we were going to go, then the relationship would end and the next man would drift into my life. Thinking about it now, most of the relationships had gone as far as they were going to go after the first couple of months, the rest of the time spent together must have just been convenience and familiarity. I know some couples who spend ten or twenty years in that mode. Thank God I eventually grew up and didn't make the mistake of staying in a comfortable but unfulfilling relationship.

I can now look back and see how my immaturity played a huge role in the relationships I found myself in. But the real question is what role did God play? I was a believer, I went to church, and I prayed—but, for some reason, I always separated my romantic life from my religious life. Maybe it was easier that way. Maybe it allowed me to avoid the tough questions, and ignore God's answers. It was only years later, when I did seek God's help in this area of my life, that I found romantic fulfillment.

When I returned to California in 1987, ready to surrender my life to God, I realized this meant my entire life—romance included. I had to believe that God knew what was best for me in this area, as in all areas, of my life. And, as always, the Lord came through for me.

I had crossed paths with Greg, the man I eventually married, at pre-vious points in my life. We had both attended UCLA at the same time in the late seventies. Although the student population at UCLA was large, the black student population was small, and we tended to travel in the same circles, so most of us knew each other. I have vague memories of Greg around campus and at dorm functions, but beyond that we didn't know or remember each other.

After I graduated I accepted a job as a computer programmer trainee with a local bank. I left that job for a position in Albany, New York. I was later to find out that Greg, still in California, started in the same position, at the same company, two weeks after I left.

But it was not time for us to meet then. I was too young to appreci-ate his quiet, studious manner and he would not have related to my youthful zest for life.

Years later God finally brought us together. I had recently returned to California and decided to attend a local meeting of the Black Data Processing Associates. I parked behind Greg and for some reason sat and watched him exit his car and head for the meeting. I felt something at the time, I can't deny it. I've heard people talk about thunderbolts and love at first sight, but that wasn't it. It was more like a jolt of recognition. I knew he was someone I wanted to know better.

After the meeting I asked him if he would walk me to my car. We ended up spending over an hour standing at our cars and marveling over our similar past. We couldn't believe that we had never met each other before that night. We talked like old friends who had found each other after years apart. It was then that it all came together. After years of traveling similar, but, distinct, paths, Greg and I joined on the single path God intended for us all along.

LOOKING FOR LOVE

"YOU WANT SOMETHING BUT DON'T GET IT. YOU KILL AND COVET,
BUT YOU CANNOT HAVE WHAT YOU WANT. YOU QUARREL AND FIGHT.

**YOU DO NOT HAVE, BECAUSE YOU DO NOT ASK GOD. WHEN YOU ASK,
YOU DO NOT RECEIVE, BECAUSE YOU ASK WITH WRONG MOTIVES,
THAT YOU MAY SPEND WHAT YOU GET ON YOUR PLEASURES."**

JAMES 4:2–3 (NIV)

What do we feed a soul that hungers for romantic companion-ship? And how long must we wait? Should we put our lives on hold until our soul mate comes? Or, should we search far and low, leaving no stone unturned until we find the companionship we are looking for? We pray to the Lord to please send us the partner we so desire, and yet we still hunger.

The question we need to ask ourselves is: How prepared are we to accept the love we seek? Have we done what is necessary to make ourselves worthy of companionship? If it *is* love we seek, then, first there are some things we need to do to get ready.

Prepare yourself for love:

- **Put past hurts and disappointments behind you.** Don't let the negative baggage you are carrying from childhood, or a past rela-tionship, get in the way of new chances for love. Do whatever you have to do to move on, and forgive.
- **Get rid of unrealistic expectations.** Let go of your ideals of the perfect mate. Don't set standards that no one could meet. Open yourself up to new possibilities—you never know who's around the next bend.
- **Do things that you enjoy.** Are you going to sit around bemoaning the fact that you don't have a mate, or are you going to get out and enjoy life? How many concerts, plays, movies, or sporting events are you going to miss because you think you need a date to go with? Instead of sitting on the sidelines of life, grab a friend, a relative, or even go by yourself. When you don't have others with you, you will make more of an effort to meet and converse with new people.

- **Try something new.** Do you always go to the same places, do the same things, see the same people? Get out of your routine. Explore new avenues. Take up a new hobby. Join a new group. Expose yourself to new situations.
- **Spend time investing in a better you.** All of us have something we can learn or some habit we should break. We may need a physical or a spiritual makeover to become the person God wants us to be.
- **Find your own way with love.** Everyone has advice when it comes to love. You have to discern for yourself which advice is worthwhile and which isn't, but for the most part you have to trust your own God-given instincts. Don't waste a lot of time listening to others. Only you and the Lord know your situation, your wants, and your needs.
- **Give your heart.** In many cases, it's not the romantic companionship we miss, as much as it is the chance to offer our heart in love. We miss the hugs and the warm touches. We miss being with someone who wants and enjoys our company. There are lots of ways to experience love. There are people, be they children, seniors, or disabled adults, who need our love and affection. There are a myriad of causes to which we can offer our support and devotion.
- **Put it in the Lord's hands.** The Lord not only knows *what* is best for us, He knows *who* is best for us. As we prepare ourselves for the love we are seeking we need to relax and know that in this area, as in all others, the Lord will deliver. Keep serving Him and doing His will. Have faith! Scripture tells us:

"YOU NEED TO PERSEVERE SO THAT WHEN YOU HAVE DONE
THE WILL OF GOD, YOU WILL RECEIVE WHAT HE HAS PROMISED."

HEBREWS 10:36 (NIV)

WHAT'S LOVE GOT TO DO WITH IT?

"WHERE HAS YOUR LOVER GONE, MOST BEAUTIFUL OF WOMEN?
WHICH WAY DID YOUR LOVER TURN, THAT WE MAY LOOK
FOR HIM WITH YOU?"
"MY LOVER HAS GONE DOWN TO HIS GARDEN, TO THE BEDS OF
SPICES, TO BROWSE IN THE GARDENS AND TO GATHER LILIES. I AM
MY LOVER'S AND MY LOVER IS MINE; HE BROWSES
AMONG THE LILIES."

SONG OF SOLOMON 6:1–2 (NIV)

Love is delicious, love is delectable, and love can even be delightfully dangerous. But love alone won't maintain or sustain a relationship. There is a difference between love, lust, and fantasy. It is a wise soul who can distinguish among the three. When it comes to matters of the heart, falling in love is the easy part, staying in love takes real commitment. Many of us think we're in love, and end up making a commitment to someone before we're ever really sure who we are.

Confronting our true selves, our selves that go beyond who we are, what we do, and all external influences is a real journey of self-discovery. When we uncover the true self, it is much easier to recognize pure love. Being able to accurately characterize what it is we feel for another requires both emotional and spiritual maturity. To get a true definition of love we can go to the Word—*1 Corinthians 13:4–8 (NIV)*:

- In verse 4 it says that love is "patient and kind." This means we should pay attention if someone we say we love is consistently short with us; has no time to be still and listen to what we say, and what we don't say. We really ought to seek someone who makes an effort to truly understand the unique ways in which we communicate our feelings.

- Verse 4 also says that love "does not envy, it does not boast, and it is not proud." We don't have to constantly brag about our mates saying "My man this . . ." or "My woman that   " Actions speak for themselves. It also means we don't have to envy other people's relationships—thinking that what they have is better or more special than what we have. This is so important because too many of us think we know what someone else's relationship is like, but the truth is, once we set aside all judgments and perceptions, other relationships can be just as trying and just as challenging as our own. And it's important to remember love means different things to different people. What one of us could deal with in a partner, another of us could never tolerate. That's why it's crucial to put God first in any relationship. It is only when we have the maturity to put Him first that we ultimately end up loving from a place that is sanctified and sacred.

- Verse 5 says love "is not rude or self-seeking, not easily angered, and keeps no record of wrongs." This tells us about "Agape Love," or unconditional love and forgiveness. It teaches us the importance of staying peaceful in our relationships, and moving on from the past. It speaks of forgiveness. How many of us can truly put the past in its place? If more of us could "Let Go and Let God" the divorce rate wouldn't be at an all-time high, nor would the percentages of disdainful, bitter separations between people who at one time claimed to be in love. If we can't move on from the past, there is really no hope of living as a Christian couple.

- Verse 6 tells us "Love does not delight in evil but, rejoices with the truth." Real love will never find joy in someone else's sorrow. Real love is always truthful even when it hurts. Real love requires that each participant be honest with the other, but more important, be honest with themselves. Honesty is not always easy. It requires the often painful process of looking deep within to the darkest parts of ourselves. It requires bringing forth the integrity to stand straight up, faults and all. Love obligates us to make an honest assessment of our wants, needs, and deepest desires.

• In verse 7 it says love "always protects, always trusts, always hopes and always perseveres." True, God-given love shields itself with expectation, always moving forward with hopes for a brighter day. True love never gives up on itself. This is where real love distinguishes itself from unions based on the illusion of love. That illusion can disguise itself in packaging and presentation. Let us love with a heart that is forever open to give and forgive, and a spirit that will never stop trying to let love abide.

• And then there is verse 8, which tells us "Love never fails—But where there are prophecies, they will cease, where there are tongues, they will be stilled; and where there is knowledge, it will pass away." The seasons will change. People in your life will come and go. But we are never to forget that love itself is pure. It is the only thing that offers us the fullness of God, the completeness of His desire for us. True love ought to be a trinity, with God at the helm. We want to express the essence of who we are mentally, physically, and spiritually. Therefore, we ought to search, pray, and use this trinity as a standard bearer when looking for love. If we are blessed, we will find a love that is like the three strands in a strong braid. One strand will represent our intelligence. Another our physical needs. The third will symbolize the spiritual fullness of who we are. God will be the knot that keeps these strands from breaking or coming apart. Always remember: True love cannot fail—pray for God to make you worthy of this kind of spiritual love. Set forth on the long, arduous, inward journey to learn who you are, and what it is you're really looking for.

ANDRIA: *That's been the challenge for me. Truly understanding who I am, with no judgments, no illusions, no justifications, and no excuses. I am certainly clearer now than I have ever been about who I am, and* what that means when it comes to love. I know, for instance, that I'm a communicator. I want, need, and actually love the process of communication. I guess that's why journalism is a good fit for me. I try exceedingly hard to search my heart and then with my mind find the words and actions that represent the deepest part of myself. This is the place from which I love.

I also know now, which I didn't acknowledge in my youth, that I am an extremely affectionate woman. I, like many others, downplayed this side of me for years. But the fact is, it is an essential aspect of my nature, which adds to my completeness. I love to touch. I express myself through touch; whether it's a big adoring hug for my children, or a comforting embrace for a friend in need, I am a person who needs physical contact.

More important, the lens from which I view my relationships is found deep within my Higher self. I am in love with only One. I am in love with God Almighty. I love others, therefore, from a place that permeates my soul. I love spiritually. I love deeply. I love, always acknowledging the Divine, which resides and resonates within my mind and heart. Yes, I love my husband. Yes, I love my children . . . but as I continue to grow in Christ, I strive to love them with the same love that the Almighty has infused in my heart. What kind of love is that? John (God's Word) says in chapter 17 verse 24:

> "FATHER, I WANT THOSE YOU HAVE GIVEN TO ME TO BE WITH ME, TO
> BE WHERE I AM. I WANT THEM TO SEE MY GLORY, WHICH YOU GAVE
> ME BECAUSE YOU LOVED ME BEFORE THE WORLD WAS MADE."
> VERSE 26: "I HAVE MADE YOUR NAME KNOWN TO THEM, AND I
> WILL MAKE IT KNOWN SO THAT THE LOVE YOU HAVE FOR ME WILL BE
> IN THEM AND I WILL BE IN THEM."

What that means for me is that I must continue to love everyone, especially my family, by letting them know of my love for God. Most of us

*have the capacity to love from this place of spiritual elevation. 1 John
3:18 (God's Word):*

> *". . . WE MUST SHOW LOVE THROUGH ACTIONS THAT ARE SINCERE,
> NOT THROUGH EMPTY WORDS."*

*So what we do, we should do in love. What we say, we should say in
love. It takes a conscious effort to do this, for it is easy to fall back into
our own egos. After all, it is human nature to want love with strings attached. If we could only love as God loves us.*

*My aspiration is endeavoring to be this kind of lover, whether it be
a lover to my husband, my children, or my friends. The challenge in love
is finding partners in life who will strive to express this kind of spiritual
love. A love that is nothing less than a blessing from above. Finding a
compatible mate who acknowledges and joyfully feeds the integral
parts of who we are can be found only through prayer, faith, honesty,
and trust. Anything else that comes along, no matter how beautiful or
bountiful or filled with promise, will forever pale in comparison to the
Trinity, which we all deserve.*

THE SPIRIT WITHIN

> ". . . LIVE YOUR LIFE AS YOUR SPIRITUAL NATURE DIRECTS YOU.
> THEN YOU WILL NEVER FOLLOW THROUGH ON WHAT YOUR CORRUPT
> NATURE WANTS. WHAT YOUR CORRUPT NATURE WANTS IS CONTRARY
> TO WHAT YOUR SPIRITUAL NATURE WANTS . . . THEY ARE OPPOSED TO
> EACH OTHER . . . THE SPIRITUAL NATURE PRODUCES LOVE, JOY,
> PEACE, PATIENCE, KINDNESS, GOODNESS, FAITHFULNESS,
> GENTLENESS AND SELF-CONTROL . . ."

> GALATIANS 5:16, 17, 22, 23 (GOD'S WORD)

Men and women have been using their charms to woo and entice
each other since the Garden of Eden. We spend many hours in the
beauty and barber shop, the gym, and, yes, the plastic surgeon's office

trying to remake ourselves into something we think the opposite sex will find attractive. Try as we might, however, none of us stays young forever. Things are going to drop, spread, and roll despite our attempts to stall the effects of time and gravity. This is true for both women and men. If you get caught up in trying to conform to what society says is beautiful you are going to be miserable and depressed at every birthday. It doesn't guarantee success in your love relationships anyway. There are lots of "beautiful" people who can attest to that. We'd be better served spending that time focusing on who it is God wants us to be.

True beauty and charisma come from inside. Like a sweet virus, they affect everyone you come in contact with. All of us know of people who aren't considered physically attractive by society's standards, but they light up a room when they walk in. They're never at a loss for companions and admirers. These people know what we wear on the inside is what others see on the outside. They joyfully let their inner light shine.

Intrinsic beauty can come only from knowing a Higher Power. God's grace surpasses our physical characteristics and our personality traits. The Lord wants to show us what is really important—our souls, and our relationship with Him. When our souls are right, we build relationships based on mutual respect rather than on physical attraction. We learn to love the total being rather than just the way someone looks or makes us feel.

If we base our relationships strictly on physical attraction, we not only lose the chance to get to know our love interest the way God intends us to—as a spiritual being—but we also are not expressing our Love for Christ in the manner in which He seeks. We never get past the outer person to see the inner one.

Sexually transmitted diseases and unwanted pregnancies are just part of the legacy of relationships based on superficial pleasure. The other part is women and men who don't like the people they've become. Their self-esteem is low because they are giving up a major part of themselves and getting little in return. For we can pretend to others that it really didn't matter—that we were just in it for the sex, but we can never quiet our inner voice enough to convince ourselves that our intimate encounters are meaningless.

We know this is not what God wants for us. God wants us to treasure and cherish our bodies—not offer them without merit on casual encounters. Scripture says in *1 Corinthians 6:18 (NIV)*:

"FLEE FROM SEXUAL IMMORALITY. ALL OTHER SINS A MAN COMMITS ARE OUTSIDE HIS BODY, BUT HE WHO SINS SEXUALLY SINS AGAINST HIS OWN BODY."

Why would we knowingly do something to hurt ourselves? We wouldn't if we truly understood the real bond that occurs when two people share of themselves. The hard work really begins when we embark on a much deeper voyage than the trip to sexual freedom. To really understand ourselves as spiritual beings, we must enter into a conversation with God. We then must discipline ourselves to sit and listen for what it is He wants to tell us. It may not be what we want to hear, but it will be what is best for us in the long run.

How do we know what God means for our relationship? If someone special in our life appeals to our physical nature, how do we get them to sing to our souls as well? Where is our help? It is clearly in the Word. Read *Galatians 5:22 and 23 (God's Word)* again:

"THE SPIRITUAL NATURE PRODUCES LOVE, JOY, PEACE, PATIENCE, KINDNESS, GOODNESS, FAITHFULNESS, GENTLENESS AND SELF-CONTROL . . ."

So, living our lives as our spiritual nature directs us results in self-control. We are mind, body, and spirit. We can pursue greater education to develop our minds. We can work out at the gym and strengthen our bodies. But it is when we seek to elevate our spiritual nature that we gain self-control. And it is when we look for a greater understanding of our spiritual selves that we are better prepared to go ahead and live our lives as the Spirit guides us to.

The Word clearly lets us know that our spirit will send up a red flag if we find ourselves involved in a relationship that is not based on the trinity of mind, body, and soul. If we cultivate our spiritual side, we'll see the warning signs. The more we walk in the Spirit, the more we'll be able to resist the desires of the flesh, no matter what those desires are. If they are contrary to the way God wants us to live our lives, Spirit will give us the power to recognize, resist, and rise above them.

WHAT YOU WON'T DO FOR LOVE

"... FOR LOVE IS AS STRONG AS DEATH, ITS JEALOUSY
UNYIELDING AS THE GRAVE ..."

SONG OF SOLOMON 8:6 (NIV)

"Love" sometimes makes us do things that we normally would not do. Love is an emotion of extremes. We can love so deeply that we become blind, or we can love so badly that we become desperate. We do all kinds of things—*in the name of love*. We will make fools out of ourselves. We will lie, cheat, even steal—*in the name of love*. We will give others the power to commit negative or abusive acts against us—*in the name of love*. We will take ourselves through changes that we know are hazardous to our health, our mental stability, our physical wellness, and our spiritual wholeness—all *in the name of love*. Maybe what we need to do when we find ourselves too in love is to pull out one of Diana Ross's old hits, and simply—"*Stop! In the Name of Love*"!

Many of us sink to the depths of desperation when a relationship ends before we want it to end. When it fails we often look for someone to blame. Sometimes we blame ourselves, sometimes we blame others. But we seldom take the time to think that maybe it is a blessing in disguise.

Some of us go to extremes trying to resurrect a failed relationship. We resort to violence, blackmail, stalking—you name it. There are even those who embrace the dark side and start "working roots," casting spells, and doing all kinds of things to get their ex-mate back. But if you've got to go through extraordinary measures to keep a relationship going, maybe you never had it in the first place.

Most of us don't go quite that far. We simply suffer, wondering what we did to deserve the pain we're in, or we burn with jealousy wondering whom our ex-lover is with now. Although we should probably be thanking God for removing someone from our life who didn't need to be there in the first place, when the heart is in pain it is hard to recognize this—much less accept it. This is the time when we are most vulnerable to *real* tragedy. For if we leave an open door into the dark alleys and capillaries where jealousy, envy, and hatred secretly hide, know this one thing: That's all the devil is waiting for—an opening. That's when he will pounce. We're warned about this in *Ephesians 4:27 (NIV):*

"AND DO NOT GIVE THE DEVIL A FOOTHOLD . . . "

In other words, don't give him an opportunity to go to work.

When we're in a state of panic and fear, we are vulnerable to attack. When we've let our spiritual guard down, we then give our own weaknesses the power to emerge, and bring forth the worst of who it is we see in the mirror. When it comes to love, better to give a failed relationship over to God than find yourself wanting someone who doesn't want you—and more important—being unhappy with the person we see in the mirror.

ANDRIA: *If he wants to leave, let him. If she's ready to walk, don't block the door. Who would want to keep someone in their life who doesn't want to be there? And why would anyone seek out dark forces in the name of love? A lot of people say this root stuff is real and it's deep. But*

I'll never for the life of me figure out why anyone would make an appointment with what the old folks call "The root doctor," in order to keep somebody from falling out of love.

The question is does it work, and should we pay any attention to it at all? My theory is the only way it might work is if the spirit is vulnerable and your constitution is weak. Anyway, believe it or not, there are folks who truly do things like taking a lock of hair while someone's sleeping or putting something in someone's food. I know of such a case now, where a young woman, I guess decent enough, is suspected by her friends and enemies of crossing over to the dark side—using spiritual power to negatively manipulate the will of a man she's been with for years. They say she has set out to negatively influence someone else's life.

Anyway, this young woman comes from a matriarchal family where for generations the women are believed to have "worked roots." It seems on numerous occasions she returns back home, usually when she and the man she's living with are having problems. The talk is, she goes back there just to get somebody to work "magic" on this man. A man who is well off, educated, and spiritually weak.

He says he's tired of the relationship, and yet he continues to open his wallet to this woman, buying her everything from new clothes to European vacations. He tells her she's the only one, but she knows he has several other women on the side. He's not exactly an angel, but it seems like every time he finds the strength to move away from her emotionally, she takes a trip back home. Every time he tries to take a few steps forward and away from her, he gets weak both physically and mentally. By the time she comes back, he's changed his mind again and has turned away from those other women, and back toward her. I suppose she loves him, in her own way, but would she necessarily go through such extreme measures if he weren't financing her life? Love is a strange emotion that will make some of us do strange things.

Older black people will tell you the only way to ward off any power *these spells might have on you is to stay strong in the Word. For just as there is good in this world, there is also evil. Don't underestimate it either. It's a force to be aware of and to always keep your eye upon.*

Don't turn your back, pretending the evil one is not of this world, for he is, as are his angels of darkness. Realize if you dabble in powers you know nothing about, you may end up opening one of its dark doors. Yes, we are all children of God, but we don't all choose to serve Him.

STAND BY ME

"AND BE YE KIND ONE TO ANOTHER, TENDERHEARTED, FORGIVING ONE ANOTHER EVEN AS GOD, FOR CHRIST'S SAKE HATH FORGIVEN YOU."

EPHESIANS 4:32 (KJV)

Don't you get tired of reading about the conflict between African-American men and women? Doesn't it get old hearing that sisters have little or no statistical chance of finding a suitable mate for a variety of reasons? Brothers are told that black women will not respect and support them in their endeavors. Sisters are told black men are threatened by their success, and will never love them the way a secure man is supposed to love a woman. We can buy into the negativity or we can accept our reality. We all know there are benefits and burdens with everything in life, including love, but the truth of the matter is we've been loving and supporting each other for centuries. Most of the time all we have is each other.

Relationships are hard for all people, black, white, yellow, or brown. And yes, we do carry the extra baggage of racism, but we also carry the familiarity of our culture. When our men say, "Baby, it's cold outside," we know they are not talking about the weather. When we tell them "Don't go there," they know we are not talking about a trip or a journey. And, if either one of us says, "I'm sticking with you, baby, like white on rice," the other knows there is someone who's going to be there if the going gets rough. Our brand of loving has always been unique. It has always been strong.

Let's be smart enough and strong enough to acknowledge the vast potential of what love can bring, and stop fantasizing about dream relationships. Love shouldn't feel forced, but know that it does require hard work. What does it truly mean to be with someone for better or worse? What does it really mean to call forth the kind of love that only God can give? It requires acceptance and generosity.

There is much to learn about loving. Even more to learn about how we ourselves love. When we acknowledge the sanctity of this emotion, and then define it for ourselves, we begin to see just how vital a role love plays in our lives. We all need to express love, and to receive it. *First Corinthians 13:1* points out:

> IF WE DON'T HAVE LOVE, WE ARE NOTHING MORE THAN
> LOUD GONGS OR CLASHING CYMBALS.

In other words—if we don't have love, we go through life making lots of noise, but never really making music.

Let life strike up the band! Let's commit right now to reach for complete love, where we are quenched and fed in ways that truly honor who we are. Often, we simply accept what is offered at the time. We accept something *less than*, or we accept the fact that we will never find what we're looking for. It's important to be able to identify *real* love, wait for that love, and then receive the love God has preordained for each one of us. This is the kind of love we want to accept for ourselves and teach others who are awaiting a blessing of the heart.

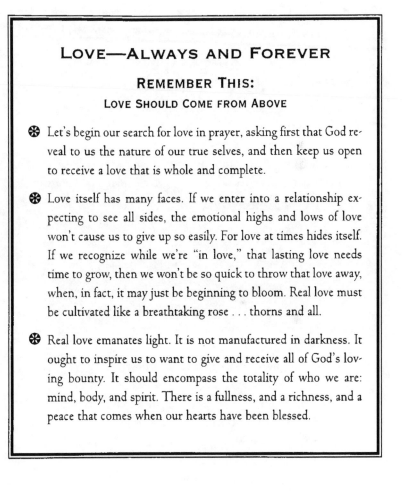

LOVE—ALWAYS AND FOREVER

REMEMBER THIS:
LOVE SHOULD COME FROM ABOVE

❀ Let's begin our search for love in prayer, asking first that God reveal to us the nature of our true selves, and then keep us open to receive a love that is whole and complete.

❀ Love itself has many faces. If we enter into a relationship expecting to see all sides, the emotional highs and lows of love won't cause us to give up so easily. For love at times hides itself. If we recognize while we're "in love," that lasting love needs time to grow, then we won't be so quick to throw that love away, when, in fact, it may just be beginning to bloom. Real love must be cultivated like a breathtaking rose . . . thorns and all.

❀ Real love emanates light. It is not manufactured in darkness. It ought to inspire us to want to give and receive all of God's loving bounty. It should encompass the totality of who we are: mind, body, and spirit. There is a fullness, and a richness, and a peace that comes when our hearts have been blessed.

LOVE—ALWAYS AND FOREVER

PRAY FOR THIS:

PRAY FOR DIVINE LOVE

Thank you, God, for the love in my life. For the love which comes from another person and for the love that grows from deep inside myself. Whether it is here now or awaiting. If it's on the way, then let me hold on to the faith that it will come—that I deserve the best love has to offer. If it is here now, let me nourish it, and have the patience to wait a little while longer, for love to bloom.

A PRAYER FOR ROMANTIC FULFILLMENT:

Dear Lord, please give comfort, as only you can,
to my longing heart.
Give me spiritual nourishment to feed the hungers within me.
Let my spirit be stronger than my flesh.
Give me the strength to wait for the love
You will send my way.
Give me knowledge so that I might know such love
when it is placed before me.
I will accept it as it is offered, because although
I know my wants,
You know my needs.
Thank You, Lord, for granting me anticipation for Love.
Please continue to fill my days with hope, as I carry
on the business of Your Kingdom,
while awaiting the love I seek.
I will wait on You, Dear God, Thank You for the
blessing that is to come.
Amen.

CHAPTER SEVEN

Marriage—For Better or Worse

"BUT EVERY HUSBAND MUST LOVE HIS WIFE AS HE LOVES HIMSELF, AND WIVES SHOULD RESPECT THEIR HUSBANDS."

EPHESIANS 5:33 (GOD'S WORD)

Just as with the love you feel for your children, the wonderful thing about marriage (if it has been sanctioned from above) is, if you put God first—are truly committed and extremely patient—love will grow to be unconditional and stand the test of time. It will also, and sometimes often, be tested.

One of the trials we consistently put our marriages through is, we judge them by a standard of loving that is not of God, but of man. We romanticize marriage based on the relationships we think our friends have with their spouses. Or maybe it comes from some warped sense that love should be the way it is in a romance novel. The truth is: Love is rarely like that, if ever at all. Is it possible? Yes, if God gives it to you. Is it probable? No. Why? Too many of us fail to put God first before we say "I do." That doesn't mean, however, that our marriages can't be nurtured into a divine place from which to love.

Complete love draws its fullness from the ideal. The ideal is the kind of love Christ has for us. Count yourself fortunate if you have found a partner who speaks to your body, mind, *and* soul. A partner with whom you share an intuitive ability to love and be loved. If you pray in earnest to the Master to orchestrate that kind of love in your life, it will crescendo with an exact pitch that utters sweet music that only you and your beloved one can hear.

Considering that some of us enter into our spirituality long after we've spoken our vows, it's a miracle that God keeps so many of our marriages together in the first place. When we haven't really put God first, we usually end up trying to find the things within our marriage that we should have found within ourselves *before* the marriage. Things like peace, harmony, and total acceptance. Our marriages today will continue to be stressed and vulnerable if we forget about God. Bottom line: If you want a whole and fulfilling marriage, bring God into the equation immediately. Because in the thick of life itself—the job, the kids, the mortgage, the bills, whatever—it's almost inevitable to focus not on what you have in your marriage, but rather on what you feel you lack.

When you're frustrated, coming up with an image of a more perfect partner is easy. But have you ever stopped to count the blessings that your spouse brings into your life, just the way he or she is? Of course, it's hard to stay focused on this when you're trying to find your own place in the world. Then your spouse may seem like yet one more person making demands on your time and energy. And, as you struggle to balance, trying to meet the needs of your family, you may wonder to yourself: Who is meeting *my* needs? Who is taking care of *me?*

But you see, a large part of finding peace once you're married is giving up the notion that someone else is responsible for your happiness. True, the person you marry should have a deep and abiding concern for your well-being, but he/she shouldn't carry the weight of making *you* happy. Only you can do that.

Too often we burden our husband or wife with the responsibility of fulfilling our every want, our every need; we accept no responsibility for accomplishing these things on our own. That's ridiculous! If you want abundance, go out and find it. If you want a more meaning-ful career—ask the Lord to reveal your calling. If you want a fulfilling home life—invite God inside, for only He can bring you joy that is unspeakable. A husband or a wife cannot do that for you. And once you've found that inner joy, it's much easier to recognize the joy that others bring you and the price you must pay to keep it.

ANDRIA: *Marriage is hard. Once you ride out the honeymoon phase, reality crashes down and you see that nothing about compromise is easy. And that's what marriage is: compromise every day. You get tired of chicken, he gets upset when you make beef. You like to go out when it's just the two of you, he always wants to invite another couple. You think you should dress the kids warmly in the winter, he thinks you're layering just a little too much. Little things? Not necessarily. On any given day, week, month, or period in your marriage, when one of you is more stressed out than the other, these little things can lead to major explosions.*

Flashback: First day of school a few years ago. Granted, I was tired, he was working like a dog, and just as I always do, I bought my daugh-ter's school shoes one size too big. I mean the girl's feet grow like corn stalks and I was not about to buy new shoes in a month. So here we are, 7:30 A.M., and she tells me her shoes are slipping off her feet. Being the resourceful mother that I am, I simply put two pair of socks on her. Matching her outfit perfectly I might add. My husband comes down the hallway, checks her out head to toe, and has a fit! "What's this girl got on? It's seventy degrees outside, and you've got two pair of socks on her." I explain, her shoes were slipping a bit, so the solution (at what's now 7:45 A.M.) was clearly to put two pairs of socks on. What was I go-ing to do, go back to the store at that very moment?

Well, honey, right there in the hallway, before breakfast, before my coffee, before all the kids, he and I practically got into a knock down–drag out fight. *He was yelling, I was screaming, the kids were crying, and then, all of a sudden, we stopped, got out of each other's face, and walked away. We realized this argument had nothing to do with two pairs of socks, but everything to do with the fact that we hadn't spent any time alone together in more than a month. I don't remember who made up first, but I'm glad we didn't let it go any further. It's important to be able to say you're sorry, even over the little things. And it's important to realize when something is getting out of hand.*

By the way, she went to school with two pairs of socks. He compromised that day, but I probably compromised about something else the next. The real key is not to compromise so much of yourself that you lose yourself or the love you vowed to keep.

A NOBLE MARRIAGE

"A WIFE OF NOBLE CHARACTER WHO CAN FIND? SHE IS WORTH FAR MORE THAN RUBIES. HER HUSBAND HAS FULL CONFIDENCE IN HER AND LACKS NOTHING OF VALUE."

PROVERBS 31:10–11 (NIV)

What's wrong with aspiring to achieve a noble marriage? After all, tradition has its place. Granted, we know the elements of matrimony have changed: Mom works and may be the primary breadwinner, Dad is expected to wash the dishes and change the diapers, Grandma and Granddad may live miles away and are busy with their own lives, but many of us still long for convention. Call it societal training, or wishful thinking, but we sometimes hold on to those visions of tradition: A father who is the primary provider for the family; a strong and supportive wife and mother; grandparents, cousins, aunts, and uncles who live near and can provide the family with a support base, and built-in baby-sitters. It is, of course, a dream for many married couples who face a reality far from that. So what do we do? How do we cope?

What happens all too often is that we sabotage the success we might have in marriage. We nag our spouse to death, trying to fit him/her into this little dream we've created for ourselves, instead of altering that dream a little to reflect the reality of relationships today. Newsflash!!! There are no "white knights," or "saints" for that matter. No man is going to rescue us. No woman is going to put her life completely on hold, and if she does she'll resent the marriage. More and more rare in families today is this thing called a single breadwinner. For the most part, it takes two incomes to make ends meet. And June Cleaver was never real! She was a TV sitcom character! Just as it was years ago, today each partner must work to keep the marriage together.

Happiness? Well, we will always strive for that, but we need to be realistic about what happiness is. It's not about the house or the car or the country club membership. It's about finding someone who is on your team no matter what. It's about giving to that person, as well as being willing to take. And oftentimes, marital bliss never enters the equation. For there are moments in a marriage when all that keeps you together is the commitment. The fact that you took an oath, and said "I do."

Lord knows it's not easy. You have a much stronger chance of making it, however, if you put God in charge of the relationship and learn what it takes to be a real husband or be a real wife.

ANDRIA: *I've been with my husband for more than half my life. Believe me, we still have our ups and downs. Times of pure joy, and then fleeting moments when it's difficult to remember why we got together in the first place.*

In the beginning of our marriage, I was into speaking my mind always and doing my thing, often with little regard for my role as wife. I thought that whole concept was something from my grandmother's era. I was extremely independent and didn't think too much about what I was supposed to be doing as a wife. I gave no thought to my responsibilities or obligations. I have matured since then.

We sisters need to confer with those in our families who've stuck it out, and are not included in the grim statistics of the divorce rate. And we need to talk candidly with our relatives who didn't stay married. They have a lot to teach us. We should also refer to the Word. The Bible clearly and quite specifically talks about marriage, and the role of a good wife. Ephesians 5:22 (God's Word):

> *"WIVES, PLACE YOURSELVES UNDER YOUR HUSBAND'S AUTHORITY AS*
> *YOU HAVE PLACED YOURSELVES UNDER THE LORD'S AUTHORITY."*

But don't start throwing this book down yet, for it goes on to say: 5:25 (God's Word):

> *"HUSBANDS, LOVE YOUR WIVES AS CHRIST LOVED THE CHURCH*
> *AND GAVE HIS LIFE FOR IT."*

Sometimes we oh-so-independent, professional, "I'm Every Woman" women need to fall back into that role for the sake of letting our men be men. Society tries to take that from them. We ought not assist. If we are always so busy taking charge and voicing our opinions (nagging!!!), then our men can't give us the very thing we say we want. I have come to understand, sometimes there is great strength in silence.

We spend a lot of time thinking about the qualities we want in a spouse, but we don't think about our own qualifications for being a good wife or husband. What are we bringing to the table? Are we ready to put our past behind and assume the role? Or is it that we want to straddle the fence; part of us wants to be a devoted spouse and the other part wants to be single with all the independence that entails. But we can't have it both ways.

One element that is necessary for a successful marriage is an opportunity for both husband and wife to have the freedom to be all they can be—within the commitment of loving each other. If we focus on that, then we're less likely to concentrate on what we see as our spouse's shortcomings. We will be more likely to examine our own behavior. We may complain about her hanging out with her friends, but if we're honest maybe we don't want to come home on Friday nights either. We may constantly belittle him for not making enough money, but then we'll own up to our own reckless spending habits. We may lament that she is not as carefree and as much fun as she was prior to marriage, but we'll also rejoice and appreciate that she takes seriously her role as wife and mother.

Scripture tells us in *Matthew 7:3–5 (NIV)*:

"WHY DO YOU LOOK AT THE SPECK OF SAWDUST IN YOUR BROTHER'S EYE AND PAY NO ATTENTION TO THE PLANK IN YOUR OWN EYE? HOW CAN YOU SAY TO YOUR BROTHER, 'LET ME TAKE THE SPECK OUT OF YOUR EYE,' WHEN ALL THE TIME THERE IS A PLANK IN YOUR OWN EYE? YOU HYPOCRITE, FIRST TAKE THE PLANK OUT OF YOUR OWN EYE, AND THEN YOU WILL SEE CLEARLY TO REMOVE THE SPECK FROM YOUR BROTHER'S EYE."

Let's shine the light back in our own faces, and in our own lives. Let's face our marriages with an attitude of gratitude, lifting them up, instead of tearing them down. Let's strive to reach marital maturity, seeing the riches and responsibilities of each blessed day together.

LINNIE: *It wasn't until my early thirties that I reached the maturity required for marriage—I was finally ready! Some people are ready in their early twenties, but not me. I must say, I'm glad I waited. I don't feel as though I missed out on anything. I enjoyed being single, and now I enjoy being married.*

The most important decision for me concerning marriage, the one the Lord led me to, was to marry for love. I had thought marrying for love was a gamble because of the vulnerability it entails. I looked at all the marriages around me and most seemed to be in shambles. I thought of all the women I knew who were going around trying to project the image of marital bliss, when in reality either they or their husbands were very unhappy. I thought of all the divorces even among what had appeared to be solid marriages. Yet, with all of this, I realized that I had to go into marriage in love and with the expectation it would last forever. I realized that marriage was more than just a piece of paper—it's a holy union—what God has joined together.

I knew right away when I met the man who was to become my husband (even though it took him a few more months to figure it out). I knew then as I know now that he was God's answer to my prayers. You see I knew that the man whom I married would be different from the guys I had dated. The traits that had attracted me to men as a young, single woman (impulsive, fun-seeking, noncommittal) were not the ones I wanted in a husband.

But also, I had some growing up to do. I had to realize what was really important in life—that a quiet night at home watching a movie could be just as enjoyable as a night out on the town. I had to be prepared to put my husband before the demands of the outside world—job, friends, family. I had to strip away layers of veneer in order to show my true self to the man I married—I couldn't pretend I was somebody I wasn't. I did all this and more with no regrets.

In return I got the husband and the marriage I wanted. My husband is the head of our house, and I must admit he handles it well. This does not mean that I can't take care of myself or a family or that my husband is more intelligent than I am. I spent plenty of years taking care of myself and I think I did a good job. I am capable of supporting a family and making the appropriate decisions, but he is the head of this family. He is the ultimate decision maker and protector of the family. It has nothing to do with income or household responsibilities. It's more a matter of leadership. It is very important to me that our son understands our family's hierarchy and respects his father's role.

But even though I wanted a traditional marriage, marriage itself still took some getting used to. After being single for many years it was not always easy to adjust to sharing life so intimately with someone else. And yes there are times even today when I wake up, look over at him snoring loudly next to me, and wonder "Who is he and what is he doing here? And, more important, what am I doing here???"

I've come to accept that I'll never change him and I know he knows he'll never change me. He's never going to empty the kitchen trash can before it overflows or stop being a packrat (he saves empty cereal boxes), and I'm never going to remember to turn off the lights when I leave a room or that he's allergic to cheese (thank goodness his allergy's not life-threatening—I would've killed him by now).

But even with his "shortcomings" and my "perfections," I know that we are good together. I don't take it for granted. Marriage, like every-thing in life, is day to day, month to month, year to year. You work on it, you reassess, and you work some more. But the commitment should be forever.

KEEPING THE HOME FIRES BURNING

"LET THY FOUNTAIN BE BLESSED; AND REJOICE WITH THE WIFE OF THY YOUTH. LET HER BE AS THE LOVING HIND AND PLEASANT ROE; LET HER BREASTS SATISFY THEE AT ALL TIMES; AND BE THOU RAVISHED ALWAYS WITH HER LOVE."

PROVERBS 5:18–19 (KJV)

Your relationship with your husband or wife differs from your re-lationship with your *man* or your *woman*. If you are lucky, your spouse will be your *man* or your *woman* (by this we mean the one who ignites your passions). If not, you may need to work on rekindling the sparks. The key word here is rekindling. You cannot rekindle a fire that never burned. You must have passion for the person you intend to marry. You must work to keep the passion alive once you are married. It's a fact that during the course of a marriage that passion is likely to wane, sometimes to the point of a vague memory, but if it wasn't there from the beginning, you have no hope of finding it.

Chances are the relationship will change once you're married and your needs may not be met quite as easily. Neither may your spouse's. But together the two of you should stay the course. One way to avoid complacency in marriage is to put God first and consistently make an effort to nurture yourself and your relationship with your spouse. Regularly spend time together in the presence of God, asking that He order your steps, guide your hearts, and bless your union. Try the following:

- **Spend Time Alone with Your Spouse.** You may have to get away from the hassles of daily living to remember what it is that attracted you to each other in the first place. This may mean an actual getaway to a cabin or hotel room, or it could be as simple as keeping kids, toys, and other disturbances out of your bedroom and retreating behind closed doors for a while.

- **Spend Time Alone with Yourself.** Getting away by yourself may provide the clarity you need to appreciate your spouse and your marriage. Here's a recommendation. Carve out some time for distance. We're not talking about moving back in with your mother so you can "find yourself." If that's what you need, that's another chapter in another book. We mean work things out so you can either take a vacation by yourself, or at the very least take a day and night away from home to be alone. Get away from the kids. Get away from the demands of work. Get away from the familiar lug who lies next to you snoring at night. Get away and just be with yourself and the Lord. If you can make this more than a catch up on your sleep session, and really consciously focus on what is right in the relationship rather than on what's wrong . . . magic will happen. You'll find yourself shifting your perspective and placing your relationship in a much more positive light than is ever possible when you're at home, caught up in the daily routine. Then, add to these verbal celebrations when you're alone. As you meditate on the positive, write these attributes down. You'll remember why you married the person in the first place.

- **Don't Compare Your Spouse to Others.** You never know a person until you've lived with him or her, and no matter how great other people seem, their clothes still get dirty and need washing, there's something around the house they either can't or won't fix, and who knows what a person is like when that individual is sick or tired? It's important not to compare our spouses to our mothers and fathers (my momma can cook better than she can; my daddy always knew how to fix a leaky faucet!); our sisters and brothers (my sister knows how to act like a lady; why can't you fight my battles the way my brother did?); our bosses (she respects my opinion more than you do); our friend's spouse (you never send me flowers the way her husband does); our children (they love me more than you do); and, every other person we know of—from athletes and movie stars to all the people we used to date. It's important to remember that our spouse is the person we married, and the only person who made a permanent commitment to us.

- **Keep Your Marriage Private.** Don't tell your friends, your parents, or even your siblings about the inner workings of your marriage. If you do, at some time or another your friends will get envious, your parents will get mad, and your siblings just might get even. Keep your business to yourself. Some people will share even the most intimate details of their marriage with friends and family. Then, long after you two have made up and moved on, they still remember. You have to be very careful whom you confide in. Even those who you think are qualified to counsel you may have ulterior motives or bad advice. Your best bet: Only talk to God about your relationship with your spouse. If you need professional help, ask God to guide you to a spiritual counselor.

- **Put Your Spouse Before Your Children.** We know that your child is part of you and your spouse is just some person you met and married, but it is the marital relationship that is the foundation of the family. One day your children will grow up and leave the nest (if you do your job right), but your spouse will be there forever.

- **Put God Before Everything.** A successful marriage is one where both parties know the requirements of true love. It takes an unending commitment to those things of the heart which drew you one to the other. A blessed marriage, one that will sustain the ravages of heartache, trouble, doubt, and disappointment, is one where love abides. *Luke 10:27 (KJV)* answers the question of how we might inherit eternal life. A blueprint for how our marriage might sustain the test of time. There Jesus answered,

" 'THOU SHALT LOVE THE LORD THY GOD WITH ALL THY HEART, AND WITH ALL THY SOUL, AND WITH ALL THY STRENGTH, AND WITH ALL THY MIND; AND THY NEIGHBOR AS THYSELF.' "

We are to love the Lord first and at least love our spouses as much as we love ourselves. If we put the Divine in charge of all our relationships, then they have no other option but to thrive, survive, and sustain us with pure love.

INFIDELITY

"NOW IT IS REQUIRED THAT THOSE WHO HAVE BEEN GIVEN A TRUST MUST PROVE FAITHFUL."

1 CORINTHIANS 4:2 (NIV)

Nothing can make us angrier than infidelity. Infidelity can make a person riled regardless of whether he or she is married. As a matter of fact, some married folk accept that their spouses play around and aren't bothered by their flings. (They just don't want to know about them!) Whereas, some single people who've dated a person for only a few months are deeply devastated by a mate's betrayal. It's a matter of the level of commitment, and of course the level of trust, as well as personal preference.

Today, we all seem to be a lot more passive when it comes to dealing with infidelity. Some women allow their men to convince them that they don't see what's right before their eyes—"Even though he has a house, a bank account, and a baby with that woman there is nothing going on between them." Yeah, right! And it goes both ways. There are a lot of blind men out there who think they know their wives, but don't really want to see what their wives are doing.

Why do women and men end up in bed with someone who is not their spouse? A wife doesn't want to admit to an unfulfilling marriage, and instead chooses to try and find joy and completion with another man. A husband has a woman on the sly, but can't walk away from the material trappings and comfort of his marriage. When we break our marriage vows, we break them for a number of reasons. Sometimes infidelity messes up a good thing, other times it serves only as one symptom of a failed union.

We know marriage is sacred, so we try to honor the commitment to our spouses and to the vows we made. It is possible, however, that in the course of a marriage we might be tempted. When we think of all we could lose for a moment of passion, we sometimes realize the price is too much to bear. That is what keeps us faithful. We're all familiar with one of the Ten Commandments found in *Exodus 20:14 (KJV)*:

"THOU SHALT NOT COMMIT ADULTERY."

But the Word also warns us in *Mark 14:38 (NAS)*:

"   THE SPIRIT IS WILLING, BUT THE FLESH IS WEAK."

It is, however, in *Ephesians 5:28 (NIV)* where we find guidance:

"HUSBANDS OUGHT TO LOVE THEIR WIVES AS THEIR OWN BODIES.
HE WHO LOVES HIS WIFE LOVES HIMSELF."

Love's what we ought to hold on to, especially in the face of temptation. We should pray for the fortitude to turn away because we do not want to hurt God, our spouses, or our children. By holding in our hearts and minds the Word, we strive to remain true.

ANDRIA: *You find someone you love. Someone you trust. Someone you're committed to building a life with, and then, just as you're busy building that life, the unexpected happens. You find out there's another woman, or maybe he finds out there's been another man.*

I have a girlfriend who tells me she'd forgive her husband if he was just "fooling around" but, if he actually went off and fell in love, well, that, she says, would be difficult to accept and put behind her.

Why? Is it that as sexual creatures, we can deal with the fact that we will one day find ourselves attracted to someone other than our spouse, but as romantics we can't handle the competition of another "love"? It would be impossible to define what we thought we had with our significant other if we had to accept the fact that the very essence of the relationship, the love, was somehow lacking. Void enough to make room for another?

I've had many a conversation about this very topic with female friends and male friends who want to come to terms with the whole concept of monogamy. The questions are many. Are we so one dimensional that we only have room enough in our hearts to let just one enter? Are we supposed to be so blinded by love that we never look at another in that special way? Are we really expected to find such completeness in the one we exchanged rings with that we never hunger or thirst in areas that go unfed?

I'm married and I still don't have any simple answers to these questions. I do, however, have a greater understanding of the commitment of marriage . . . of the vows we stand and speak before God. I understand that sometimes we have to forsake that which our human selves desire, and lift up that which our spiritual selves know to be acceptable in the sight of man and God. No one wants to be the "other," which means that we each have to commit to the person we're with during the good times and the bad, and pray for the strength to live that commitment even in the midst of marital hardship.

If we can stick it out, if we can ride the tide and stay committed to the commitment of marriage, we then give ourselves the benefit, even through the roughest of times, of assessing the strength of our relationship—a relationship that should be based on honesty, to ourselves and to one another. We need to really look at who we are, our wants and our needs. Own up to them, and then assess whether or not our significant other has the capacity to allow us the freedom to express who we are. Too often, we give up, run off, and search for someone who we think will make us happy. But then we might end up in the same situation all over again. Happiness really occurs by knowing your innermost self. By listening to God within, we seek to understand what happiness is for us.

Fulfillment is more likely in a marriage that allows you the freedom to express yourself in ways that honor who you are. This need for personal liberation is a cornerstone in a loving relationship—one that gives us the strength to hang in there knowing that whatever the challenge, this too shall pass. But if we are in a marriage that binds the very essence of our individual expression, eventually love itself requires that we look the relationship squarely in the face and then decide if hanging in there will ultimately strengthen us and the love we hope to have.

MAY THE CIRCLE BE UNBROKEN

"WHAT THEREFORE GOD HATH JOINED TOGETHER,
LET NOT MAN PUT ASUNDER."

MARK 10:9 (KJV)

Now, we're not suggesting that everyone who's married is with the right person. Some of us make grave mistakes during the selection process. Then, when we find ourselves trapped in a bad marriage with no way out, we close our eyes to our own desperation, and enter the land of denial. We choose to ignore the warning signs, and there are *always* signs. Maybe he is abusive and unfaithful. Maybe she is not emotionally mature enough to handle the responsibilities of marriage and parenthood. Maybe he really wants to be with another man. Or, maybe she's just not right for him, and he's not right for her either.

So what are the qualities you should look for in a potential partner and expect from a spouse?

- **Mutual Respect.** Each partner has to respect the other's time, talents, and thoughts. Your partner should not belittle you or take you for granted. Respect should be shown, not just when others are present, but even when it's just the two of you. A person who hits you or talks badly to you does not respect you. A partner who always keeps you waiting or constantly puts his or her needs before your own, does not respect you. And a mate who puts down or diminishes your talents and accomplishments does not respect you.
- **Similar Morals and Values.** Partners should share a common sense of what's right and what's wrong. It may be tempting to overlook a partner's moral indiscretions, but eventually it will eat away at the marriage. If children are involved, it becomes even more important for spouses to share values, since parents are responsible for teaching morals and values to their offspring. A partner who breaks the law—either man's laws or God's laws—is going to bring stress and strain to the marriage.
- **Support.** Partners should support each other 100 percent, whether it's physical, material, or spiritual support. This is possible only if there are mutual respect and similar values in the marriage. Spouses can and will disagree on things, but once a compromise is reached,

both partners should lend their full support. Be it disciplining their children, starting a business, or tackling some obstacle from the outside world, spouses need to present a united front. If your spouse does not unite with you, you are not married in the true sense of the word. In the Gospel According to Matthew, Jesus speaks of marriage, saying:

" 'FOR THIS REASON A MAN WILL LEAVE HIS FATHER AND MOTHER AND BE UNITED TO HIS WIFE, AND THE TWO WILL BECOME ONE FLESH. SO THEY ARE NO LONGER TWO, BUT ONE . . ' "

MATTHEW 19:5–6 (NIV)

- **Shared Beliefs.** It goes without saying that partners should share a belief in God, in the power of prayer, and in the importance of faith. But, those of you married to nonbelievers, or fence-straddlers, take heart. Scripture tells us in *1 Corinthians 7:14–15 (NIV)*:

"FOR THE UNBELIEVING HUSBAND HAS BEEN SANCTIFIED THROUGH HIS WIFE, AND THE UNBELIEVING WIFE HAS BEEN SANCTIFIED THROUGH HER BELIEVING HUSBAND. OTHERWISE YOUR CHILDREN WOULD BE UNCLEAN, BUT AS IT IS, THEY ARE HOLY. BUT IF THE UNBELIEVER LEAVES, LET HIM DO SO. A BELIEVING MAN OR WOMAN IS NOT BOUND IN SUCH CIRCUMSTANCES; GOD HAS CALLED US TO LIVE IN PEACE."

So where do you draw the line? How much of yourself do you give to a marriage that doesn't seem to be nurturing you or your mate? Maybe it's time to go when standing by your spouse becomes detrimental to your health and well-being. While we marry until *death do us part*, we are not expected to stay in marriages that are killing us, either literally, figuratively, or spiritually.

No matter what, always put God first. Seek His advice before making any decisions about your marriage. It requires prayer and faith to know when a marriage is salvageable and when it's not. Some will tell you to give up and get to stepping. Others will tell you to hang in there at all costs. But only God can tell you what to do. But if you do seek the advice of another, make sure it is with someone whom you trust, and know has your best interest at heart. Talk to those who will be quick to love, and slow to judge.

Above all else, as it is written in *1 Thessalonians 5:17 (KJV)*:

> "PRAY WITHOUT CEASING."

Listen to that voice within and let it guide you. Know that God will comfort and protect you whatever decision you make. He will make a way.

A PARENT'S ADVICE

"APPLY THINE HEART UNTO INSTRUCTION, AND THINE EARS TO THE WORDS OF KNOWLEDGE."

PROVERBS 23:12 (KJV)

Our perspective on marriage is often shaped by our parents' views and opinions. Sometimes we end up repeating our parents' marriage. We may seek the same type of man our mother sought. We may expect our husband to be like our father. We seldom realize just how much our parents' ideas about marriage shape our own convictions until years later we remember what they said. Staying ever aware of the influences our parents have on us helps us keep all of it in perspective.

ANDRIA: Advice My Father Gave Me About Marriage

We know that money can either make life easier or more difficult. It is the same within a marriage. My father gave me and my college girl-friends a bit of advice a long time ago that I'm convinced has helped me sustain my marriage to this day. He told us, "No matter how in love you fall, no matter how much togetherness you want in your relationship, no matter how much you share with your man . . . always, always have your own money."

Having money can sour a marriage to the point of illusion, so you imagine the union is better than it is. Not having money can sour a marriage to the point of divorce. That's why my father said to make sure I always had my own bank account. That way I wouldn't be looking for my husband to dig into his pockets every time I wanted something for myself. And I would have the financial security to do what I needed to do, when I needed to do it.

1 Timothy 6:10 (KJV) warns us,

"THE LOVE OF MONEY IS THE ROOT OF ALL EVIL,"

so why give it any authority over your relationship? One way to devalue the role money can play in a loving relationship is by lessening the need to constantly have to justify its use. My advice: keep a joint bank account that takes care of all the bills you incur together. But also have your own account. Just like you have a life together, you also are two individuals, separate and apart from one another. I think it puts a strain on your relationship when you give money more power than it deserves.

Keep money in its proper perspective. It's nice when you have it, but not necessary for love. If you each contribute fairly to taking care of the priorities (saving money and paying bills), then what else is there to talk about? Deal with your own money and be generous and trusting enough to let him deal with his.

LINNIE: Advice My Mother Gave Me About Marriage

It wasn't so much what she did say as what she didn't say that I appreciate. You see, my mother never told me I had to get married. I know of women whose parents sent them to college to find a husband—the old M.R.S. degree. But my mother wanted more for me. She encouraged me to build a life for myself before getting married.

Some women think the highest honor their daughters can attain is being some man's wife. Some mothers start dreaming of their daughter's wedding when she is still in preschool. Not my mom. She was not negative about marriage, she just didn't see it as the be-all and end-all for her daughter. "Travel," she'd tell me, "enjoy life, you've got plenty of time to settle down."

Even when I turned thirty, that age where most parents start to freak out if their daughters aren't married, my mother still didn't quiz me about my marriage prospects. I think if I had told my mother I would never marry she would have accepted it.

But there was one thing my mother did make clear to me—not to have a child out of wedlock. She would not give in on this issue. Her stance was the same when I was thirty as it was when I was fifteen—don't bring a baby into the world unless you're married. I gave birth fifteen months after my wedding. To my mom this was still cutting it close!

So to whom do we listen when we seek advice on marriage? Our parents? Our friends? Our ministers? Our therapists? While they all may have our best interests at heart, they are not, and should not, be part of our marriage. But God is. If we have listened, God has led us to the right man or woman for us. If not, only God can help to make the situation right.

We join together as a couple to serve God and build a family. We stand together against the outside world. We move through life in unity, letting God prepare our way. We go to the Word, which says in *Mark 10:8 (NIV):*

" . . AND THE TWO WILL BECOME ONE FLESH. SO THEY ARE NO LONGER TWO, BUT ONE."

MARRIAGE—FOR BETTER OR WORSE

REMEMBER THIS

✸ Marriage is compromise every day. So pick and choose your battles with your beloved. Not everything needs to be an issue on which you stake your relationship. Like a mighty oak, learn when to stand firm, and when to bend. And never stake your inner happiness on anyone else. Ultimately, it is your relationship with God that brings you joy. Therefore, do not burden your spouse with the responsibility of meeting your every need.

✸ Examine the lens through which you view your marriage. Is it from a perspective of gratitude and abundance, or presumption and lack? As a marital exercise, make a commitment to concentrate on your spouse's strengths rather than on his or her shortcomings. Start by doing this three days a week and then proceed from there. Examine your own shortcomings in an ongoing effort to achieve harmony.

✸ Turning to others for advice or romantic fulfillment can be dangerous. It can lead to outside judgments or influences. Instead, carve out special time on a regular basis for you and your spouse. Just as you need to feed your body food to maintain a balanced diet, your relationship needs quality and uninterrupted time to stay strong against the distractions of the world.

MARRIAGE—FOR BETTER OR WORSE

PRAY FOR THIS:

LORD, IF IT BE THY WILL, LET THIS MARRIAGE THRIVE.

We only want a relationship the Lord wants us to have. Pray for a sound marriage, one that will survive the ravages of attack, and the grim statistics of divorce. Pray for peace together or apart.

❀

THE MATRIMONIAL PRAYER

Lord, I want this man so much. I want only to feel his touch.
I want to savor his love. I freely offer him mine.
Only if Your eyes are smiling on this union will we each
know the Divine.
Two becoming one is my prayer. Only with Your blessings
can this marriage work. Protect us
from any darkness which might lurk.
Only through Your guidance can we find completeness.

Me with him—him with me—and us with Thee.
Please, God, show me how to be the woman he seeks.
Teach him how to fulfill my needs. Let this union
stand strong.
Keep us from temptation, keep us from harm. Lord, feed me
where he cannot. Nourish his
manhood so that he goes not without.
Only You can heal the holes. Please, dear God,
bless our souls.
Keep me true to him, and him to me. Forgive us both our
selfish inequities. Make this
marriage sacred. Make this marriage sound.
Help us to learn forgiveness. Help us to put the past behind.
And if it pleases You, dear Lord, use us for Your service.
We thank You for joining what no man can put asunder.
Thank You for bringing us one to the other.
And if it be Your will, please keep us together until such time
when You say so. Lord, bring us great joy and do,
Lord . . . let love abide. Amen.

CHAPTER EIGHT

Children and Parenthood

"SUFFER THE LITTLE CHILDREN TO COME UNTO ME, AND
FORBID THEM NOT; FOR SUCH IS THE KINGDOM OF GOD.
VERILY I SAY UNTO YOU, WHOSOEVER SHALL NOT
RECEIVE THE KINGDOM OF GOD AS A LITTLE CHILD, HE
SHALL NOT ENTER THEREIN. AND HE TOOK THEM UP IN
HIS ARMS, PUT HIS HANDS UPON THEM,
AND BLESSED THEM."

MARK 10:14–16 (KJV)

Having a child, whether it's born to you, adopted, or just latches on, is one of the things in this world that can knock you to your knees—either from love, worry, disappointment, or utter confusion about what to do next. Parenting doesn't seem to be getting any easier. Our children are exposed to more of life at an earlier age than we were. They seem to be developing faster both mentally and physically. But what about spiritually?

Most adults would agree there seems to be a moral and spiritual void in many of our children. Could it be because we are not teaching them God's laws? Our elders say with each generation, children will grow wiser, yet weaker. The Bible talks about this too. We are seeing all too tragically the evidence of this today. Therefore, as parents, whether these children are born to us or not, we must be wise enough to raise them as *Proverbs 22:6 (NAS)* suggests. We must

"TRAIN UP A CHILD IN THE WAY HE SHOULD GO, EVEN WHEN HE
IS OLD HE WILL NOT DEPART FROM IT."

If we give the children of today that which we were given yesterday, when they are adults they will have a strong foundation to stand upon. They will have strong spiritual armor as they go out to battle the challenges, conflicts, and temptations of a not so forgiving world.

We can't raise our children right without giving them the spiritual tools to sustain them when they're grown. We can't do it all on our own. We can't hold on to them and keep them from the world. We've got to send them forward. So let's do so with God at the helm. Let's center them in prayer and faith, giving them more to grasp than a pair of Nikes and a video game. Let's show them the way to the Lord, because it's the only way. All the programs and all the money in the world can't help our children if we don't at least try to save their souls. Right now they're languishing in the emptiness—not just African-American kids, but most of today's youth.

But it is *our* children who must constantly confront a world which labels them as "lazy, promiscuous, unintelligent, and violent." And almost everything in *their* world reinforces this—*their* music, *their* television, *their* movies. Then, there are the statistics that constantly make headlines. They are told they have a better chance of going to prison than to college, or of becoming an unwed parent before the age of twenty. This then is the dilemma of today's black parent—raising kids who can stand up for themselves—be assertive and self-assured—without ending up a statistic.

LINNIE: *Of all the things I've tried to tackle in life I must say that motherhood is one of the toughest for me; it is also the most rewarding. I have been blessed with a bright, energetic child who is not and has never been afraid to test his limits. I must admit that I've had some sleepless nights worrying about this. For I've already seen the labels that are attached to black children at an early age.*

A white child and a black child can exhibit the exact same behavior and it is described differently. A white child is energetic, a black child is hyperactive. A white child is assertive, a black child is aggressive. A white child has a short attention span, a black child has Attention Deficit Disorder. A white child has a reading problem, a black child has a learning disability. And it goes on and on. The antics of white children are seen as cute and typical of their age group, whereas the same antics when carried out by black children are seen as predelinquent and leading to future violent and inappropriate behavior.

This was really brought home to me a few years ago when a black child—six years old—was accused of savagely beating an infant. There were folks calling for putting this kid away and throwing away the key! I'm surprised some of our more conservative, racist brethren didn't call for the death penalty. The kid was six years old! If he had been blond and blue-eyed I don't think we would have seen such vigilante justice on the part of the public or the prosecutors in the town where he lived.

Now true, he did a despicable thing and he is obviously a very troubled child—but he's still a child! It is unfortunate, but not inconceivable, that a six-year-old does not know right from wrong. A six-year-old could hurt an infant while "playing" with him. I'm not saying that is what happened. All I'm saying is that a six-year-old is a very young child himself. And in this particular case, I do believe it was the child's race that caused all of the calls for his imprisonment.

It's a fact—society sees us, particularly our males, as prone to violence. Even worse, they see young black males as future inmates. In society's eyes, it's only a matter of time. And it's not just racism these children face. The number of children killing each other is totally out of control. For many parents this is their prime concern—more important than the racism their children encounter. These parents are afraid to let their children leave the house! Even to go to school.

All of this is enough to make parents want to throw up their hands. Instead we should fall on our knees. We have to surrender our children to the Lord because only God can be with them always. We also have to pray that our society will pay more attention to what we are doing to our children. Easy access to guns; profanity and lack of morality in their entertainment sources; low expectations and discrimination against minority and poor children; family members and neighbors who wash their hands of them—we all share the responsibility and the blame. God holds us all responsible for our children. In Matthew 19:14 (NIV), we read:

> "JESUS SAID, 'LET THE LITTLE CHILDREN COME TO ME, AND DO NOT
> HINDER THEM, FOR THE KINGDOM OF HEAVEN BELONGS
> TO SUCH AS THESE.' "

FAITH OF OUR FATHERS

"HEAR THIS, YOU ELDERS; LISTEN, ALL WHO LIVE IN THE LAND. HAS
ANYTHING LIKE THIS EVER HAPPENED IN YOUR DAYS OR IN THE DAYS
OF YOUR FOREFATHERS? TELL IT TO YOUR CHILDREN, AND LET YOUR
CHILDREN TELL IT TO THEIR CHILDREN, AND THEIR CHILDREN
TO THE NEXT GENERATION."

JOEL 1:2–3 (NIV)

The challenges facing the children of today are indeed daunting. Sometimes we may wonder why people bother to have children given the state of the world. But when we feel this way, it helps to remember the children born during slavery and how their parents must have felt.

Imagine knowing that any child you had would never be yours, but would instead belong to someone else who could snatch that precious life from your arms and sell her. Imagine knowing that it didn't matter how bright your child was because she could never be taught how to read or write or ever hold a decent job. Imagine knowing the abuses and brutalities that awaited your children. And yet, with all of this, our ancestors, locked in bondage, kept having babies. We know they did because we're here today as proof. And what was it that kept them going? It was their religion and their hope for a brighter future. It was their faith. Faith that things would be just a little better for their children, and their children's children—by and by. Which brings us to today.

ANDRIA: *I tuck my three children in safely at night. And I thank God. I lovingly rub their backs and relish in the moment. And sometimes, there in the darkness, when I'm watching them sleep, the reality of just how much we've endured as a people comes to me as bright as the moonlit sky shining through their bedroom windows.*

I am reminded of the horrors of slavery, and the dismal future the children of our ancestors faced. Maybe today, our babies are more protected from the ravages of racism. But sometimes it seems as if life is more frightening now. We are allegedly living in an enlightened world, and yet there are so many examples of painful disregard for our past and for our children. We too should echo to each generation, "Never again."

I once did a news story on an antiques dealer up in New Hampshire. His shop was in a tiny little bedroom community, where so called "Yuppies" moved to get away from the hustle and bustle of Boston. New Hampshire is a beautiful place with many beautiful people. It is also a state many refer to as the whitest state in the Union. A reputation most likely gained because of the relatively few minorities who choose to live there.

The fact is all the more poignant considering the shop owner, who was displaying black memorabilia in his store window. Some of it was humorous. Some—thought-provoking. And some, unbearably painful.

He had among his "precious" collection an authentic Ku Klux Klan out-fit, and he asked me if I was interested in purchasing it!

The controversy surrounded the fact that this man was actually re-producing certain pieces of so-called art. He had a poster displayed in his front window. He said he had sold hundreds of them. He was actually reprinting from the original. The poster was a black-and-white photo of about sixteen of the sweetest little brown babies you'd ever want to see. Some were crying, some were laughing, some were curled up like angels sleeping. The caption underneath read: "Alligator Bait."

To this day, when I think about it, I weep. When I asked him why he was reproducing and trying to sell so many, he said he didn't necessar-ily think it was right, but he had no choice. It was a business decision. He needed to recoup his investment. The original, he said, cost him $250.

When our children awaken every morning, this is the world into which we send them. There is but one sure way to equip them to deal with life's inequities as well as life's opportunities. That way is to teach them to lean on the Lord. No matter what confronts them, whether it be a bully in the playground, a bully in the office, or a windfall of blessings, we've got to give our children practice in calling His name, and guide them in being watchful for His answers.

Many of the problems that faced slave parents still haunt us today. There is little difference between the child of yesterday who had a shortened life span because of the abuses of slavery, and the child of today who has a shortened life span because of gang violence, drugs, or neglect. There is little difference between the child of yesterday who could not attend school or learn to read because it was illegal, and the child of today who can attend school but still can't read. And there is little difference between the child of yesterday who could look for-ward only to toiling in fields for no wages, and the child of today who can look forward only to no job or one with low wages.

But because of the faith and perseverance of our ancestors, there *are* many children today—those you don't hear much about—who are beating the odds. They are living fruitful, productive lives and making a positive contribution to their community and society as a whole. Thankfully, many of our children fall into this category. Someone—a parent, a teacher, a coach, a neighbor—took the time to teach these children the things they needed to learn for growth and survival. Somewhere in their development these children were put on the right path, God's path.

TEACH THE CHILDREN

"AND THOU SHALT TEACH THEM ORDINANCES AND LAWS, AND SHALT SHOW THEM THE WAY WHEREIN THEY MUST WALK, AND THE WORK THAT THEY MUST DO."

EXODUS 18:20 (KJV)

Parenthood can give you an appreciation for all the people who spend their time trying to keep children on the right track, trying to teach them. What do you teach a child, other than reading, writing, and arithmetic? There are a lot of things that children need to know in order to survive and succeed, and it's not all in books.

Not only do we need to teach our children how to pray and how to have faith, they also need to know who God is first hand and His purpose in their lives. There are basic things we should do to bring our children closer to God.

- **Teach them the Ten Commandments.** Even the youngest of children can understand this basic set of rights and wrongs found in *Exodus 20:1–17* and *Deuteronomy 5:6–21.* Review each of these with your children.
- **Give children a Bible at an early age.** There are Bibles for all age groups. The New Adventure Bible (Zondervan Publishers) is for

teens and young adults. Some have colorful pictures and are written for children. There are even Bibles interpreted especially for black children, such as *The Holy Bible with Songs and Illustrations for Children of Color,* Thomas Nelson Publishers.

- **Let children know that God is always there for them and they can turn to Him for forgiveness and help.** You can't always be there for your children, so they need to develop their own relationship with God. You want them to know they can turn to God when they have problems instead of turning to the temptations of the world. Teach your children the Twenty-third Psalm, and help them to understand the comfort they can always find within its words.

- **Take children to church and let them participate.** Years ago children were expected to sit through adult church services. Today many churches have nurseries or activities for children during worship service. And most churches have Sunday school, where children can learn about God and religious doctrine.

- **Have children baptized or christened and select worthy godparents.** Dedicate your child to God from birth. Select God-fearing people who will take their role as godparents seriously.

- **Teach children prayers to say before going to bed.** Children need to know they should thank God for the day before their heads hit the pillow and they should pray for the coming day before they fall asleep. If nothing else, all children should be taught "The Lord's Prayer," found in *Matthew* 6:9–13.

- **Teach children verses to say before eating.** Children should never take for granted God's grace. Food on the table is because of His grace. Through the habit of bowing their heads before ever taking a bite, children are reminded to be thankful for their food and know that it is there only through God's blessings.

- **Emphasize to children the need to pray for others (compassion) and give to others (charity).** A child with compassion will respect the rights of others and help those who are in need. A child who can empathize is more likely to be understanding as an adult. A child with a sensitive heart will give from it more freely to help others.

- **Teach children to appreciate the wonder of nature.** Help your child to treasure all that God has created and to find solace in nature. When children learn to respect the resources of this earth, they will always live with an appreciation for the planet, and protect it more vigorously. Showing them God's awesome power in their external surroundings gives them a pathway to access their internal relationship with Him. In nature, they can then listen for the still small voice within.

- **Most important—pray with your children.** Get on your knees with them when they say their prayers at night. Sit at the table with them for the family meal and say your verses together. Take them to the altar with you at church. Let your children see that you yourself have an intimate relationship with Christ. Let them know you believe!

SPARE THE ROD

"EVEN A CHILD IS KNOWN BY HIS ACTIONS, BY WHETHER HIS CONDUCT IS PURE AND RIGHT."

PROVERBS 20:11 (NIV)

A man or woman of integrity. An adult with light. A person who does what he or she says and doesn't just talk about it is nine times out of ten a child who was brought up right, or as the old folks say— God-fearing. So when we begin to understand that the children we raise today will be the same way as adults, we see more clearly why it is so very important to live by example, and show our children "the way they should go." We need to emphasize and reward behavior that reflects our morals, our values, and our goodness. We ought to discipline our children when their behavior goes against the grain of who we say we are, and who it is we want them to become.

Somehow we have granted our children rights that used to belong only to adults. We let them make decisions they are not mature enough to handle. We let them spend freely money they do not earn. Where we once believed that children should be seen and not heard, we now let our children run rampant in supermarkets, show disrespect to the sales staff in department stores, and whine and cry the "I wanna, I wanna, I wanna" blues all over the shopping mall.

Today's pop psychologists say to "reason" with your children. Make them a part of your decisions. Give them a vote when it comes to family affairs. That's all fine, well, and good between the pages of some how-to book. In practice, however, it has failed to make the translation between yesterday's parental generation of *"Do what I say"* and today's parents' permissive *"Let's give our children space to be themselves."* What has emerged in too many cases are children who are desperate for discipline.

We know the Bible says in *Proverbs 13:24 (NIV)*:

"HE WHO SPARES THE ROD HATES HIS SON, BUT HE WHO LOVES HIM IS CAREFUL TO DISCIPLINE HIM."

And unfortunately, many parents interpret this to mean it is all right for them to mentally or physically abuse their children; too many tragic headlines reflect this reality. But there are also tragic headlines that reflect the reality of children raised without discipline. Children should never be abused, but they do need to be given structure. They need to be held accountable for their actions at an early age to save them from trouble ahead. The Word makes this painfully clear in *Proverbs 19:18 (NIV)*:

"DISCIPLINE YOUR SON, FOR IN THAT THERE IS HOPE; DO NOT BE A WILLING PARTY TO HIS DEATH."

We all want our children to have strong self-esteem as well as a strong sense of right and wrong. We want them to stand tall with pride, and kneel low with humility. The challenge is how to bridge the gap between the two.

ANDRIA: *It's not that I consider myself an expert. I don't. I'm still working very hard at the toughest job on the planet. Sometimes I feel I don't have patience enough, energy enough, or insight enough to transfer all of my life lessons to my children. For I want desperately to live by example. I want the three of them to grow up being the kind of people that will make a difference in this world. I want them to grow up understanding fully that this world owes them nothing! In fact, it's just the opposite. They've got to make a contribution the world will remember.*

My grandmother would say to me time and time and time again, usually on the heels of a tongue lashing or a switch whipping, "I'm gonna always love you. But I've got to raise you so that other people will love you too." When I was younger, I would walk away, lip synching her words. I knew they were coming, and I was tired of hearing them. Now that I have children of my own, I find myself saying the very same thing, and understanding the depth of meaning in these simple words.

How do we begin to raise our children so that other people will love them? It's a difficult process based on moral simplicities—truth, honesty, responsibility, and respect. If we can live the things we admire, if we can instill in our children a sense of accountability, then we've made tremendous progress in leading these precious lambs into an adulthood where they can stand tall and be proud of who they are. Especially when they look in the mirror. Ultimately, we are all known by our actions, whether our conduct is *pure and right*. Even our children.

Another lesson we ought to remind ourselves of from time to time is that children are just that . . . children. We on the other hand are supposed to be the adults.

LINNIE: *Scene: My son and I are in a restaurant. We're about to order breakfast.*

Him (after thoroughly reviewing the children's specials on the menu): *Mommy, I want five silver-dollar pancakes, a waffle with a happy face, fwench fwies, and a Dr. Pepper with no ice.*

Me: *Honey, if you want the pancake breakfast it comes with a sausage and an egg only. If you want the waffle breakfast it comes with bacon and an egg. You can't have both.*

Him: *But, Mommy I don't want a sausage, or a bacon, or a egg. I want five silver-dollar pancakes, a waffle with a happy face, fwench fwies, and a Dr. Pepper with no ice.*

Me (getting irritated and quieter): *Precious — You can get the pancake breakfast or the happy face waffle — not both! And you need some fruit and milk instead of french fries and Dr. Pepper!*

Him (getting irritated and louder): *But Mom-my, I don't want fwuit or milk. I want five silver-dollar pancakes, a waffle with a happy face, fwench fwies, and a Dr. Pepper with no ice!*

The waitress arrives:

Me: *He'll have the pancake breakfast with milk, but can we get french fries instead of the sausage and the egg???*

Him: *No, no, no — Mom-my! You got it wong — I want five silver-dollar pancakes, a waffle with a happy face, fwench fwies, and a Dr. Pepper with no ice.*

Something is "wong" with this picture. Until I was around thirteen I don't ever remember having anything to say about the food that I ate. Food was just placed before me. I ate it or I didn't. And if I didn't eat it there were no substitutions or replacements! And I wouldn't dare voice an opinion about what I did or did not want to be served!

I guess children today are allowed to express their opinions, wants, and desires more so than the children of yesterday. It's a fine line that I, like many parents, walk. We want to encourage our children to have minds of their own, but we try to remember that they are still children. It is our responsibility as parents and guardians to make the right decisions for them.

When I am in doubt about what to do in a particular parenting situation, I often think back to my own childhood and wonder what my parents would have done. This never ceases to amaze me because for years I thought my parents knew little about adequate child rearing. But, of course, getting older and having children of my own has reversed this opinion.

Like many parents, I find myself doing and saying things the same as my parents did. And while I never forget that my child is not a carbon copy of my husband or myself, and we're not carbon copies of our parents, I think there's something to be said for the old-fashioned discipline that has been passed through the generations.

IT TAKES A SANCTUARY

"AND ALL THY CHILDREN SHALL BE TAUGHT OF THE LORD;
AND GREAT SHALL BE THE PEACE OF THY CHILDREN."

ISAIAH 54:13 (KJV)

We all are responsible for raising and teaching children, whether they are our own or someone else's. We can't save our own children without saving others' too. Maybe we think we have enough money and resources to keep our kids surrounded by all that is good in life. We sacrifice and send them to the best schools, lead them to the right friends, and provide them with safe extracurricular activities. We use all our resources to place our child on the right path. But someday the very child we are trying to protect will come in contact with someone who wasn't raised right. Someone who wasn't taught respect for others, or themselves.

So when we see any child in trouble we need to do whatever we can to help him. It may mean volunteering our time and talents, calling a social service agency on the child's behalf, or, at the very least, writing a check for an organization that supports children. We need to provide a place where children can rest. Where they can release the pressures of the world. What better place than the church?

ANDRIA: *Church was the stage on which my life unfolded. Mine and my sisters' real-life drama. We played our parts well. You see, our roles as members of the first family at church were clear. It wasn't always an easy act either. Sometimes we just wanted to act up! When you're a P.K., trouble was something you were always tempted by—even came hairline close to it a time or two—but trouble was also to be avoided.*

I remember a time when I was nine years old. After school, I deviated for just a few minutes and went to the Jewish deli on the corner of Crown Street and Nostrand Avenue in Brooklyn. I knew I was supposed to go straight home, that was the deal. But I had this thing for the french fries there. The owner, Pesach, always made them just right. Crinkle cut with a little salt. Then he would put a big scoop in a brown paper bag. I didn't even need money because my father had set up a lunch account for me and my sister there. Besides, all the kids went to Pesach's after school. Just this one time, I thought, why couldn't I?

After I left the deli, just when I was crossing the street, about to dig into my little greasy brown paper bag with the perfectly salted french fries, a loud series of bangs blasted in my ear. The next thing I knew I was running, all the kids were running. I looked around and one of the boys from school had set off some firecrackers. I looked up, and in the window above were some church ladies, yelling down to us: "Get on out of here now! You're all gonna be in for it."

Well, I don't even remember where I flung my fries, I just remember holding on to my book bag and running till I ran out of breath. I stopped running when I reached my house on President Street about eight blocks away. There I was, out of breath, my head to the pavement, my hands on my knees, my socks in my shoes, my heart thumping ready to explode, and the front door opened. There was another loud noise, the sound of my father's voice, and the sting of his hand on my butt. One of those church ladies hanging out the window on Crown Street had recognized me, and had called ahead to my house.

For the longest time I didn't understand my father's actions. And I certainly didn't understand that busybody woman, who surely must have known I would never have set off firecrackers. My young mind told me, I was the victim here. It was simply a case of being in the wrong place at the wrong time. But my father didn't see it that way. He told me if I had gone directly home as I was supposed to, my butt wouldn't be hurting. He grabbed me, brought me inside, got his belt, and gave me two good hits. One from him, and one from the church lady.

You see, my lesson from that was one of honesty and of honor. I wasn't honest enough to come straight home, and I had compromised the honor of my family because someone else called them about my troubled path. Rarely do we even hold up the characteristics of honesty, honor, or respect anymore. But my family did. Back then the collective church family did. No, I didn't set fire to a building or steal from the store. I hadn't even been a member of the firecracker gang. But I also didn't do what I was supposed to do. Being in the wrong place at the wrong time has certainly changed the fate of many a youth. Should I have been punished in that manner? Perhaps not. But who knows what other roads I might have veered off had it not been for people like the church lady on Crown Street and my father's willingness to apply instant discipline.

Our churches can provide sanctuary for our youth. And, not just on Sundays. Tutoring, after-school activities, rites of passage programs, mentoring—these are just some of the ways churches around the country are helping in their congregations and communities. We need to do more. We need to get back to the days when church members took seriously their role as guardians of the children.

SAVE THE CHILDREN

"YOU WILL KNOW THAT YOUR CHILDREN WILL BE MANY, AND YOUR DESCENDANTS LIKE THE GRASS OF THE EARTH."

JOB 5:25 (NIV)

We will continue to have children, just as our ancestors did, because we realize just as they did, that our children represent our hope for the future, and will carry on our cultural traditions. With God's help we will work to save our young people from succumbing to the challenges of the world.

How do we save our children? First, we have to pray for our young people. We live in a society that labels them and cuts them down, telling them they can't. We have to constantly tell them they can. We must arm them with spiritual fortitude. That spiritual armor is the Word. All of what we need is written in the Bible. If we can be conscientious students ourselves, we can pass on to our children the unwavering truth about God's promises and God's ways. So when life gets tough, and it will, when challenges abound, and they are surely to come, the rock we must have our children stand upon is God. Our children should be able to turn to God in prayer, just as we do. *He is the foundation we must give them.* A foundation that will never falter.

CHAPTER EIGHT—CHILDREN AND PARENTHOOD

REMEMBER THIS

❀ Children are to be given love and the Lord. We can't raise them right without prayer and faith. Give your children verbal ammunition that brings God closer to their everyday living experience. When they say, "I'm lucky," tell them, "No, you are blessed." When they say, "Nobody at school likes me," tell them, "God loves you." When they feel defeated or frustrated and say, "I can't," let them know, "It doesn't matter, because God can do everything, but fail." You can truly

"DO ALL THINGS THROUGH CHRIST WHO STRENGTHENS YOU."

PHILIPPIANS 4:13

❀ Teach your children to call upon the Lord for help. Whether it's a bad dream, a fear of failure, or a tough test in school, pray with them. Open up the Bible with them. Go down the index and show them how to find the book of Psalms. Make the twenty-third chapter, verse 1 (KJV), your special saying in times of trials and tribulations:

"THE LORD IS MY SHEPHERD, I SHALL NOT WANT."

Help them to believe it.

- Our churches have the ability to provide sanctuary for our children. Let's provide our churches with the resources to be there for our youth. Implement tutorial and mentoring programs at your church. When you think of giving to a charity—give to your church. Don't be afraid to offer your special talent as a one-shot deal or an ongoing support service. Just think: If each parent would give just a small something, we would have churches that offer big possibilities for our young people.

CHILDREN AND PARENTHOOD

PRAY FOR THIS:

LET ME ALWAYS RESPECT THE ANOINTMENT
OF BEING A PARENT.

Our families must stay strong if we are to survive. We are merely the keepers of God's flock . . . Let us be passionate parents and guardians—strong enough to live as examples, brave enough to show our children the way.

A PARENT'S PRAYER

Dear Heavenly Father, I come to give thanks for this
wonderful gift of life You have bestowed
upon me: Lord, I thank You for my child.
I pray, Dear God, You will make me worthy of this gift.
Lord, teach me how to be the best parent I can be.
When I am tired, give me strength.
When I am bothered, give me patience.
When I am confused, give me right answers.
And, when I have done the best I can do,
remind me You are with me, and I am never alone.
Dear Lord, please protect and guide my child.
Protect him/her from the evils within and without;
When he/she is hungry, give him/her nourishment,
When he/she is lost, show him/her the way,
When he/she is in trouble, give him/her safe harbor,
And, please, Dear Lord, whether I am present or not

Surround him/her with Your Love, Your Peace,
and Your Guidance.
We surrender ourselves to You as we travel this journey
of life together. Amen.

CHAPTER NINE

A House Is Not a Home

"BETTER A DRY CRUST WITH PEACE AND QUIET THAN A HOUSE FULL OF FEASTING WITH STRIFE."

PROVERBS 17:1 (NIV)

Status comes in many forms in America. Too often we judge a person's station in life by what kind of car he drives, the kind of job she holds, the mate he or she has, how much money he or she makes, and the kind of house the person buys. But long ago, Aurealia Jane Smith Hall told her grandchildren often, "Pray for a home, not a house . . . anybody can buy a house, but only God *can give you a home."* A home is something you're blessed with and create together with God by the way you respect it, protect it, and nurture those who reside there. A house may cost millions, but a home is something you can't put a price tag on.

The place where we close our doors to the outside world is a place we should honor as a private retreat. Our home is where we cry and laugh, where we live and love. Our home, therefore, must be a place of harmony and balance. Our home is a fortress, the one space we should be able to withdraw to and be alone with our loved ones, and alone with God.

Protect your space as if you were protecting your life, for negative energy you allow in can permeate it like a bad headache that won't go away. If you want your home to be one of love, then don't feel pressured to let people inside who don't love you. If you want your peace and quiet there, don't let negative vibes pass through. Make sure those who enter are loved ones you want to be a blessing to and who can be a blessing in your life in return.

LINNIE: *There have been occasions when I have unsuspectingly allowed negativity into my house. A few years ago I allowed my home to be used as a meeting place for a group to which I belonged. I hadn't really wanted to do this but some of the members begged me because there wasn't anyplace else to meet—or so they said. So I hesitantly agreed to allow them to meet at my house once a month.*

I'm from the old school that says that anytime someone comes to your house, for whatever reason, you have food available. Since these people were coming to my house after work, I knew they would be hungry so I'd usually have something prepared for them. I would have it laid out just as though I were entertaining. They never offered to chip in or bring anything, but it was okay with me, because in my mind they were guests.

The meetings went okay for a few months, but soon personality clashes became apparent and I started to have doubts about the viability of the group. A couple of the people were downright hostile to myself and several others, and yet they kept coming to the meetings.

I got to the point that I didn't look forward to the meetings and I certainly didn't want to break bread with some of those folks—especially my bread in my house!

But the clincher was when the very ones who had asked to use my house said, "Why do we always have to meet here anyway?" Well, that was it for me. I decided right then and there that I would have no more meetings at my house after that and I didn't. Of course, the group disbanded soon thereafter.

On another occasion I had a Christmas gathering for family and friends. One guest felt compelled to voice her opinion, rather loudly, about her disappointment with God and religion and those who believed. This was a lightning rod to some of the other guests, who quickly seized the opportunity to debate with her (which was probably what she wanted in the first place). As I overheard some of her blasphemous remarks I wondered how such darkness had found its way into my home.

Fortunately, I had said a prayer for peace before the party and knew the ravings of this confused soul were unimportant. So I prayed for this woman and went about my business. Scripture tells us in 1 Peter 3:9–11 (NIV):

> "Do not repay evil with evil or insult with insult, but with blessing, because to this you were called so that you may inherit a blessing."

For

> "Whoever would love life and see good days must keep his tongue from evil and his lips from deceitful speech. He must turn from evil and do good; he must seek peace and pursue it."

What I learned from those experiences is to be careful whom I allow in my house. I now realize I don't have to have anyone in my home I don't want there. It may mean I entertain less but that's okay, because I am now particular about who enters my space. I realized that my home is for the relaxation and enjoyment of those I love and respect. And, if negativity does slip in uninvited, I know the God of peace still reigns in my home.

IS THIS AS GOOD AS IT GETS?

"AS GOODS INCREASE, SO DO THOSE WHO CONSUME THEM. AND
WHAT BENEFIT ARE THEY TO THE OWNER EXCEPT TO
FEAST HIS EYES ON THEM?"

ECCLESIASTES 5:11 (NIV)

We've all heard the saying—"keeping up with the Joneses." We know there will always be people who have more than we do and people with less. And yet, we still get caught up in the trap of competing with others for material things. We measure our success by our possessions. We measure our station in life by where someone else may be.

We all know people who have to call all their friends the moment they drive a new car off the lot. And, let it be a luxury car (never mind the fact that they're struggling to pay for it) well, then, they have to parade all over town to show off their "good fortune."

But maybe it's not a car we're bragging about. Maybe it's designer clothes, jewelry, our job, our husband, our children. Taking pride in our families and our accomplishments is one thing, but lauding them over others is quite another. Usually this is done by insecure people. The more insecure they are, the more they brag.

This is never more evident than when it comes to where we live. Some people lose friends instantly just by moving into a bigger house, or their longtime friends don't visit because they can't stand the idea of someone they know having something they perceive as better than what they have. Some people all of sudden have newfound friends who invite themselves over and into their lives. (Of course we know from Chapter Four these aren't real friends anyway.)

When you experience this kind of reaction from folks, or you yourself get caught up in the cycle too, know that no matter what your house looks like, no matter what the square footage, no matter what the neighborhood—the important thing is you make God a part of your home. Scripture tells us in *1 Corinthians* 12:31 *(NRSV):*

" . . STRIVE FOR THE GREATER GIFTS. AND I WILL SHOW YOU
A STILL MORE EXCELLENT WAY."

ANDRIA: *Have you ever been to someone's house and as soon as you walk through the door it's like you've walked into the pages of some decorating magazine? I'm not talking about going to someone's home that is gorgeous beyond belief. I'm talking about being in someone's house that's masquerading as a home. Here's the difference: A home is where you express the essence of who you are.*

A home reflects the basics of your personality. It reveals as much about you as you do when you speak with words. This is why—whether you're in a condo, a fifteen-room mansion, or a rented motel room—it's so important that you pray for God to give you a home, and not just a house.

I have a dear friend who sank several years of her life into designing a fabulous new house. Just the right piece of land. Just the right architect. She is very talented in her own right and could have been working in any of several professions, but instead answered a higher calling to be a mother to her children and a wife to a very successful husband. So she literally spent a couple of years married to this project, supervising even the most minute details.

There was picking the tile (imported, of course), selecting the windows (there are many), and then there was all the frustration a job like this brings. There's no question, when she finally moved in, she moved into one of the most incredible houses I've ever seen. But even now, she admits, it was just a house. Phenomenally built, but when you went through the huge wooden doors, conspicuously missing was all the warmth you would expect inside.

Here's the story: She spent so much time building up someone else's dream, she put hers on hold. She forgot to consistently put God first, *and instead put forth every material effort, so the spiritual element was absent.*

Three years later, she no longer lives there. Most people can't figure out how she could ever have left such a grand place. But I understand without reservation. Today, she's spending more time getting to know God and is focusing on her own dreams, aspirations, and divine purpose. She's the first one to tell you, the size of your home doesn't matter. What matters most is that you are able to find peace at home and with God. Now she lives in a much smaller, but lovely, condominium. And when you step inside, you truly feel the warmth and generosity of her spirit and her home.

HOW TO MAKE YOUR HOME A RETREAT

". . . SHE WENT INTO THE FIELD AND HAS WORKED STEADILY FROM MORNING TILL NOW, EXCEPT FOR A SHORT REST IN THE SHELTER."

RUTH 2:7 (NIV)

In our quest to have it all we may end up having nothing. This is a dilemma many of us are struggling to work through. Especially those of us who were fooled into thinking we could have it all. Career, marriage, parenthood, community service, hobbies, family obligations—these are just some of the demands of today. When we do finally make it home after a long day at work, our second shift of cooking, cleaning, and tending to our family begins. You can have it all, but not at the same time, and having it all comes with a price: We have little time to enjoy the home we've worked so hard for.

We know something has to give but what? *Luke 16:13* tells us that we cannot serve two masters. We know to start with God first, but then what? If we are married with children, we tend to choose between our career and our family. If we are single, we tend to choose between our career and our social life. But the reality is we have to take care of ourselves before we can take care of others. Most of the time we feel guilty if we steal a little time for ourselves. Before we start beating ourselves up because we don't have time to mow the lawn, cook apple pies, or iron a shirt—let's think of ways to reflect and relax. Let's implement a daily regimen that starts with Divine acknowledgment and intervention.

- **Establish priorities.** Ask God to

  "ORDER MY STEPS IN THY WORD . ."

  as it says in *Psalms 119:133 (KJV)*. Instead of being at the mercy of calendars and datebooks, let God take the lead in your life. Take time every day for prayer and meditation. As you relax and reflect, ask for direction. Prayerfully determine what you should accomplish each day, each week, each month. But don't plan too much! God has a way of moving our plans aside and showing His will to us. When He does this, we have to be ready to go with it.
- **Find solitary time.** Sometimes you need it to hear yourself think, and sometimes you need it to hear God's answers to your prayers. And while you may not be able to get to a tropical locale where you can lie on the beach and wait for an island guy to bring you Margaritas, at the very least you can take a walk or go somewhere—a lake, the mountains, or even a park. Go commune with nature and listen for your inner voice. And if you can't get to an outdoor location you can create an inner sanctuary in your home. If nothing else try a leisurely bath. This is the simplest form of relaxation. But who can relax with kids banging on the bathroom door? Try a fragrant bath at *midnight* (as long as you're not too tired). The quiet will soothe you as much as the warm, aromatic water. You might feel just as rested as if you've had a full eight hours of sleep.
- **Learn to say no.** Will the world really come to an end if you don't sweep the floor, take the trash out, wash the clothes, or have the kids in bed by eight? Must you serve on every committee or re-

spond to every request for your time or talents? Is the phone call coming in so urgent, you can't let the machine pick up and then return the call later? While we all need some structure in our lives, every now and then, especially when you're too tired to do one more thing, you've got to let it go. Remember, all of what you put off will be right there waiting for you when you're relaxed and better able to deal.

• **Leave your job at work.** You can't live and breathe the job. Even if you are in a profession that requires you to be on call, you've got to find a way to get away from it on occasion. One problem is that we think faxes, beepers, computers, and cell phones leave us no excuse but to be available, but that's only if we give in to them. If you know there's someone else to handle potential crises, leave your beeper on the dresser (on vibrate!). If you have an answering service, check it twice during your day off, not every hour. You must make yourself take the time. The world won't stop without you.

• **Inform your family of your rights.** Your family can love you to death. They can sit back and allow you to work your fingers to the bone serving and pleasing them! They may never consider that you need time off from family responsibilities. Take it! Time off and time for yourself mean when you get back to life—back to reality— you'll come back being a better you! More patient, more loving, and more energy to face another day of giving it all you've got!

• **Above all else, take time to pray.**

ANDRIA: *My issue is, I try to give all I've got—all the time.*

My doctor, my friends, my husband, even I myself have often been a bit befuddled about my weight. Yeah, I lost twenty-five pounds when I was at the height of professional stress. But, thank God, He's delivered me from all that. So why then am I still moving at warp speed and thin as a rail? All my closest and dearest friends have expressed their concern for me. They think I do too much. They think I don't eat enough. They think I need to slow down. They're right.

While Linnie and I were still penning this book, I told her what some of my friends and family members were saying. A couple of them even wondered if I had an eating disorder. I don't. Right then and there, Linnie shared with me (in her not-so-subtle way), that my problem had nothing to do with my food intake. (I have the potential to really pig out.) She said, "Andria, your problem is you never slow down. You don't know how to relax. You just don't ever stop." She asked me why I found it necessary to do at least five things at the same time. Why couldn't I simply read a book, do my nails, sit and think, or hold a conversation without trying to do all these things at the same time? She spoke, and I saw the light. I dubbed my condition Perpetual Motion Sickness. Linnie dubbed it my version of PMS. We had to laugh about it, but it's not really all that funny. I think a lot of people suffer from this same condition. We feel that just because we can do something, we ought to do it. We believe that having the ability to juggle means we should always perform at that level.

To give you an example, at the time I was writing this very story, Linnie and I were in serious crunch mode. We were on deadline to hand in these revisions to our editor within twelve hours. Linnie was on the West Coast, I was on the East. It was six o'clock. I was stressing. I was writing, but I stopped in the middle of it all to go cook dinner for my family. And what had I taken out to prepare? A seven-pound lamb roast! My plan: Wash it; season it with some rosemary and fresh garlic; throw it in the oven for two hours, make potatoes au gratin, from scratch of course (one of the kids' favorite dishes), and some fresh cabbage and corn muffins.

Of course, while I was in the kitchen, just getting started cooking (never mind it was a school night and dinner wouldn't be ready till 8 P.M.), I called Linnie. You know, I figured I'd update her on my progress with the manuscript while I was seasoning the lamb. Maximize, maximize, maximize!

I told her, "I'll be back on the computer in about two and a half hours, once I cook, feed the kids, clean the kitchen, and get them in bed. Then I'll e-mail you more of the document."

Linnie started cracking up, then she raised her voice. "Girl, what is wrong with you? This is why they have delivery! This of all nights is a Pizza Night, and you're about to cook a lamb roast? Get real." I did. I put the meat in the refrigerator and made hot dogs.

I hugged her over the phone that night for calling me on my PMS. I had obviously fallen off the wagon. I guess she managed to get through to me what others had been trying to tell me for quite some time. She opened my eyes to something I needed to finally acknowledge. Maybe I should start support groups all over the country for people like me. You know, in the middle of a crowded room I can stand up and proclaim, "Hi, I'm Andria Hall, and I have PMS—Perpetual Motion Sickness." On second thought, I just need to take this little problem of mine to the Lord in prayer. My first step to healing is to acknowledge my problem. My second step toward recovery is to make sure I tell all my friends. They'll call me on it if I continue to go over the edge. My third step to transformation is regular prayer, and to live the daily regimen we expose above. Read it and be delivered.

A SHELTER IN THE TIME OF STORM

"WITH WISDOM A HOUSE IS BUILT. WITH UNDERSTANDING IT IS ESTABLISHED. WITH KNOWLEDGE ITS ROOMS ARE FILLED WITH EVERY KIND OF RICHES, BOTH PRECIOUS AND PLEASANT."

PROVERBS 24:3–4 (GOD'S WORD)

If you truly want to make your home a sanctuary, an escape from the pressures of the world, then take some time to bring a few spiritual touches to your fortress. Invite God into your house. Make a permanent space for Him. Let Him fill every nook and cranny of your home.

- **Remember your ancestors.** Make room for them too by including their memories and traditions. Say grace before you eat, the way your daddy used to say it. Set places at the table with Grandma's china or Auntie's silver. Place Grandpa's pipe on the mantel.
- **Clean and organize your house.** We've heard all our lives that cleanliness is next to godliness, but sometimes life gets so hectic, things start to pile up, the kids make a mess, and before we know it our space has gotten out of control. Organize! Get rid of some of the clutter. Your attitude at home will be so much better when your house is orderly. We're not talking about passing the white glove test—but just having everything in its place with some semblance of neatness will clear your space and your head.
- **Include plants and flowers.** Bringing some of nature inside is one way to remind us of God's greatness, making a home more spiritual. Flowers and plants can really liven up a home. Some, such as fern, philodendron, and spider are easy to grow and require little maintenance. And don't wait for someone else to bring you flowers, you might be waiting a long time. Every once in a while, treat yourself to a single rose or an arrangement of white lilies. You deserve them. After all, if you don't consider yourself special, who will?
- **Display family photos and artifacts.** Pictures of our relatives and ancestors keep us connected to our family tree. Photo albums filled with snapshots of friends and family are treasures which induce lasting memories. Make a scrapbook of letters and cards from loved ones, or try framing a piece of jewelry that once belonged to a family member.
- **Include magazines, books, and periodicals that speak to your culture and spirituality.** Generations of black households have

had our magazines, *Jet* and *Ebony* in particular, on the coffee table for years. Today we include *Essence*, *Black Enterprise*, and other periodicals that speak to our experience. We also have books that uplift us spiritually, especially in our bedrooms. We read them upon waking or before retiring for bed. And there is one more thing. Just like in a hotel room, there should always be a Bible. You never know when you'll need to go to the Word. Some of us read it every day without fail, others find we only really open it when we're in crisis. No matter what, God wants us all to rely on His promises. Home should, after all, be the place we come to for solace and comfort. The Bible will always give you both.

- **Finally, let peace and joy settle into every room.** Once you've prayed to the Lord that He give you a home, not just a house, one way to make sure you literally feel it as a home is to fill it with things scripture refers to as both precious and pleasant.

HOME COOKING

"SO HEAP ON THE WOOD AND KINDLE THE FIRE. COOK THE MEAT WELL, MIXING IN THE SPICES; AND LET THE BONES BE CHARRED."

EZEKIEL 24:10 (NIV)

Black folk have always had an affinity for good, down-home cooking. Maybe it's because for so long we had to take pleasure in the small things in life like a good meal. But more than that, the kitchen was a place where we could gather and swap tales as well as recipes. Who among us over the age of thirty can't remember sitting in somebody's kitchen as a child snapping fresh string beans. You can't do that with the frozen or canned varieties!

We love to entertain. We honor the tradition of breaking bread together. We enjoy pampering our friends and relatives, which in our culture means serving them fine down-home cuisine. We don't often choose to share a table with people we neither like nor respect! But, if you are a friend, we will pull out our finest table linen and serve you the best food we can afford. Some meals are meant to be cooked the old-fashioned way. They are cooked not only for their taste and appeal but, in some cases, for therapeutic purposes. These are the basic recipes that we've been using for years. They soothe us when we're feeling stressed. They take us back to a simpler time. They make us feel a camaraderie with those who have gone before us. Something special happens when you are in the kitchen cooking something the way your mom, dad, or grandmother used to cook it.

ANDRIA: *Certain things put me right back in my mother's kitchen. One of them is macaroni and cheese. Forget the packaged stuff, this recipe is the real thing. Now I don't know about you, but it's just not as mouthwatering when you cut a piece of macaroni and cheese, as it is when you get one of those big metal stirring spoons out of the top kitchen drawer, and scoop out a creamy, hot, heaping helping of it. But be forewarned, when you do, it's either gonna burn your tongue if you eat it too fast, or bust your gut, if you eat too much. When you cook Momma Honey's Macaroni and Cheese, you've got to make it on an empty stomach. That way you have even greater incentive to get this recipe right. Plus, you'll enjoy it that much more.*

MOMMA HONEY'S MACARONI AND CHEESE

$1^1/_2$ cups grated extra-sharp Cheddar cheese
(my mother always uses CrackerBarrel)
2 cups small elbow macaroni—(my mother always uses Mueller's)
about $2^1/_2$ cups whole milk, maybe a little more
1 teaspoon salt
enough pepper to see it in the mix
a pat of butter
enough paprika to turn it slightly pink

just a pinch of flour
a wooden spoon for stirring
by no means use an egg—not necessary

So here's what you do. First of all, try to find yourself a nonstick quart-size pot, 'cause with this recipe you stir in the cheese as you go. The only thing worse than eating too much macaroni and cheese (which I do every time) is trying to clean the pot. So nonstick is definitely the way to go. What my mom taught me to do is to grate the cheese first. (Hide it from the kids though, otherwise you'll never end up with enough. Almost all kids were mice in their last life.)

Anyway, put the grated cheese into a bowl and set it aside with a dish towel on top to camouflage it. Then, boil up the water, and put the pasta in (but don't let it overcook). Remember: it's going to cook in the oven too. Mushy is not what you're going for here. After the pasta is al dente, done but still firm, drain it and throw it back in the same pan, but turn the fire off for a while. Add the grated cheese to the piping hot noodles, and stir with the wooden spoon until it's all melted. Just when it starts to get gooey, turn the stove back on to medium heat. Make a little hole in the middle of the elbows and pour the milk in. The level should be just over the elbows (not yours). Stir and then let it sit while it gets hot again.

Now, throw in the salt, pepper, butter, paprika, flour, and stir it all up, making sure it's nicely mixed. Once it starts to bubble just a bit, turn off the stove, and pour it all into a shallow baking dish. Sprinkle more paprika on top and let it brown in the oven for about 15 or 20 minutes on 400°. Remember: don't eat it right away, lest you burn your tongue. This is not a difficult recipe, but you may have to try it a couple of times before you can get it right every time. It's a texture thing, you know. Creamy, not curdy. Loose, not tight. In no time, you'll be able to call yourself a seasoned macaroni and cheese mom. Even if you don't have any kids! Enjoy!

Of course, these recipes that have been passed down through generations aren't concerned with calories or fat. Many of us remember growing up with a coffee can on the stove to collect bacon grease. The grease would be strained and used for frying at a later time. Unfortunately, some of our relatives who used all that fat ended up with heart trouble, hypertension, or cancer; you just know that all that fattening food was bad for them. You can't eat like that every day, it'll kill you. Today, thankfully, we look for healthy alternatives: steamed vegetables instead of those cooked with ham or salt pork. We prepare stir-fry or fresh salads. So when we do indulge in that fried chicken, we don't have to worry about paying such a hefty price.

LINNIE: *My aunt Faye (who really isn't my aunt but my mother's best friend, which is why I call her aunt) knows her way around a kitchen. While she has embraced the cooking technology of today—microwaves, blenders, and Cuisinarts—she still has fond remembrances of the kitchens she grew up in, and the way they did things "back then."*

She talks about "ice boxes" versus refrigerators and the days when bacon was sold by the slab and you had to ask the butcher to slice it for you. There were no frozen foods or box cake mixes in the house when she grew up. Women in those days seemed to find time for canning, baking, and making sumptuous stews.

When I talk to Aunt Faye about cooking and what to have on hand in the kitchen, I realize that whatever cooking I think I'm good at is woefully inadequate compared to the way she cooks and the ingredients she uses. I accept that my sweet potato pie and peach cobbler will never taste like hers.

She talks nostalgically about neck bones, hog maws, ham hocks, salt pork, and pork rind. These are the things they kept in their kitchens long ago, not the ten brands of mustard and frozen piecrusts we modern women cherish. And while I will never give up premade salads, every now and then I put on some neck bones and greens.

It fascinates me to hear her talk about our tradition of using all the parts of an animal. She speaks of growing up where folks went out to their yard, killed their own chickens, and cooked everything but the feathers—the liver, the heart, the neck, and some people even used the feet. Once the meat was off the chicken, the carcass was used for soups and broths.

Fried chicken always takes us back. Back to church socials, bus trips, and family get-togethers. In shoe boxes tied with string or in greasy paper bags, fried chicken never seems to lose its appeal, whether hot or cold. When we think about how we got over as a people, we remember the many fried chicken dinners bought and sold in our communities. These dinners helped build churches, buy uniforms, and keep many black restaurants in business.

Health concerns dictate that we not eat as much fried foods as we used to, but every now and then you've got to fix yourself some "real" fried chicken. Not baked chicken, or chicken with the skin taken off— real fried chicken. This means using a cast-iron skillet, just like Mama and Grandma used, and a brown paper bag to put your flour in. Remember this cooking process is like a communion, so you have to do it the right way. A plastic bag would probably work just as well, but it may not conjure up childhood memories for you. Find that brown paper bag to shake the chicken in!

Here's my recipe for frying chicken. I call it:

BABYFACE BROWNED FRIED CHICKEN

7 to 8 chicken pieces

2 eggs

3 cups flour

salt and pepper

cooking oil (we all have our favorite brands)

to spice things up a bit, use some seasoning salt, rosemary,

and paprika

You know the first thing you do with your raw chicken—wash, drain, and pat it dry. We don't need the USDA to tell us that. The eggs, no more than two, are used for your batter. Lightly beat the eggs with water, or milk if you want, but just a couple of teaspoons. If you've got about seven to eight pieces of chicken you'll need about three cups of flour. Throw it in that brown paper bag. Add the seasonings and—shake it up, baby! Heat enough oil or shortening in your cast-iron skillet to cover the chicken at least halfway. Dip the chicken pieces in the egg mixture and then put them in the bag with the flour and shake some more. When the oil is hot (test with a few drops of water—if you don't know what this means, stay away from cooking with hot oil), place the chicken pieces in the skillet.

So now the question is how long do you cook the chicken? I once had a friend ask me that question. We know that undercooked chicken will make us sick. I think my friend was looking for a time, but my reply was "Until it's brown." "What shade of brown?" she asked. Now this was a tough one. She was obviously not a cook, so I had to say something she could relate to.

"Well," I said, "not Sinbad brown—that's too light, and not Wesley Snipes brown—that's too dark. I got it! Babyface brown—that's just right."

Now some folk think that being able to cook "soul" food or "home cooking" will get and keep a man. Experience shows us that a man's gonna do what he's gonna do, regardless. But tell a brother you're gonna fix him some chicken with red beans and rice and watch his reaction. You may not be able to keep him, but you sure will get his attention for a while.

HOME IS WHERE THE LORD IS

"... HE BLESSES THE HOME OF THE RIGHTEOUS."

PROVERBS 3:33 (NIV)

Houses may come and go, but we want a home that will withstand the winds of change. A home we take with us wherever we go. A home that is our refuge at the end of a busy day. There was a time when everyone, young and old, knew they were expected to be home in time for dinner—hands washed and sitting at the table ready to say grace. The commitment was made so we could catch up and keep up with one another. That time was sacred.

We're so busy these days. Our homes have become way stations, where we stop in between trips, or hotels, where we come only to sleep. We pass each other in the hallways and on our way out the door. We don't bother to entertain much because who has the time to prepare a meal or clean up?

Then we wonder why we can't find peace and why we all seem so disconnected. We plan and look forward to expensive vacations where we can "find ourselves," where we can have "quality time" together. Well, if you can't "find" yourself at home, why are you wasting time and money on rent or mortgage? Your home, like you, doesn't have to be perfect, but it should be comfortable and spirit-filled. When you walk through the door and kick your shoes off, you should feel an inner joy. Don't settle for less.

It is not the walls, or the furniture, or the size of the rooms that make a house a home. It's the love you bring to everything you do inside. Whether it's playing Monopoly with the kids; pulling up weeds in the backyard, lovingly, albeit at times grudgingly; doing your tenth load of laundry; or placing a meal on the table made with your hands and from your heart. A home should put you at peace. That means indulging all your senses so that home not only *feels* like home but *smells* like home and *looks* like home too.

Sometimes we might feel tempted to lock ourselves and our cares away when we're at home, closing out the rest of the world. And while the temptation may be strong, let's remember even in our effort to protect our personal space, to still extend our kindness to those whom God has sent.

"DO NOT FORGET TO ENTERTAIN STRANGERS, FOR BY SO DOING
SOME PEOPLE HAVE ENTERTAINED ANGELS
WITHOUT KNOWING IT."

HEBREWS 13:2 (NIV)

CHAPTER NINE—A HOUSE IS NOT A HOME

REMEMBER THIS

❀ Before you unpack one single box in a new home, make sure to bless your space. If you've already moved in, rededicate it to God. Recite the "Prayer for the Home" that follows, or say your own. Pray that the Lord gives you a home . . . not just a house.

❀ Consciously control the energy that enters your sanctuary. If you don't want someone in your home, don't feel compelled to extend an invitation. A piece of everyone's spirit is always left behind. Energy cannot be contained. Make sure you feel comfortable with the people you allow inside your home.

❀ Surround your spirit at home with things that make you feel comfortable and secure. Whether it's a loved one's picture you've framed and mounted, or items stocked in the kitchen cabinets, honor yourself and your family with memories that invoke peace, and food that keeps you healthy, smiling, and coming back for more.

A HOUSE IS NOT A HOME

PRAY FOR THIS:
LORD LET OUR HOME BE WHERE YOU RESIDE.

If God is not invited into our home, peace will never be a permanent resident. We must dedicate not just our lives but our living to God as well. Let that living not be in vain.

❧

PRAYER FOR THE HOME

Dear Heavenly Father, we thank You for this sanctuary which
you have provided us and ask you to bless this home
and its inhabitants.

Bless the land this home was built upon. May it be as solid as
the rock of Gibraltar. May it be fruitful and abundantly
giving—rooted in sanctified soil. Protect all you have
placed here from the ravages of nature, whether it be
floods, fires, storms, or earthquakes.

Bless the rooms of this home. From wall to wall, from door to
door, from floor to ceiling—permeate this home with
Your presence. Let our activities in each room be those
You would find worthy.

Bless the living areas. Let them provide comfort to us after
a hard day's labor when we long for rest. Let them provide a
respite to us during those times when we need spiritual
renewal. And let them provide a place for us to celebrate the
joys of life. Surround us with what we need to uplift our
spirits; however, let us always remember, material things
will come and go, but Your love is forever.

Bless the bedrooms. Watch over us as we sleep and grant us peaceful slumber. Let us greet each new day in this home with joyful expectation.

Bless the kitchen. Allow us to lovingly prepare and serve meals in this home. Give us the sustenance we need to nourish our bodies as well as our souls.

Bless those who visit this home. May they leave all adversity and strife at the door and enter with a spirit of peace and good cheer. Let them respect our surroundings and know that in *this* house we serve You.

And, Dear God, *bless those who live in this home.* Thank You for giving us shelter. We pray that You will always find us worthy of this home. Let Your spirit reside with us forever. Amen.

CHAPTER TEN

Jobs, Careers, and Callings

"COME UNTO ME, ALL YE THAT LABOUR AND ARE HEAVY
LADEN, AND I WILL GIVE YOU REST. TAKE MY YOKE UPON
YOU, AND LEARN OF ME; FOR I AM MEEK AND LOWLY IN
HEART, AND YE SHALL FIND REST UNTO YOUR SOULS.
FOR MY YOKE IS EASY, AND MY BURDEN IS LIGHT."

MATTHEW 11:28–30 (KJV)

Many of us labor daily at jobs we neither like nor enjoy. We pursue careers we think will bring us fame or fortune. We spend our lives with people we don't respect, doing things that don't bring us any sense of fulfillment or peace. We go to work each and every day just for the paycheck. Mind you, there's nothing wrong with getting paid for your efforts but too many of us set out on that never-ending quest for money or status only to find that both are fleeting. We define ourselves by our job titles and when something happens at the job to rock our world, we don't know who we are anymore, or where we belong.

Some of us will spend decades dedicating ourselves to a company or a boss. For a while, we'll feel good about ourselves, which boosts our self-esteem, but ask anyone who's made it to the top if they feel it's all been worth it, and their answer might surprise you. If we forgo our relationships with family and friends, making ourselves available to the job 24-7, then maybe we've given up too much. If every word out of our mouths is about the job and we end up with no outside life, maybe we need to find a life that's more meaningful. Many people put off getting married or having children so they won't be encumbered as they attempt to climb the ladder of success. Later, they say, they'll settle down, but does later ever come?

Some of us labor at jobs that are beneath our skills and abilities. We don't take the necessary steps to advance and move out of the position because we're comfortable. We live for the weekends, spending our money on shopping and hanging out just so we don't have to think about the job. By Sunday evening, we start getting depressed and by Monday morning we've hit the ground running . . . running toward Friday when we're off again, and away from the j-o-b.

Others—those of us who are open to God's blessings, no matter how they come—ask and perhaps find the strength to answer our callings. We then dedicate our lives to doing the work God would have us do.

A calling is one of God's richest blessings. We've all heard, "God is not through with me yet," which means you've got something to give that this world needs. Following your calling means you've refused to edit your potential by staying put on a particular road. Many times that road is so familiar, it's hard to change direction. We just want to stay there because that's what we've been doing for the past ten years. But it's when we take the fork in the road . you know, the one less traveled, that we ultimately find our good. To do so, we must be willing to break the vocational paradigm and simply go for it!

God has called all of us *His* children, which makes us soldiers for Christ. That means the individual talents we've been blessed with need to be cultivated and utilized for a greater reason than simply fattening our bank accounts. Following the voice of a Higher calling means taking on the difficult burdens, but also accepting the wonderful benefits that await each of us if we only listen.

THE AMERICAN DREAM

"AND WE DREAMED A DREAM IN ONE NIGHT, I AND HE; WE DREAMED EACH MAN ACCORDING TO THE INTERPRETATION OF HIS DREAM."

GENESIS 41:11 (KJV)

Many of us spend decades in the workplace striving for our shot at the American dream. We work by someone else's rules on how to make it—how to succeed—how to find real job security. And then, the rules change. When we realize there is no such thing as job security anymore, we become disillusioned. We see that the American dream is a picture someone else painted.

With the glass ceiling firmly in place, and layoffs becoming an everyday occurrence regardless of the economy, we need to wake up from the dream. Maybe it's time to change the picture. Maybe it's finally time to ask God what He has in mind. Be prepared, though. When we get to the point where we're willing to listen, there may be pain involved. It most certainly means moving past our comfort zone, and into God's possibility zone.

Think about Moses for a second *(Exodus)*. We've all heard the story about him. He was once royalty; the adopted son of a Pharaoh. Then, through a series of unpredictable events, he was cast out of Egypt and wandered through the desert until he finally found a place to settle. He married, had children, and spent decades tending someone else's sheep.

Moses got curious one day, and decided to check out a natural phenomenon—a bush of fire that refused to burn out. He discovered it was the Spirit of God. That Spirit directed him to follow his calling: to go back to Egypt and lead a group of slaves out of bondage. Moses couldn't for the life of him figure out why God had chosen him. He said he couldn't be the one, after all he was an outcast, and on top of that, he tended to get tongue-tied when he had to speak. But despite his insecurities, the cries of the Israelites in bondage superseded his desire to stay where he was.

You see, sometimes God leads us where we don't want to be in order for us to realize our potential. This means we have to get comfortable with the uncomfortable. It most certainly means going deep within to see not with our own eyes, but with Spirit sight.

The American dream is in many cases an illusion. Waking up from that may mean we are forced to reinvent who we are. While we may not be comfortable with that at first, once we put our faith in God we will find reassurance in Him. Better that, than putting our trust in someone else's definition of what our potential truly is.

LINNIE: *I never felt a sense of welcome from the corporate environments I worked in during the seventies and the eighties. It was always apparent the establishment was the domain of those who did not look like me or think like me. From the ethnic jokes that were always on the tip of somebody's tongue, to the unabashed racist and sexist behavior, there was no question of the sense of entitlement and superiority felt by many in that environment. I remember thinking that my uncles were ten times sharper than most of the men I came in contact with, but of course the opportunities hadn't been there for them. It was a private club. A few of us were able to sneak in, but we were always reminded that we were only visitors. I think America suffered for this and so did those companies.*

I always felt there had to be something more than what the corporate world had to offer. I longed for warmth and it offered coldness; I longed for diversity and it offered sameness; and most important, I longed for spirituality and it offered practicality. I was the square peg trying to fit into the round hole. But what was I to do? After all, the whole point of my education and training was to secure a corporate job and climb the career ladder.

And so, I did what others did before me, and what many are still do-

ing today—I gritted my teeth, held my chin up, and forged ahead. I was tough when I needed to be tough, charming when I needed to be charming, and crafty when I needed to be crafty. But the problem was, this wasn't me. I was only doing what was necessary to hang on in corporate America.

So, behind the closed door of my office, or in my car at lunchtime, I would pray to the Lord to show me a better way. Many times I prayed to God to remove the turmoil that was around me in the workplace. And He would. I also knew I had to take God with me when I attended meetings. So I would say a prayer beforehand, and He would walk in with me. If I led the meeting, my favorite prayer was a short one I created for myself: "Lord, guide me as I lead this meeting. Let my words be brief, yet persuasive. Let my message be received as it is given. And please, Lord, let those who attend come with an open heart and mind. God bless us all. Amen."

I couldn't have made it in that world without God on my side. And as I matured, I learned not to be as concerned about the environment itself, but to concentrate on what I could learn from it and how I could grow—both professionally and personally. But eventually, I realized I could never find the spirituality I longed for in a corporate environment. I realized I needed to use the skills I had learned in corporate America to serve God.

It became easier for me to do this after my son was born. After his birth I reexamined my priorities and the American dream was no longer something I wanted to pursue. My husband helped by reminding me I could not serve two masters: my career and my family. Something had to give. I decided to go with my family.

I started by working part time and then I began consulting for nonprofit organizations. This allowed me the flexibility of working from home and having lots of time to spend with my son. I started working for my church and was able to use many of the skills I had learned in corporate jobs. This led to the formation of my own company, partnered

*with my longtime friend Andria—This Far By Faith Enterprises. Through
our company, we use our skills and resources to spread the word of the
importance of faith in God. At last, the Lord has led me to spiritually fulfilling work!*

DOOR CLOSERS

"DO NOT WITHHOLD GOOD FROM THOSE WHO DESERVE IT,
WHEN IT IS IN YOUR POWER TO ACT."

PROVERBS 3:27 (NIV)

It seems no matter how far up the ladder of success you get, there
will be someone who doesn't want you there, doesn't think you deserve to be there, who will do what he or she can to get you out of
there! They are Professional Door Closers, using their positions as
owners, managers, or supervisors to keep others from reaching their
fullest potential. They are shepherds whom God has put in charge of
His flock, but who have turned their backs on the sheep that were
placed in their care. Instead of mentoring, they alienate and promul-
gate their intentions. Instead of assisting where they can, they "withhold good from those who deserve it."

Look at *Jeremiah 23:1–4 (God's Word)*:

" 'HOW HORRIBLE IT WILL BE FOR THE SHEPHERDS WHO ARE
DESTROYING AND SCATTERING THE SHEEP IN MY CARE,' DECLARES
THE LORD. 'THIS IS WHAT I, THE LORD GOD OF ISRAEL, SAID TO THE
SHEPHERDS WHO TAKE CARE OF MY PEOPLE: "YOU HAVE SCATTERED
MY SHEEP AND CHASED THEM AWAY. YOU HAVE NOT TAKEN CARE OF
THEM, SO NOW I WILL TAKE CARE OF YOU BY PUNISHING YOU FOR
THE EVIL YOU HAVE DONE," ' DECLARES THE LORD. 'THEN I WILL
GATHER THE REMAINING PART OF MY FLOCK FROM ALL THE
COUNTRIES WHERE I CHASED THEM. I WILL BRING THEM BACK TO
THEIR PASTURE, AND THEY WILL BE FERTILE AND INCREASE IN

NUMBER. I WILL PUT SHEPHERDS OVER THEM. THOSE SHEPHERDS
WILL TAKE CARE OF THEM . ' "

When we get a chance to help others advance, God expects us to
do just that. Maybe that is why He has allowed us to assume a leadership position in the first place. Unfortunately, so many labor to keep
folks "in their place." It seems this kind of insecure behavior is an
equal opportunity trait in both whites and blacks. But the wounds cut
much deeper for African Americans when it's one of their own.

Our elders realized the success of our people could not be measured by the few of us who made good in their day. The teachers, the
preachers, the doctors, and the dentists. For even they, like most of us
now, were only one closed door removed from their poorer relatives.

Today, some of us talk about our lesser-achieving brethren as
though they deserve their lot in life. We forget what our elders
knew—"There, but for the grace of God, go I." We think we have
made it, not because of God's merciful intervention, but based on
something we did on our own. We not only look down on those at
the bottom, we sometimes feel threatened by those who could be our
peers.

For decades, while most of us were pained at being "the only
one," others of us thought it a privilege. Some began to feel safe with
that distinction, wearing it as some strange badge of honor. And if
they see more African Americans gracing the halls of the establishment, they actively push to close the doors they themselves only recently walked through.

ANDRIA: At first, you don't want to admit it's happening—that a fellow
African American would single you out because of your race. I mean,
how could an African-American supervisor not be different than corpo-
rate-minded white males. They are, after all, bringing to the table their
life experiences. It was because of these trials and tribulations, we think,

they cannot help but bring a sense of justice, fairness, and fair play. They know how hard it is for professional blacks trying to make it in white America. They most assuredly understand, deeply and personally, the feeling of being overlooked, not because you can't do the work but because you don't fit the profile and refuse or don't know how to play the politics.

I guess I got comfortable, at one point in my career, thinking I had arrived. I had paid my dues. It was no longer about politics, it was about the work. I thought I could simply do my job, live my life, and be accepted for who I was—a child of God. Funny thing happens when you get comfortable. There's always somebody waiting to see you squirm. Just as Jesus tells us in John 15:20–21 (God's Word):

" . . IF THEY PERSECUTED ME, THEY WILL ALSO PERSECUTE YOU .
INDEED, THEY WILL DO ALL THIS TO YOU BECAUSE YOU ARE COMMITTED
TO ME, SINCE THEY DON'T KNOW THE ONE WHO SENT ME."

When you are committed to serving God and not man, if you refuse to have two masters, you will most certainly be singled out!

Who knows for sure why I was targeted? Maybe to send a clear message that just because I was African American, there would be no playing favorites if the boss was also black and female. Maybe it wasn't about me at all, but about someone wanting to prove to their superiors they could be as tough as they were.

I guess it's hard for some, when they finally reach a level of achievement, not to want to close the door so they can't get pushed out. The problem is: No one else can get through. Or, maybe these Professional Door Closers are being used to minimize our collective power and presence on the corporate landscape.

One thing's for sure, this divide and conquer game manifests itself so often in corporate life today that a pattern is now emerging. Many of our successful African Americans who have made it to the top also make a habit of moving into a position of power and then singling out either *a black male or a black female of whom to make an example. Instead of changing the rules, they simply play by the same rules the big boys do. Why is it these professional blacks employ the tactics used against them to keep them from achieving?*

Too many of us leave our spiritual selves at the door when we walk into our offices. More of us should wear it on our sleeves while we're at work. If we did, there would be more harmony and less discord. We would realize that God's kingdom is infinite and there is more than enough for everybody. Collectively, we would prosper and business would grow.

SOUL SURVIVOR

"WE WEAR OURSELVES OUT DOING PHYSICAL LABOR. WHEN PEOPLE VERBALLY ABUSE US, WE BLESS THEM. WHEN PEOPLE PERSECUTE US, WE ENDURE IT. WHEN OUR REPUTATIONS ARE ATTACKED, WE REMAIN COURTEOUS . . ."

1 CORINTHIANS 4:12–13 (GOD'S WORD)

Whether a manual laborer or corporate deal maker, we all toil. Most of the time we are recognized and rewarded for our efforts. But sometimes we are confronted with competitiveness, envy, insecurity, or just plain evil by people who choose to sabotage us on the job. For the most part, it's called office politics and it's everywhere—from major corporations to the smallest of church offices. Sometimes it becomes a battle for the soul.

So what must we do to survive hostility in the workplace? Leaving the job is an obvious answer, but maybe, for whatever reason, changing jobs is not an option for us. If this is the case, try this as a faith exercise:

- Place anyone who is creating disharmony at the job in God's hands. We must pray for them. *1 Samuel 12:11* reassures us that

God will deliver us out of the hands of our enemies so we can be safe on every side. Holding a person up in prayer can yield amazing results. An enemy will eventually turn and become an ally, or God will simply move the person out of your way.

- **Make sure your own spiritual life is strong.** When we know we are doing the right thing, when we know we have cleaned up our "spiritual act," we can then use Divine radar to hone in on what really is the problem at work. Go through a spiritual checklist: Am I treating everybody right at the office? Not just those who can help me, but also those whom I can assist? If I'm complaining about unfair wages, am I living up to my responsibilities toward my employer? Am I really giving my all for the eight to ten hours when I'm working? If God can trust me with someone else's wealth, won't He then give me my own?

- **Look at the bigger picture.** Why are things happening the way they are? Remember: Through God, all things work together for good. If you are experiencing a challenge, it is for a reason. No one can keep you from your good *except* you. Stay open even in the midst of the storm. Know you are walking a path which will ultimately take you from where you are to where you need to be. Divine order prevails.

- **Ask the Lord to take control of the situation.** "Lead me, Lord," should be your daily prayer. God can guide you through the land mines on the job. He can order your steps so you won't falter. *Matthew 10:19* reminds you that He can tell you what to say and when to say it. We, however, must ask the Holy Spirit to work through us and take charge.

- **Remember our Faith Formula.** Even life on the job is "Divinely Inspired." If you've decided to live this concept, then you must apply the Faith Formula in every aspect of living. Employment is no exception. Let go and Let God. Wait on the Lord. Know that He will lead you to your good. Live your faith.

Surrender + Belief + Patience = Faith

It may not be easy, especially if you're faced with challenges in the workplace. But you can always call on God, and know that even in the most difficult of circumstances, He protects and provides.

ANDRIA: *Anyone who's faced workplace hostility and strife knows it is a personally and professionally agonizing time. That's certainly how it was for me. Sabotage, back-stabbing, not knowing whom to trust or whom to confide in. My course of action was to make a decision.*

My soul had grown weary. I had become tired of the pace, tired of the politics . . . tired of jumping through hoops. During its worst, I practically lived on my knees. It was a spiritual struggle, but eventually, my prayers were answered. I decided I would no longer degrade my ability, nor the profession I had worked so long and hard in, by being anyone's scapegoat for success. I would not continue to participate in the old divide and conquer game.

My grandmother always used to tell me, if God puts you somewhere, no man (or woman) can take you from there. If God closes a door, He always opens a window. Well, it was only the grace of God, His mercy—His wisdom and His never-ending sense of Divine timing—that ultimately removed me from the situation.

I have to admit though, coping was nearly unbearable. We all have our stories of painful politics and sabotage in the workplace. But when I finally accepted just what was going on, I turned even more to God for His guidance. It's times like these when we need to become more of a Christian. It's not easy, and it requires heavy-duty prayer.

So every morning, instead of getting off the elevator and cursing the place I dreaded being, I decided to bless it. Each day, instead of spewing thoughts of venom and disdain for those in charge, I blessed them. Every day, I would pray at my desk for protection and ask the Lord to give me strength and wisdom to hold out until He said it was time to go.

I realize now that I actually contributed to my own torture. It's important to own up to the role we play when we're facing hard times. You see, God never wants us more attached to any one thing than we are to Him. I was fighting with my will, thinking, "If I just do this, or if I just do that . . ." Well, after fighting as much as I could, I gave in and it was only when I surrendered my attachment to the results of the outcome that I found my freedom.

That freedom came one summer night while I was in bed, exhausted, twenty-five pounds thinner than five months before, and incredibly stressed. I opened up the Bible, as so many of us often do, letting the pages fall where they may to receive the message I was meant to read that night. I found myself at the book of James. It's a small chapter, only five pages. Normally I would have been too mentally drained to tackle an entire book, but within these five pages my soul found surrender in James 1:2–4 (God's Word):

> "MY BROTHERS AND SISTERS, BE VERY HAPPY WHEN YOU ARE
> TESTED IN DIFFERENT WAYS. YOU KNOW THAT SUCH TESTING OF
> YOUR FAITH PRODUCES ENDURANCE. ENDURE UNTIL YOUR TESTING
> IS OVER. THEN YOU WILL BE MATURE AND COMPLETE,
> AND YOU WON'T NEED ANYTHING."

After reading from James, I finally released my will unto His. It didn't matter anymore what anyone else thought about me, my abilities, or my standing in the workplace. What mattered was that I could now rejoice in the midst of my own misery. I was being tested in different ways, and according to the Word, that meant it was time to celebrate. The more I stayed in the Word, the greater strength I found in my faith. 2 Peter 1:5–7 (God's Word):

> ". . MAKE EVERY EFFORT TO ADD INTEGRITY TO YOUR FAITH; AND
> TO INTEGRITY ADD KNOWLEDGE; TO KNOWLEDGE ADD SELF-CONTROL;
> TO SELF-CONTROL ADD ENDURANCE; TO ENDURANCE ADD GODLINESS;

TO GODLINESS ADD CHRISTIAN AFFECTION; AND TO CHRISTIAN
AFFECTION ADD LOVE."

I was now in love with the moment, no matter how difficult. I no longer needed to tread water. I was able to freestyle and still stay afloat. Just as scripture guides us to be thankful for all gifts, to count it all joy. In Philippians 4:11–14 (God's Word), it says:

". . . I'VE LEARNED TO BE CONTENT IN WHATEVER SITUATION I'M IN.
I KNOW HOW TO LIVE IN POVERTY OR PROSPERITY. NO MATTER WHAT
THE SITUATION. I'VE LEARNED THE SECRET OF HOW TO LIVE WHEN
I'M FULL OR WHEN I'M HUNGRY, WHEN I HAVE TOO MUCH OR WHEN
I HAVE TOO LITTLE. I CAN DO EVERYTHING THROUGH CHRIST
WHO STRENGTHENS ME."

The next day, I went to work, content if I stayed, content if I left. Happy if either outcome was on my terms or not. Two weeks later, I was gone . . on my terms. I surrendered to His direction for my life.

When we move out of the way, that's when the Holy Spirit is free to act on our behalf. We always need to remember that if we are challenged, it is for a reason. Some fights we need to fight. God has somewhere for us to go, something for us to do. It is by enduring these tests that we grow into a state of preparedness as we reach our next level of spiritual immaturity. (We never fully grow-up in faith, become an adult with nothing else to learn. There is always another lesson.) As we grow, we are free to move on to greater heights.

What is clear to me now, which was so cloudy then, is that if I had stayed where I was, I likely wouldn't have written this book or started a company with Linnie. Every challenge prepares us for the road ahead. Who knows? Maybe I wouldn't have been strong enough spiritually to step out on faith, doing what the Lord really wanted me to do.

If I hadn't been tested, I don't know if I would have had the strength for all that lay ahead: a shift in my career, my status as a work-at-home mom, an entrepreneur, and committed Christian professional. I'm not sure I would have had the endurance to help start a company dedicated to changing the lives of individuals and getting them to seek out their own greater talents for a grander purpose. Had I not surrendered, I never would have survived. It was only in surrendering that I found real power. Not the kind of power an insecure boss has over an employee, but the kind of power the Lord has over our lives.

ANSWER THE CALL

"WITH THIS IN MIND, WE CONSTANTLY PRAY FOR YOU, THAT OUR
GOD MAY COUNT YOU WORTHY OF HIS CALLING, AND THAT BY HIS
POWER HE MAY FULFILL EVERY GOOD PURPOSE OF YOURS
AND EVERY ACT PROMPTED BY YOUR FAITH."

2 THESSALONIANS 1:11 (NIV)

We are all given gifts from God. Gifts that we should use to serve others and the Lord. Our goal ought to be to determine what our gifts are and how we can bring them forth to let our light shine. And if we're not in touch with our inner voice, it is impossible to listen for direction. We've all heard questions coming from deep within, the ones that say to us: "*Why are you wasting your talents on this job?*" or "*Why aren't you pursuing what you really love?*" But we are often so blinded by what the world tells us we should be doing, that we can't listen to what we've been blessed to be *able* to do if given the chance.

Sometimes we know what our gifts are but choose not to use them. We think we won't be prosperous or fulfilled if we pursue our gifts as a vocation. Or, we are insecure about ourselves so we hold back, thinking we're not quite good enough to share our talents with the world. But displaying the colors God has uniquely dressed us in is incredibly joyous, for it is a vivid display to the world of just how good God can be.

Gathering up our talents, giving all we have, and then expecting to receive joy, compensation, and peace from a job well done is all but missing in the workplace. We step up to the plate each and every day, head out to the j-o-b to answer the call, but the call is becoming more impossible to answer. Our work environments are increasingly demanding, giving less and less in return for our efforts. We are left feeling exhausted and depleted. More and more of us are finding our spiritual gas tanks on "Empty," as we go to work everyday wondering if we really are making a difference.

If you're having strong feelings that God has more in store for you, that He's not through with you yet, then you are already on a path of self-discovery and service. The next step is in acknowledging that God has a calling for each of us. Finding your passion and purpose in life is attainable.

Ask God to open your mind and heart to what He wants to reveal to you. Tell Him you want to be of service to others. Look objectively at your life and ask the following questions:

- If I could do anything just for the love of it, without being paid, what would it be?
- What is the one thing I've always wanted to do?
- What am I really good at?
- How can I best please God with my talents?
- When my life is over, what do I want to be remembered for?

LINNIE: *I never considered myself a writer even though I've been writing all my life. I remember poems and stories I wrote when I was a small child. Writing was a way for me to overcome my shyness. Even when I was too timid to express myself verbally, I could write my heart out and let my feelings flow.*

During much of my adult life I've kept journals where I've documented my pains, triumphs, and pleasures. I also wrote short stories, poems, and articles, but still didn't consider myself a writer. Then I looked back on some of my early goals and objectives from long ago and there it was—back in 1978 I wrote that I wanted to be a published writer. But it was still not something I pursued. It was a back-burner, "maybe someday," kind of dream. And real life wasn't about chasing dreams. It was about making money. Oh, how wrong I was!

Well—here I am a writer! It's been a long road to get me where I need to be. I know that all of my experiences have led me to this point. I am now old enough to realize the value of following your dreams. I am comfortable enough to let go of old ideas about career goals and success.

Now my writing is God-inspired. I feel as though I am the messenger and He is the muse. I write not just for personal fulfillment but to spread the word. I have moved writing to the forefront of my life, as He has guided me to. I am so thankful that He never gave up on me.

We may feel that we aren't able to pursue our calling. We have to pay the bills and put food on the table. The realities of life may make us feel foolish and irresponsible if we decide to follow a path others perceive as trivial. Stepping out on faith can be a scary thing no matter how much we believe. But this is the requirement if we are to answer our calling. We must pray to God for His guidance, and then we have to go for it!

ANDRIA: I'm beginning to think that when God speaks to us when we're young, we hear Him more clearly. Children always seem to have a closer relationship with God. When we grow up, we're too spiritually immature to know that it's Him talking to us.

I, like Linnie, have always had something to say on paper. When I was in high school, my good friend Evelyne inspired me to write poetry. So I began to write down my emotional, social, and political perceptions in images. This as I was sweetly entering womanhood. Then I wrote

about a fireman—how the lure of love was so enticing and so dangerous. (What did I really know back then about love?)

I also kept a diary; a secret journal of my hidden heart. Then, when
I came home from college that first summer, I left my things in the car
overnight because I was just too tired to unpack and woke up the next
morning to find that someone had broken into my blue Datsun. They
didn't take the portable stereo I had packed up in the backseat. They
didn't take my Pentax camera . . . they didn't even take the suitcases I
had piled one on top of the other. What they took could never be replaced. The only two things missing were my diary and the little
wooden/wicker stool my grandmother gave me when I was four years
old. I was so wounded and violated that I have not kept a personal journal since. That loss almost kept me from writing again.

But by my junior year, after giving up on majoring in special ed and
sociology, I finally found my true love . . . creative writing. That was
where I was sure my talents lay. I could wax poetic about the meaning of
life, and say things in fantasy I could never acknowledge in reality. But
then the reality of having to get a job and eat hit me like books falling
off a shelf. How on earth would I support myself as a writer? But after my
boyfriend (now my husband) kept encouraging me to go into journalism, I finally relented and said, "I know, I'll become a television reporter,
make my money that way, and then I can afford to write that novel."
Well, as you sit reading this now, you tell me: God was talking to me
back then, was I simply not hearing what He was saying?

I spent eighteen years as a journalist. I love and value all I have
done in the past and look forward to what I will do in the future. I've won
awards, but now seek recognition on a much deeper level. I have come
to understand who my audience really is. And one day, I hope to measure up in His rating book. To God I give the glory, and now . . . I'm writing, and I'm writing about Him. I could never have done that in television
news.

I made the decision to follow my calling and I'm blessed because of *it. I pray I can be a blessing to others. After all, that's what our living should be about. How about you? Do you have a purpose? Is the Universe leading you in a more Divine direction? That's a question that you should ask yourself. Maybe the time has come for you to be able to hear God's answers.*

THIS LITTLE LIGHT OF MINE

"NO ONE LIGHTS A LAMP AND PUTS IT UNDER A BASKET. INSTEAD, EVERYONE WHO LIGHTS A LAMP, PUTS IT ON A LAMPSTAND. THEN ITS LIGHT SHINES ON EVERYONE IN THE HOUSE. IN THE SAME WAY LET YOUR LIGHT SHINE IN FRONT OF PEOPLE. THEN THEY WILL SEE THE GOOD THAT YOU DO AND PRAISE YOUR FATHER IN HEAVEN."

MATTHEW 5:15–16 (GOD'S WORD)

It's when our very livelihood is threatened that we sometimes feel most alone, and this is when we should turn to the scriptures to find solace and direction. This is when we should take comfort in the fact that the Divine is indeed at work in all things. Someone else may have evil or self-serving intentions for our lives, but God turns evil into good. He has the power to turn a crisis into a calling.

How do we know when He is calling us to pursue something different? It takes practice. Sometimes His voice will come to us, and we'll call it a "hunch." At other times, we'll feel moved to do something, and call it "inspiration." These are all ways in which we receive our direction from the Lord. He is vast and infinite. God can talk to us any way He pleases! It's up to us to pay attention. So start developing your inner ear now. And look for the signs. He wants our lights to shine.

"IN THE SAME WAY, LET YOUR LIGHT SHINE BEFORE MEN, THAT THEY MAY SEE YOUR GOOD DEEDS AND PRAISE YOUR FATHER IN HEAVEN."

MATTHEW 5:16 (KJV)

CHAPTER TEN—JOBS, CAREERS, AND CALLINGS

REMEMBER THIS

❋ **SEEK YOUR CALLING.** The world awaits what you have to offer. Ask God, what it is He might like to tell you. It doesn't have to be a formal, heavy-duty talk. Just open up the dialogue. Keep reaching out to Him. In *Proverbs 8:17 (KJV)* it is written:

"I LOVE THOSE WHO LOVE ME, AND THOSE WHO SEEK ME EARLY SHALL FIND ME."

Notice scripture says "*early.*" Call His name, ask Him for His guidance. Ask Him to tell you what it is He would have you to do. Where it is He would have you to go. If you do this first, your way will be made easier.

❋ **MONEY IS NOT THE GOAL. SERVING OTHERS IS.** When we know this, prosperity prevails. How does God want you to serve? Carve out some time for listening. Let God know what questions you'd like answered. Go somewhere quiet with pen and paper in hand. Say a prayer of praise. Thank Christ for His suffering so that you have access to the Father, and then be still. Don't think with your head, instead write down whatever comes into your heart. Try isolating that part of your body. Actually visualize words being written across your left chest. Then, as you are writing, ask God, "Am I getting it right?" Give yourself time to find a rhythm with this. Don't rush it. Carve out at least half an hour. Do this as many times as you feel you need to, and then review the words you were moved to write down. Then act on them!

PRAY FOR THIS:
LORD, LET ME SERVE

When we understand that the point of our journey is not to have, but to do, our total perspective shifts. We give rather than focus on receiving. We open ourselves up to God's will, and because of His grace and mercy, He rains down upon us an abundance of blessings.

PRAYER FOR GUIDANCE AT WORK

Lord, I humbly come before You. I thank You for
hearing my call.
I need Your protection now. In the workplace, I need it
more than ever.
In every decision, guide me toward Your will.
Please teach me to take Your hand.

Help me to be still. Please lead me down Your path and
Should I come to a fork, let me not panic and
wonder if I'm lost.
Instead, gently remind me that You are my Divine compass.
You would never leave me in this wilderness alone.
As I seek out a livelihood,
I remember Your promise to provide. You said
You'd never forsake me so I remain ever at
the ready to do Your will.
Your word says to come before the throne as a little child.
So I bow my head. I throw open my arms to You.
Then, I can reach out to others.
Let not politics nor pride keep me from being of service.
I am here to do Your good works.
And if I can be so honored, let them see Your brilliance
through my compassionate laboring.
Then we will all be able to say, Amen.

CHAPTER ELEVEN

Crossing Raging Waters

"... THE LORD HATH HIS WAY IN THE WHIRLWIND AND
IN THE STORM, AND THE CLOUDS ARE THE DUST OF HIS
FEET. HE REBUKETH THE SEA, AND MAKETH IT DRY ...
THE LORD IS GOOD, A STRONG HOLD IN THE DAY OF
TROUBLE, AND HE KNOWETH THEM THAT TRUST IN HIM."

NAHUM 1:3–4, 7 (KJV)

It seems no matter how enlightened we are, how in tune we are, or how righteous we think we are, there will be times when we find ourselves deep in troubled water. When the raging waters draw near we frantically search for something to hold on to. We look for a lifeline.

Some of us look to other people to rescue us. We worry our friends and family with our problems, hoping to make our burdens their own. Others find temporary solace with drugs or alcohol. Maybe it's cocaine or Prozac or Jack Daniel's, anything as long as it temporarily numbs the pain. Still others are in denial—they pretend they don't see the water rising around them. But many fall on their knees, throw up their hands, and say, "Lord help me."

And He will. Maybe not when we want it, or the way we want it, but scripture tells us in *Psalms 9:10 (NIV):*

"THOSE WHO KNOW YOUR NAME WILL TRUST IN YOU, FOR YOU,
LORD, HAVE NEVER FORSAKEN THOSE WHO SEEK YOU."

We trust that God will lead us to calmer waters. We pray to our Father:

"PEACE BE STILL."

It makes no difference if you are turning to the Lord for the first time or if you are a constant caller—He will hear your cry. Sometimes we don't know what to say or how to say it, but rest assured—He will hear your cry. Or maybe we've rejected Him for most of our lives and hate admitting that we need Him now. Don't worry—He will hear your cry.

Challenges, disappointments, grief, problems, frustrations, we all have them. Don't even think about navigating through them without the Lord. Let Him be your rock, your armor, and your anchor.

HIS EYE IS ON THE SPARROW

"FOR, LO, THE WINTER IS PAST, THE RAIN IS OVER AND GONE. THE
FLOWERS APPEAR ON THE EARTH; THE TIME OF THE SINGING OF
BIRDS IS COME, AND THE VOICE OF THE TURTLEDOVE
IS HEARD IN OUR LAND."

SONG OF SOLOMON 2:11–12 (AMPLIFIED)

The lyrics go like this. "I sing because I'm happy. I sing because I'm free. His eye is on the sparrow, for I know He watches me." When we give our cares to Him, there is a certain freedom we receive. When we survive one of life's storms, there is a joy, because then we truly understand God is here for us in a practical sense. There is a special place where we can enter unto His rest. This is where peace and love abide. This is where our spirits can forever reside, even if our bodies, minds, and hearts are elsewhere. We know that whatever happens He is there.

The meaning of life is change. Some of us deal with these changes better than others. Still, throughout our lives, we have a hard time adjusting to anything that upsets our world. Most times, forced change is for the better, but how do we participate in ensuring this? We live the Faith Formula: Putting God first, we *surrender* into prayer each and every situation we're confronted with; we have the *belief* that God will fix it and the *patience* to allow the Divine to do what is best. We accept God's grace knowing that this change will work together for the good of all concerned.

It's hard, when we're young or vulnerable, spiritually ignorant or emotionally trapped, to understand that we have all been placed on the path that was meant for us. It's even harder to accept this as a universal truth when we see that some paths are fraught with pitfalls, dangers, toils, and snares, while others appear strewn with roses. But nonetheless, when we train ourselves to view our circumstances with spiritual illumination, then we will more often view things with God's light rather than with the light of man.

ANDRIA: *When I was six and my sister was eight, my mother left my father for just a few short weeks. My mother's relationship with my father was difficult. There were many marital issues she was forced to deal with that no woman should ever have to endure. My dad was confronted with an onslaught of professional challenges and responsibilities, more than most men could ever handle. The demands of a needy church pulled him in too many directions. It eventually pulled their marriage apart. She desperately needed to get his attention. Her brief departure was meant to be a wake-up call that their marriage was in real trouble. But when she tried to come back, circumstances had changed. Life had put all of us on a different path. I sometimes wonder what would have happened* to each of us—my mom, my dad, my sister, and me—had we all lived to-gether.

At that time, I had no other friends who lived with their dads and were raised by their grandparents. I still saw my mother often, but I went through a particularly tough time when I was between twelve and six-teen, trying to reconcile my love for my mother and my feelings of mater-nal deprivation. At that time, I viewed our relationship based on how oth-ers wanted me to feel. Especially a few of my father's female friends (whom, of course, I now realize were desperately trying to become my stepmother). Sometimes I took these emotions out on my mom when she would visit. I would reject her, saying I was expecting a friend to stop by, or wanted instead to be with one of those other women my father re-ally liked. I see now the pain I must have caused her. I'm sorry I didn't fully know it then. I see now that it was the glare of others' opinions of what a family should be that influenced my behavior. My sister and I were made to feel the strain of coming from an unconventional family. But all the while, God's light brilliantly cast a glow on all of us, protecting my sister Akosua and me, and preparing us for the long journey ahead.

My childhood lacked nothing, and as far as I'm concerned, every step of the way has been Divinely planned and beautifully executed. It wasn't meant for me to be raised in a traditional home. I wouldn't be who I am today if I had been. There's just no second guessing God as to how our life unfolds.

I have grown to understand the concept of God's Divine plan. I won-der if my parents have too. I know that my father continues to carry an all-too-heavy burden about the whole thing. I believe he still feels re-sponsible, inadequate, and negligent in many ways. To this day, he is constantly trying to compensate for what he thinks was a less than ideal childhood for my sister and me. To him, I say, I loved my life.

My mother, I believe, has her own disquieting thoughts too. I think she often wonders what life would have been like, had she been there day to day. I, of course, am a mom now too, and understand her feelings *of loss about not watching us grow up as closely as a mom would want to. To her, I say, I'm grateful we are so close now, because this is when I need you most in my life. For all of us, our path was the one we each needed to walk. Our life was the one He planned for us. Our love is the gift He gave to us.*

The blessing in all this is the promise that His eye really is on the sparrow. I know He watched over me. He watched over us all, moving each of us from where we were then to where we need to be at this very moment, all for His glory and Divine purpose. I accept the road that was put before me. As a child, I walked it gingerly. Now, as an adult, I boldly go forward in faith knowing He precedes me.

I am spiritually grounded. I don't believe in regrets—only lessons. I am anointed with a family of my own. If I can get over all that has happened in the past, and actually thank God for giving me the life He did, then my prayer is that both my parents are over it too. And whatever mistakes I make with my children will be forgiven.

I'm not saying my parents live with constant guilt for the way things turned out. They don't. I'm not saying they think about the past and kick themselves on a regular basis now. I'm just saying that I know how much they love us both, and in an odd way, still love each other. Maybe you come from a family where divorce has created old scars too. But in everything we must witness the Divine. So let's all rejoice in how far we've come letting love heal past hurts and carry us toward our good.

Part of accepting good is getting comfortable with the fact that we will never have the power to determine just how life will turn out. We will never be privy to the complete game plan. God is not a football coach. He doesn't huddle us together in the lockers, give us the entire strategy for tackling life's problems and then tell us: "*Now go out there and kick some butt.*" No, God won't reveal His full set of details to any one of us. Instead He offers His illumination on a need-to-know basis. *Amos 3:7 (KJV)* says:

"SURELY THE LORD GOD WILL DO NOTHING, BUT HE REVEALETH
HIS SECRET UNTO HIS SERVANTS, THE PROPHETS."

He gives us only what we can handle at the time. So instead of
putting our faith in just those things we can see, let's try putting our
faith in what we know is there, especially if it is beyond our limited
view of the horizon. Let's remember that He sits on high. He can
guide us where we cannot see.

WHEN DARKNESS COMES

"... THE DARKNESS IS PASSING AWAY AND THE TRUE LIGHT
IS ALREADY SHINING."

1 JOHN 2:8 (NIV)

If at no other time in our lives, in times of grief and sorrow
we turn to the Lord. And our God—our *magnanimous* God—
doesn't hold it against us that we haven't called out His name earlier.
He is right there with us during the dark times, offering solace and
comfort.

Losing a loved one is one of the hardest things in life. But if you
live long enough you are going to experience it. Since none of us
knows when our time will come, we have to express our love for those
closest to us continuously. We don't want to wait until it is too late
to let them know that we love and appreciate them. We want to have
the peace that comes with knowing that all was said and done. This
will allow us to ride the waves of sorrow better. As the old church
song goes, "Give me my flowers, while I'm yet living, so that I can see
the beauty that they bring."

If our loved ones have passed on, instead of grieving, we can concentrate on honoring their memories. We can remember what they
stood for and what we learned from them. We can also pay homage
to them by living our lives the way they would want us to.

When faced with the darkness of grief we can better cope by accepting the following:

- **You are never alone.** When your comforters have gone home, when those closest to you have gone back to their lives, alone, in the stillness of the night, know that you have a God when your grief and emptiness may be more than you can bear, know that He knows the extent of your sorrow.
- **Honor the memory of your loved ones.** Don't let their lives be defined by sadness and pain. Remember the good times. Celebrate the joy they brought you. Live life with integrity, honesty, and faith.
- **Take comfort.** Death does not end the relationship you had with your loved one. Love is eternal. We cannot be separated from love just as we cannot be separated from God. This world offers us only temporary shelter, but love and God will endure.

LINNIE: *I am blessed in that I was grown before I experienced the loss of a close loved one. My mother's sister Rosa and her husband Will J. Brown, Jr., died within two years of each other in the late 1980s. They were both in their fifties when they died—and I felt at the time as if I lost them too soon. I now know that anytime would have been too soon.*

Since they weren't blessed with children, my brother and I were like their surrogate children. They lavished us with much love and affection. But, more important, they gave us their time.

Aunt Rosa was quiet, yet strong. Many say I am a lot like her in both appearance and personality. Her husband, Uncle Brown as I called him, was the greatest man I have ever known. He wasn't a perfect man, but he was a good man—a black man from the old school—proud, responsible, and committed. He laid many of the bricks of my foundation. Whenever he would impart his words of wisdom he would always address me by my first and middle names. "Linnie Rachelle . . ." he would say in his strong deep voice . . . and I knew to stop what I was doing and pay attention.

After their deaths I had the grim task of disposing of their belong-ings—closing down their home. It wasn't pleasant, but there are some things in life we must do. We find strength in knowing God is with us in the dark times as well as in the good times. These are the times we lean on Him.

Unfortunately, these times can also bring out the ugliness in fami-lies. Relatives and friends start clamoring for the deceased one's assets like ants at a picnic. But with God's help, I managed to stay focused and strong during this period. I also felt the spirits of my aunt and uncle telling me what I needed to do and how to do it. They constantly re-minded me that they picked me for the task because they knew that I could do it.

Of all of my responsibilities, the hardest for me was going through their personal possessions. One of the last things I did was to go through their wallets. This felt like such an invasion of privacy that it was a few months before I could bring myself to do it.

After sorting through long-canceled credit cards, pictures, and a driv-er's license, I found, tucked in the crevice of Aunt Rosa's wallet, one half of a worn, tattered dollar bill. I knew exactly where to find the other half . . in his wallet. I carefully and respectfully reunited the dollar, just as God re-united them in Heaven.

FORGIVENESS

". . . FORGIVE, AND YOU WILL BE FORGIVEN. GIVE, AND IT WILL BE
GIVEN TO YOU. A GOOD MEASURE, PRESSED DOWN, SHAKEN
TOGETHER AND RUNNING OVER, WILL BE POURED INTO YOUR LAP.
FOR WITH THE MEASURE YOU USE, IT WILL BE MEASURED TO YOU."

LUKE 6:37–38 (NIV)

We cannot cross life's rivers of sorrow safely if we are carrying heavy baggage. No one's heart is strong enough to hold on to past wrongs. It is, however, big enough to be a vessel for God's love. Forgiveness and love are so closely related. In order to forgive, you must love the Lord enough to obey His command.

"AND WHEN YOU STAND PRAYING, IF YOU HOLD ANYTHING AGAINST ANYONE, FORGIVE HIM, SO THAT YOUR FATHER IN HEAVEN MAY FORGIVE YOU YOUR SINS."

MARK 11:25 (NIV)

LINNIE: *I've noticed that as I age the number of people whom I perceive as having done wrong by me is diminishing, probably because I've also noticed the older I get, the less I remember. I can barely remember what happened last month, never mind last year. It makes it hard to hold a grudge against somebody if you can't remember what they did to you.*

Some people say they can forgive but not forget, but for me it's the reverse—I can forget but not forgive. I will keep someone on my enemy list even if I can't exactly remember why. I know this is ridiculous!

Forgiving can be the hardest thing in the world to do. It's easier to write the person off as someone not deserving of our concern. It's easier to curse those that hurt us. It's easier to put ourselves on a pedestal and look down on all those who have wronged us.

But then we remember in Romans 3:23 (NIV) *it says:*

"... *FOR ALL HAVE SINNED AND FALL SHORT OF THE GLORY OF GOD.*"

So I guess all of us need forgiveness for something. At some point we have wronged someone whether we admit it or not. They may be struggling with how to forgive us.

I have found a way to help myself forgive. I visualize my enemy list.

I see the names on the paper. I see myself take the paper to the ocean and let it float away. My enemies are gone. I have nothing to be mad about.

But what about those who do irreparable harm to us either mentally or physically? It is not as easy to let them float away. Many times these are people who were close to us at one time. Because of this it is harder to forgive them. And the hardest to forgive of all are those we once loved who turn against us.

It is only through prayer that we can find the inner strength that we need to forgive in these cases. We need to pray for ourselves and for those we don't want to forgive. We pray we will one day forgive them, and we pray they will move closer to the light so they won't hurt anyone anymore. We might have to pray this same prayer for a night, a month, a year, or a lifetime.

It's a good feeling not to be mad at anyone about anything. It usually doesn't last long though because Man, unlike God, will disappoint. When this happens we have to remember that Christ died for our sins and that forgiveness is the cornerstone of our religion. We have to rise above the hurt and the anger.

. I'm still working on this forgiveness thing. I remember Peter's question to Jesus:

> " 'LORD, HOW MANY TIMES SHALL I FORGIVE A BELIEVER WHO
> WRONGS ME? SEVEN TIMES?' JESUS ANSWERED HIM, 'I TELL YOU,
> NOT JUST SEVEN TIMES, BUT SEVENTY TIMES SEVEN.' "
>
> MATTHEW 18:21–22 (GOD'S WORD)

This is what the Lord tells us! Keep on forgiving. Who am I to do anything less?

I have noticed that when I take the high road I am able to move past a negative situation quicker. It's much easier to navigate the roads of life without carrying the baggage of unforgiveness.

Many of us never realize the hypocrisy of saying: "I can forgive but I can't forget." This is where we sometimes bind our spiritual progress. This is where we give rise to the opening up of old wounds and the swelling of past hurts. But can you imagine if Jesus had held on to all the memories of people who had done Him wrong? Certainly, He never would have made the choices He did. We know He chose His disciples. Did He not single out Judas to fulfill his calling? Jesus knew even then, Judas would betray Him. Even on the cross He cried out to God:

> " ' . FATHER, FORGIVE THEM; FOR THEY KNOW NOT
> WHAT THEY DO . . . ' "
>
> LUKE 23:34 (KJV)

If we learn to truly forgive, we will notice that in time the details of betrayal, hurt, disappointment, and loss will fade, and just as surely, our hearts will expand to accept those who have failed us or let us down.

WHERE PEACEFUL WATERS FLOW

"HE MAKETH THE STORM A CALM, SO THAT THE WAVES THEREOF ARE STILL."

PSALMS 107:29 (KJV)

The road can get so bumpy at times—so difficult to negotiate that we begin to think our troubles and problems define us. When the outside world attacks, this is the time for us to go to our Father in secret. Others call us a failure. But God calls us a doer. Others say we have no talent. But God says we're one of His children. Others will try to tell us who we are. But God sees who we want to be.

Growing into our fullest selves means we must learn to ride the tide. Sometimes the tide will be high—other times it will be low.

Don't make the mistake of thinking you will ever have yourself so together that you won't have to cross the raging waters. For it is written
in *John 16:33 (KJV)*:

"IN THE WORLD YE SHALL HAVE TRIBULATIONS."

We are all familiar with this. The Bible is filled with stories of
challenge and difficulty. And while we may have heard somewhere
that Jesus said, in this world there will be trials, why is it we never remember the rest of what He said? We never read on any further in
that verse. The next phrase reads:

"BUT BE OF GOOD CHEER FOR I HAVE OVERCOME THE WORLD."

If you're a Christian, you know that Christ died for our sins. But
what does

"I HAVE OVERCOME THE WORLD"

mean? It means Christ conquered all of our problems so that we
would not have to bear them ourselves. It means He willingly accepted the burdens and deficiencies of the flesh, so that we could live
in the spirit.

Think of life as an overture. This is its rhythm. There will be
times when we welcome its melody . . . smooth, steady, and beautiful.
There will be other times when we cover our ears to its harshness, its
intensity, its irregular notes. But no matter the lyrics, no matter the
chorus, no matter the song—we will never have to endure it alone.
When we fully accept that the Greater One is indeed inside of us, we
never have to fear the score the orchestra plays.

ANDRIA: *We get so bogged down worrying how to meet the next challenge that we forget to put Him first in all things.* Ephesians 6:18–20
(God's Word) *says:*

"PRAY IN THE SPIRIT IN EVERY SITUATION. USE EVERY KIND OF
PRAYER AND REQUEST THERE IS. FOR THE SAME REASON, BE ALERT.
USE EVERY KIND OF EFFORT AND MAKE EVERY KIND OF REQUEST FOR
ALL OF GOD'S PEOPLE. ALSO PRAY THAT GOD WILL GIVE ME THE
RIGHT WORDS TO SAY. THEN, I WILL SPEAK BOLDLY WHEN
I REVEAL THE MYSTERY OF THE GOOD NEWS."

I've decided at least to try to consult with God on everything. From how will I pay my mortgage this month to how do I tell the kids one of their best friends is moving away. I figure if I had to pay for this kind of Celestial therapy, I'd never be able to afford it. Fortunately, it's free to all of us. I can either accept the written truth that He will supply my every need, be a comfort to me, heal me from sickness and disease, and rain down so many blessings that my storehouse (if I had one) couldn't hold them. Or . . . I could be out here and go it alone. There really is no in between for me with the promises of the Word. I'm not saying I've got this faith thing down pat. I'm just saying that many of us travel this journey putting our faith in things we can see, built by man. I'm at least going to try my best always to put my faith in Him. You know, walk by faith not by sight.

When we take a look out here in this cold, cruel world, the things we see aren't giving many of us too much hope. That's why, as the old gospel song goes: "My hope is built on nothing less, than Jesus' blood and righteousness."

Now I'm not so spiritually naive to think that no matter what the problem, God's going to e-mail me with just the right quick-fix solution. No—pennies from Heaven don't just rain down when you're broke. Publisher's Clearing House doesn't miraculously show up at the door at the very moment the landlord is having you evicted. I know that's not how Divine doctrine works; we all have to do our part. For the Word says faith without works is nothing, and patience goes hand in hand with belief. Guess I'll keep praying for my patience, and hopefully, God willing, my faith will continue to increase.

Faith is like a flower. It grows and reveals itself as it is nurtured and appreciated. How then do we participate in the unveiling of our own belief in God? We are instructed by the Word to watch what's in our hearts. Pay close attention to what it is you honestly feel, because what we find deep inside ourselves will ultimately manifest itself in our lives. How does it do that? By the words we speak. Choose, there-fore, what you say very carefully. The mouth is a powerful instrument.

"MAKE A TREE GOOD, AND THEN ITS FRUIT WILL BE GOOD. OR MAKE
A TREE ROTTEN, AND THEN ITS FRUIT WILL BE ROTTEN."

MATTHEW 12:33 (GOD'S WORD)

".. YOUR MOUTH SAYS WHAT COMES FROM INSIDE YOU. GOOD
PEOPLE DO THE GOOD THINGS THAT ARE IN THEM. BUT EVIL PEOPLE
DO THE EVIL THINGS THAT ARE IN THEM."

MATTHEW 12:34–35 (GOD'S WORD)

" .. BY YOUR WORDS YOU WILL BE DECLARED INNOCENT, OR BY
YOUR WORDS YOU WILL BE DECLARED GUILTY."

MATTHEW 12:37 (GOD'S WORD)

It's critical to watch what we say. Faith begins, first in our hearts and then reveals itself by what we utter with our tongues. Start speak-ing faith today, and watch your actions and belief follow.

- **Even if you have doubts, don't express them.** If you're not quite sure you will receive a healing or a blessing, be able to pay a bill or find a job, by no means voice your fears. Instead affirm that you will, rather than you won't. Don't look for proof; remember He-brews 11:1 (KJV):

"FAITH IS THE SUBSTANCE OF THINGS HOPED FOR,
THE EVIDENCE OF THINGS NOT SEEN."

• **Train yourself.** Begin by speaking what it is you *want* to believe, then the Father in Heaven will reward you with increased faith. Don't speak words of untruth, words of sickness, despair, hopelessness, and defeat. If you need fortifying, go to the Bible. You will find example after example of how we've already been delivered through the promises of God. Find scriptures to stand on, and then when you're feeling heavy-laden, use the Word as your comfort and guide. That's why they call it the Living Bible!

AMAZING GRACE

**"FOR BY GRACE YOU HAVE BEEN SAVED THROUGH FAITH; AND THIS
IS NOT YOUR OWN DOING, IT IS THE GIFT OF GOD—"**

EPHESIANS 2:8 (RSV)

It is the challenges we face that make us stronger and hopefully wiser. The successes of life are refreshing—they boost our self-esteem and make us feel good—but it is the problems, the disappointments, and the frustrations that we learn the most from. Scripture tells us in *Romans 5:3–4 (KJV):*

".. WE GLORY IN TRIBULATIONS ALSO, KNOWING THAT
TRIBULATION WORKETH PATIENCE, AND PATIENCE EXPERIENCE;
AND EXPERIENCE, HOPE."

It's hard to be thankful for our tough times. But we must thank *Him* for the lessons of life whether they are learned through joy or pain, because no matter how calm the tide, at some point, trouble will find a way of opening up the flood gates. Our life preserver is God.

LINNIE: *Sometimes it is not our own trials that become the turning points of our lives. It is those of our loved ones:*

I was ten years old when my brother Carlton was born. After being an only child for so long I was ecstatic to have a sibling. Because of our age difference I think I was often more maternal toward him than sisterly. I felt protective of him and I loved and cherished him more than anything. I watched him grow to be a personable and bright young man, and the years did not diminish our bond.

I was proud, but not surprised when he was accepted at UC Berkeley. He was on the path that I wanted for him. He was headed in the direction I envisioned for him. I tried to help him any way I could with his college expenses but I noticed by his second year his expenses were growing and he seemed to be spending a lot of time hanging out. I wasn't overly concerned because I remembered my own college days and knew that partying was a part of college life. I hoped that he, like me, would know where to cut it off—when to hit the books. Then came the news I didn't want to hear   . he was no longer a student at Berkeley. He was enrolled in a junior college trying to get his grades up. I was upset and shaken, and this was just an omen of what was to come.

We can be so blind when it comes to those we love. Looking back, I realize that had it been somebody else's brother, someone else's family, I would have suspected what was going on from the beginning. The erratic behavior, the money problems—I had experienced enough of life at that point that I should have known what my brother was facing. It happens in so many families. It cuts across all racial and economic lines. But, I would wager that the majority of families faced with this problem are initially shocked and surprised.

The realization of my brother's drug problem cut through me like a knife. I had suffered through career disappointments, dissolved relationships, money woes, and more, but nothing had affected me like this. I felt as if my heart were being ripped out. My beloved brother, whose life

I had many times cherished more than my own, was traveling through hell and I couldn't save him. I couldn't protect him as I always had.

A part of me wanted to shoot him—put him out of his misery as you would a wounded animal. Another part of me wanted to grab him and hold him close as I had done when he was little and had a bad dream. I wanted to make the hurt go away. His and mine.

While all this was happening, I was newly married and didn't want my husband to know just how much I was hurting. I didn't want to frighten him so I would go in the bathroom in the middle of the night and silently weep for hours. One night he came in and lifted me from the bathroom floor, held me, and told me what I didn't want to hear—that I had to let go of my brother. But how could I do that?

I started reading books on addictions and I called support groups. Everything I read and everyone I talked to focused on me. I began to hear terms like co-dependent and enabler. I couldn't understand why the focus was on me—I wasn't the one with the problem.

Of course I prayed. Prayed as I had never prayed before. I prayed for God to show me how to save my brother—how to put him back on the path I wanted for him. The answer I got from God was not the one I wanted to hear. The Lord told me, as my husband had, that I had to let go.

My brother, who was by then deep in the throes of despair, called me collect one Saturday morning. "Come pick me up," he said, as casually as if he needed a ride from the movies. "I'm tired of living like this, come get me." My ecstasy was short-lived and turned to concern as I pondered what I would do with my drug-addicted brother. I couldn't just bring him home as if nothing had happened.

I kept him on the line and called a counseling center. The counselor told me my brother needed help and that he could get someone to pick him up and take him to a meeting as a first step. I told this to my brother and he said he wasn't interested. "After all," he said, "I don't know these

*people." That is when the chain broke. I hung up the phone and released
the line and my brother. I felt better than I had felt in weeks. As though
a load had been lifted.*

*I finally realized there was nothing I could do to save my brother.
Again in my life I was faced with surrendering to God. I not only let go of
my brother's drug problem, I let go of his life. I knew I could face what
was coming. It was about me, not him. About my going on with my own
life and letting him live whatever was left of his. Later that night, I was
awakened with the feeling that my brother had hit rock bottom and that
he had died. But the funny thing was I accepted it. I had faith that whatever happened I would be all right.*

*The phone ringing early the next morning didn't surprise me. I knew
it was the news about my brother. His voice on the other end of the line
however did surprise me. "Linnie," he started, "I just wanted to let you
know I'm all right." My heart stopped. He continued: "After you hung up
yesterday I ended up at a bus stop. I didn't have any money, but when
the bus arrived I told the driver I needed help. She said, 'I'll help you,
son,' and she took me downtown to the Union Rescue Mission free of
charge. When I got off the bus she wished me luck with putting my life
back together. Late last night the people at the mission took me to a
church where I accepted Christ as my Savior and was baptized. Then
they brought me back and put me in a treatment program. I just wanted
to let you know I'm off the streets."*

*Yeah! I sing because I'm happy! I know all about God's amazing grace!
I know my brother did die that night, but I also know that by accepting
Christ he was reborn. God placed an angel in his life—the bus
driver—when he needed her. God did what I could not do—He saved him!*

*Today my brother is a married family man with a successful career. I
am so proud of him. He took God's hand, picked himself up, and climbed
out of the pit step by step. He didn't ask for any help from me as he
struggled with recovery—"I got myself into this," he said, "I'll get myself
out." He hasn't forgotten where he's been and who saved him. He says*

that when he was struggling the Lord kept reminding him of his up-bringing—the things he had been taught, the people who had believed in him. This gave him the strength to get back on the right path.

I still love him fiercely but in a different way. He has his life and I have mine. I no longer feel responsible for him. That is the way God intended it to be. Try as we might we can't live someone else's life.

This experience brought me closer to God, and I am thankful for the lesson and thankful for the pain. Through the pain, I was led to surrender. Through surrender, I was led to faith. Through faith, I was led to grace.

I will never forget what the Lord did. Sometimes I am sitting on the freeway in the middle of traffic and I have to put a shout out: "Thank You, Lord!" Or, I'm in my laundry room folding clothes and all of a sudden I drop to my knees, look toward heaven, and say: "Thank You, Lord!" Or I'm in church and I think of how great God is and I cry out: "Thank You, Lord!" I don't know about you, but I know firsthand about God's grace and mercy.

HE'LL MAKE A WAY

**"THE LORD WILL GIVE STRENGTH UNTO HIS PEOPLE;
THE LORD WILL BLESS HIS PEOPLE WITH PEACE."**

PSALMS 29:11 (KJV)

We spend so much of life focusing on our problems and challenges. We worry about ourselves, our families, and the world at large. When a problem is solved, instead of rejoicing, we move on to the next problem. Our minds are like radar constantly scanning the horizon looking for that which is bad for us or bad to us.

Scripture tells of the futility of worry in *Matthew 6:34 (NIV):*

"THEREFORE, DO NOT WORRY ABOUT TOMORROW, FOR TOMORROW
WILL WORRY ABOUT ITSELF. EACH DAY HAS ENOUGH
TROUBLE OF ITS OWN."

Instead of always worrying about the obstacles and problems we face today, we need to thank God for all that we have overcome, individually and as a people. You might be hitting that glass ceiling now, but years ago the *only* job you could have had at that company was sweeping floors. You might want a better house now, but years ago you wouldn't have been allowed to even *walk* in the neighborhood where you currently live. You may not have a million dollars today, but you've got more than your mama or daddy *ever* had.

Sometimes it's just a matter of the picture *you* paint of life. Some people cast a dismal tint on everyone they come in contact with. We all know people whom we talk to on the telephone and, afterward, we're depressed and angry. Their conversation is so negative that whatever good mood you might have been in is long gone after speaking with them. A typical conversation:

You: (calling to share some good news) Hi, how are you? Guess what?

Other Person: Oh, it's you. I guess I'm okay, I don't know—I've had better days.

You: What's wrong? Are you sick?

Other Person: Yeah, sick and tired of being sick and tired.

You: Huh?

Other Person: Oh, nothing seems to be going right for me these days.

You: I'm sorry to hear that. Do you need help?

Other Person: No, I don't need anything. It wouldn't make a difference anyhow.

You: Well, now I'm worried about you.

Other Person: Oh, don't worry about me. I guess I'll be all right. You said you have some news?

You: Never mind. It's nothing.

Other Person: Okay.

This person has succeeded in spreading his or her negativity to someone else. For our own well-being, we should limit our exposure to such people. But sometimes we are the ones spreading ill will too. We don't mean to do it, it's just why should someone else be happy when we're miserable? Why shouldn't we let the world know about our troubles?

We don't think about how far we've come. How we've grown. We think about what we don't have instead of being happy with what we've been blessed with. We need to stop right here, *right now*, and thank the Lord for blessing us. We all can find something to be thankful for. It's like the song says: "The Lord is blessing me right now." It may be as simple as waking up in the morning, or eating a good meal, or seeing a loved one's smile. These are all blessings and we should be thankful. And even in the toughest of times when it's hard to find the good in a situation, just remember: God always makes a way. He always has, and He always will.

CROSSING RAGING WATERS

REMEMBER THIS

- **HE IS WITH YOU IN BAD TIMES AS WELL AS GOOD.** Don't be afraid to call on Him. When you are troubled, turn to Him first. He knows you better than anyone else. He can help you when others can't. The song says, "He knows just how much you can bear"; that's because He's holding you in His arms in times of trouble. Just fall back and relax and let Him carry you.

- **FORGIVE SEVENTY TIMES SEVEN.** *Matthew 18:21* confirms you can never forgive too much. Forgive others just as God forgives you. Don't carry around the heavy baggage of unforgiveness. It will keep you from moving forward. Lighten your load. Forgive and forget.

- **THE LORD IS BLESSING ME RIGHT NOW. REJOICE!** Celebrate the little things. Don't take blessings for granted and don't spread negativity. Remember *Proverbs 28:20 (NIV)*:

  "A FAITHFUL MAN WILL BE RICHLY BLESSED . . ."

  Remain faithful!

CROSSING RAGING WATERS

PRAY FOR THIS:

SAFE CROSSING

When the waters are rough, and the sea of life is churning around us, all we want to do is make it to the other side. But sometimes we have to linger in the water before we know we need help to make it over. We reach for His hand and He is there, gently pulling us safely to the shore.

❧

PRAYER FOR SAFE CROSSING

Heavenly Father, sweet Master of my deliverance,
I thank you for my safe crossing. Lord, I
praise You through these troubled waters,
for You are my bridge to calmer times.
Sweet Jesus, You promised never to leave me alone.
I have come to take You at Your word. When darkness falls,
let me not be afraid, but instead
embrace the ocean that I must cross.
Through the depths I will survive, for I am swimming
toward the light.
When peaceful waters flow, let me remember it is only
through Your amazing grace that I can
now bask in the ebb and flow of life.
Change is good. I am the sparrow and You the Watcher,
Your eyes forever follow my every move.
If You can clothe the lilies of the field,
I am reminded—You will take care of my needs too.

And I thank You once again, for the calm before the storm
and even for the storm itself,
for it is in my crossing that I emerge stronger
and more fulfilled.
I run swiftly into Your everlasting arms.
Thank You, Father.
Amen.

CHAPTER TWELVE

A Place Where My Soul Can Find Rest

"WHEN JACOB AWOKE FROM HIS SLEEP, HE
THOUGHT, 'SURELY THE LORD IS IN THIS PLACE, AND I
WAS NOT AWARE OF IT.' HE WAS AFRAID AND SAID, 'HOW
AWESOME IS THIS PLACE! THIS IS NONE OTHER THAN
THE HOUSE OF GOD; THIS IS THE GATE OF HEAVEN.'
EARLY THE NEXT MORNING JACOB TOOK THE STONE HE
HAD PLACED UNDER HIS HEAD AND SET IT UP AS A
PILLAR AND POURED OIL ON TOP OF IT. HE CALLED
THAT PLACE BETHEL . . ."

GENESIS 28:16–19 (NIV)

Jacob believed Bethel to be the gateway to Heaven. He had a dream that a staircase there went from earth and reached all the way up, where the angels of God would come down and then return. Certainly, to find God we must access our own spirit, we must find Bethel within our very essence. Our search is to discover this passageway. A constant requirement is to replenish the soul. We know the world is not equipped to offer us the comfort and solace we need to survive. The world makes demands of us and gives little in return. How do we find the peace we yearn for?

Where is God and where do we go to learn more about Him? How do we serve Him? Should our search be solitary or should we find others who believe as we do? The answer is God is everywhere. He is with us when we are alone. He is with us when we are with others. Only He can "restoreth our soul."

So many are now hearing the call. So many are now turning to Him. People ask themselves why? Is it the impending arrival of the new millennium? Is it the aging of the baby boomers? Or has He become the latest fad?

We need to know that God is not "New Age" or "Old Age," He is eternal. His laws have lasted throughout the ages. If we are turning to Him more today, it is because we have realized that He alone is the way.

Many of us start our search for God at church. Perhaps because that is where we first met Him. Others start the search for God on their knees. This is where we want Him to meet us. But wherever we seek Him, He will appear. He will lead us to the still waters.

The Twenty-third Psalm serves as a guide for those who want to access God. There is no better way to describe what God does for us than what is found in the Word. Let the words speak to your soul:

"THE LORD IS MY SHEPHERD; I SHALL NOT WANT.
HE MAKETH ME TO LIE DOWN IN GREEN PASTURES:
HE LEADETH ME BESIDE THE STILL WATERS.
HE RESTORETH MY SOUL:
HE LEADETH ME IN THE PATHS OF RIGHTEOUSNESS
FOR HIS NAME'S SAKE.
YEA, THOUGH I WALK THROUGH THE VALLEY OF THE
SHADOW OF DEATH,
I WILL FEAR NO EVIL: FOR THOU ART WITH ME;
THY ROD AND THY STAFF THEY COMFORT ME.
THOU PREPAREST A TABLE BEFORE ME IN THE PRESENCE
OF MINE ENEMIES:
THOU ANOINTEST MY HEAD WITH OIL; MY CUP RUNNETH OVER.

SURELY GOODNESS AND MERCY SHALL FOLLOW ME
ALL THE DAYS OF MY LIFE:
AND I WILL DWELL IN THE HOUSE OF THE LORD FOR EVER."

PSALMS 23:1–6 (KJV)

ROCK OF AGES

"... THE LORD IS MY ROCK, AND MY FORTRESS, AND MY
DELIVERER. THE GOD OF MY ROCK, IN HIM WILL I TRUST. HE IS MY
SHIELD, AND THE HORN OF MY SALVATION, MY HIGH TOWER,
AND MY REFUGE, MY SAVIOUR ..."

2 SAMUEL 22:2–3 (KJV)

In years past, the rock that sustained American life was the church. Even today, while its foundation might be a bit worn and cracked, the church is still a vital institution that touches the lives of many of us. For African Americans, church was the only dwelling where they could gather—the only place they were accepted.

When other places relegated us to the back doors, we could always walk in the front doors of our black churches with pride. Respect there was both given and received. When we were limited to menial positions, beneath our abilities in the outside world, we could always go inside our churches and "let our light shine."

No doubt, the culture, character, and generosity of the church is rich and nurturing, but over the past two decades some of those in charge of our churches have become comfortable. They are resting on the laurels of successes obtained during the civil rights movement. But where are our successes today? Many parishioners are disillusioned.

In fact, some are now so jaded that instead of steady worship at one particular church, they wander from pillar to post searching for a church where they feel at home, while others have stopped going to church altogether. Something is ripping apart the cohesiveness of the black church. Something within the religious culture at large is not speaking to the hearts and souls of a generation. Maybe those of us who grew up in the church can remind those who didn't, and those who are younger, what church really ought to be about.

LINNIE: *I love going to church! I really love being in the house of the Lord. I love good singing and good preaching. I like to see my people dressed up in their Sunday finest, especially the good sisters in their hats. A special feeling comes over me when I enter a church for Sunday morning worship. A feeling I haven't been able to replicate anywhere else. Sure, I hear people say, "You don't have to go to church to pray, God is everywhere," and I know they are right. But there's something special about being in a congregation of fellow worshipers that always seems to restore my soul. Going to church on Sunday always seems to make my week go a whole lot better.*

I admit I used to wonder about those folk who go to church every Sunday and seem so involved in the church. There was a time for me, especially during my twenties, where I probably went many months without attending church. I didn't lose my faith or belief, it just seemed like going to church didn't fit into my schedule at the time. There were many Sunday mornings spent "lying in," just being lazy, or having something else to do. But I usually managed to get myself to somebody's church eventually—usually at the first sign of stress or trouble.

I think most of us remain close to the church in one way or the other. If you grew up in a church, and by that I mean participated in church activities as a child, it's never too far away from you. It is a major influence that stays with you always. But we hear that many young adults stray away from the church and don't come back until they're middle-aged. I don't know if it's the church's fault for not trying harder to retain the younger people, or their fault for not having time for the church.

My own experiences within the church have shown me that there is much room for improvement. It's easy to become disillusioned—preachers seem to be concerned only with building wealth and power, parishioners want to maintain the status quo and not look at new ideas, and the communities around the church suffer for lack of programs and role models. But, I have also seen the church at its best—offering hope to the downtrodden, feeding the hungry, providing shelter for the homeless, and giving youth an alternative to life on the streets.

I will not give up on the church, I will fight to make it better. We all have to work to make sure our churches continue their appointed mission. Scripture tells us in Ephesians 4:16 (NIV):

> *"FROM HIM THE WHOLE BODY, JOINED AND HELD TOGETHER BY EVERY*
> *SUPPORTING LIGAMENT, GROWS AND BUILDS ITSELF UP*
> *IN LOVE, AS EACH PART DOES ITS WORK."*

When we all come together, young and old, to serve and praise God, a good time is had by all. The singing, the shouting, the clapping, carry us to another level of fulfillment. When we truly let the Holy Ghost take us over we are able to release and may find ourselves dancing in the aisles.

Scripture says in *Psalms 95:1 (KJV)*:

> "O COME, LET US SING UNTO THE LORD: LET US MAKE A JOYFUL
> NOISE TO THE ROCK OF OUR SALVATION."

This is what we do at church. We sing and praise and pray. We strive to carry these feelings with us throughout the week. We don't want just a "Sunday Morning Experience," as if it were a concert or fashion show, we want an everyday Gospel, because we serve an everyday God.

He is *always there* for us—24/7. We don't have to get dressed up in our Sunday finest and sit in magnificent buildings to have access to our God. We serve Him when we make our lives a testament to Him.

We can do this on our own, and we can do this in the house of the Lord—at church.

We have unlimited access to God because of Christ's sacrifice. That means when Jesus died so we would have a chance at eternal life, He also gave us carte blanche access to walk with God, to talk with God, and to call Him our own. Yes, the Spirit resides within, but, thank God, we can also go outside ourselves—to church—to feel His power and love, which are unparalleled anywhere else.

But when we go into the house of the Lord, let's do so with a spirit of thanksgiving and service. And let's remember, when we come together to praise Him, to thank Him, and to ask Him for His guidance, we do so as individuals who are a part of an organization. That's called fellowship.

ALL CHURCH FOLK AIN'T RELIGIOUS

"AND LET US CONSIDER HOW WE MAY SPUR ONE ANOTHER ON TOWARD LOVE AND GOOD DEEDS. LET US NOT GIVE UP MEETING TOGETHER, AS SOME ARE IN THE HABIT OF DOING, BUT LET US ENCOURAGE ONE ANOTHER . . ."

HEBREWS 10:24–25 (NIV)

Church is where we come together with other believers to worship and praise the One Power who is greater than ourselves. Whether Baptist, Methodist, Pentecostal, or Catholic—we all come to church for at least this one reason. There is nothing like being in the house of the Lord. It doesn't matter how big the church, for the promise in *Matthew 18:20 (NIV)* is simply this

" . FOR, WHERE TWO ARE GATHERED TOGETHER IN MY NAME, THERE AM I WITH THEM."

When we commit ourselves to the place where He abides, we find joy and completion. But it is also inevitable that we will find human

trivialities and imperfections in our fellow churchgoers. It is unfortunate that so many of us turn away from the church because of this.

Church members are charged with being soldiers of the cross.
Some soldiers go to church faithfully every Sunday and are themselves
the very definition of a dedicated fighter for Christ. The men who deacon, the women who usher, the living saints who dutifully mix up
batches of homemade cakes to sell every Sunday after service, can be
the most loyal, generous, loving people you could ever have come into
your life. But some church folks can't open their hearts that wide. Instead of fighting for Him, they come to church fighting for themselves. They don't seem to be spirit-filled at all. They can barely manage a *good morning* let alone a *praise the Lord.* These folks will sit in a
certain pew every Sunday and dare anyone else to sit there. Or they
sit in church gossiping throughout the service about their fellow
parishioners.

These people are coming to church because it's habit. They've
been doing it for years. They couldn't tell you what the last sermon
was about if their souls depended on it. And they seem to have a
strong suspicion about new people, especially if they're younger. This
might just be one of the reasons why some young people have a hard
time fitting in.

Church folk are no different than anybody else and churches are
pretty much like mini corporations. There's a lot of bickering and pos-
turing in churches and there are many revelations and miracles too. It
happens no matter the denomination—no matter the race. Many
times people who assume leadership positions at church have never
been in a position of power before. They don't receive the respect they
deserve on their jobs and therefore demand it from those who worship
with them.

The maintenance man who all day has taken orders and cleaned
up after others may get to be a head deacon at church. The veteran
teacher who should have been assistant principal by now, but instead

has been passed over time and time again, may get to be chairwoman of the usher board. *He* takes his role very seriously at church. *She* assumes the position with great dedication. But sometimes that serious dedication causes people to feel a little too sanctified. They take their roles at church so seriously that they can become abusive and dictatorial.

Power has a funny way of making even the best of us feel insecure. Many of the folks who have held positions in the church for two and three decades are determined to keep these posts at all cost. They believe their self-worth as a person is tied to whatever position they hold at church. The one thing in life they have to look forward to is dying with that title sealed in the church record books and resolutions.

Most of our good sisters and brothers have no problem passing the mantle when the time comes. But many don't. They let their egos get in the way of progress. They forget what is written. *Ecclesiastes 3:1,6 (KJV)*:

"TO EVERY THING THERE IS A SEASON AND A TIME TO EVERY PURPOSE
UNDER THE HEAVEN . . . A TIME TO GET, AND A TIME
TO LOSE; A TIME TO KEEP, AND A TIME TO CAST AWAY."

They forget that it is all for His glory anyway—that any power they have has been given to them by God. *Ecclesiastes 3:14 (God's Word)*:

"I REALIZE THAT, WHATEVER GOD DOES WILL LAST FOREVER.
NOTHING CAN BE ADDED TO IT, AND NOTHING CAN BE TAKEN AWAY
FROM IT. GOD DOES THIS SO THAT PEOPLE WILL FEAR HIM."

Their worry should not be, "What will happen if I'm not here to take care of things?" Instead their joy should be, "God knows I've tried. Let someone else be a blessing to the church too."

Young people—take heart. There is room at the inn. There is a place for you. Our churches need your energy, your ideas, your time, and your talents. God needs more soldiers for His army so that others who don't know His Son might be given His name and address. You see, church is where Christ abides.

What's right with the church should be renewed, and what's wrong should be rethought. What's right with the church is God. He has never changed. He has always been right there. Calling us back to worship. What's right is that now there is a moral and spiritual imperative crying out for all of us to join together in lifting up the power of God. That power is in the Word, and church is where we can always go to hear the Word.

PREACHERS OF THE WORD

"BUT EVIL PEOPLE AND PHONY PREACHERS WILL GO FROM BAD TO WORSE AS THEY MISLEAD PEOPLE AND ARE THEMSELVES MISLED. HOWEVER, CONTINUE IN WHAT YOU HAVE LEARNED AND FOUND TO BE TRUE. YOU KNOW WHO YOUR TEACHERS WERE. FROM INFANCY YOU HAVE KNOWN THE HOLY SCRIPTURES. THEY HAVE THE POWER TO GIVE YOU WISDOM SO THAT YOU CAN BE SAVED THROUGH FAITH IN CHRIST JESUS."

2 TIMOTHY 3:13–15 (GOD'S WORD)

Despite the deficiencies of some who lead the church, despite the passivity and ineffectiveness of some of our church leaders, the church is invincible. God's omnipotence prevails. We just have to come together, ask for His supreme intervention, and move forward with what we know needs to be done.

And when we need answers we can turn to the Book—the ultimate authority—the Bible. For no matter how far we try to get away from it, we always come back to it. The words give us structure and guidance. They help us to look beyond the pulpit and the pews to move us toward positive change.

We are all human, which means all of us are flawed, but as the

Word says, we should at least strive to be Christ-like. The Bible says that's defined as:

- Holy—*Luke 1:35*
- Righteous—*Hebrews 1:9*
- Good—*Matthew 19:16*
- Faithful—*Isaiah 11:5*
- True—*John 1:14*
- Merciful—*Hebrews 2:17*
- Patient—*Matthew 27:34*
- Compassionate—*Luke 7:1*
- Loving—*John 13:1*

Being Christ-like means claiming the victory even before the fight. It means putting Him first in all things. It means seeing the Divine no matter how cloudy the skies. It means loving our family, our friends, the boss at work or the stranger on the street, without expectation and without condition. Sometimes it appears pointless, knowing we'll never reach perfection, but the only thing we can do is keep trying.

Let's try hard to hold on to our religion long after the doors of the church are closed. Trying and falling short are far better than not trying at all. With God, effort counts for something. That's what His mercy is all about. Those of us who want to worship God in His Holy Temple should strive to rest on the assurance that not only will He be there, but the men and women whom He has chosen to serve will do so with a clean heart. For where else can we gather in spirit together as one—lifting our voices in praise; opening our hearts to His message, and expressing the rhythm of our culture? Where else can we really rock!

ANDRIA: *Whenever I go back to the church where I grew up, a feeling comes over me from the moment I walk through the baroque wooden doors. Surprisingly, I am comfortable, even though things have* *changed. It is familiar, even though there are many new faces. I am shel-tered by this feeling—for I am at home.*

And as soon as the choir starts marching around the velvet pews singing, "We've come this far by faith . . ." *I get a chill. I don't know if everyone feels it and I'm not quite sure I can describe the inner emotion, but even now I hear them. My body feels them. They sing louder—*"Lean-ing on the Lord . . " *Sometimes thirty, forty, or fifty voices strong. They sway and they march and they lift their souls in perfect harmony, perfect pitch, perfect blending.* "Trusting in His holy word." *This is when I begin to notice that others too are moving. They involuntarily reel and roll, waving their hands, their heads, their hips, and their hopes.* "He's never failed us yet." *That is how church starts and builds and then booms into a crescendo of Christian acclamation. This is Sunday morning worship service. A spiritual high unattained by alternatives. Unmatched when you release and let the Spirit come in.*

But on Monday . . sometimes the very same people with whom we shared this holy communion can't seem to sustain the Christian princi-ples we all say we are striving for. Sometimes those people are us. We become afflicted with a spiritual amnesia every other day of the week but Sunday. We leave the sanctuary, and put our religion on hold.

You see all church folk ain't religious. Sometimes they just go through the motions. They let the Lord move in their lives on Sunday while they're wearing their wide brim hats and their high heel shoes to match. But then they go home, release their feet, and let down their hair. They justify the darker parts of themselves. They might beat their kids or curse their husbands.

Sometimes it's the minister who lets the Lord guide him only in the pulpit. Once he steps down, takes off that robe, and hits the streets of the community he has committed to serve, he becomes a pontificator in-stead of a coordinator . . a talker, instead of a doer. He wonders how to make things happen instead of taking action and then letting God light the way. I'm not speaking of these things because I'm looking to judge.

That's not my job nor my intention. I have a love and respect for most ministers. I speak of these things because someone ought to.

My father is a preacher. I sincerely believe he was called by God to do God's work. My grandmother used to tell the story about how her father looked at him in the crib when he was just six weeks old and said, "Aurealia, this boy's going to preach." My dad went into the pulpit on November 28, 1954. He was twenty-six years old. He's been preaching ever since. His first sermon was: "An Ambassador for the Lord."

When you think about it, that's what we all are. All of us who accept Jesus Christ as our Savior. All of us who understand those deep-seated feelings that never stop gnawing at us. We are all called to do more. We are all ambassadors for Him whether or not we acknowledge that role. But all too often, we think that it's the minister who stands up there on Sunday mornings who will be our ticket into Heaven. That he will ensure our seat at the table.

So many church folk think they can buy or bribe their way into the pearly gates by doing everything for the men of the cloth. They buy them clothes, cook their food, and wipe their brow before a bead of sweat ever drops off their forehead. It's almost like being in the presence of a superstar. They forget that Christ is the only superstar. The preacher is merely a servant.

I'll tell you what my father often says when he's up in the pulpit preaching: "Serve your Master, not your pastor." That's the bottom line, but so many church folk don't get that. It's kind of like how we as a people tend to view our secular heroes. We get so caught up in celebrity that we forget celebrity doesn't necessarily bring respect, and being well known doesn't automatically make you a role model. It's the same for our ministers. It is so important, for our own salvation, that we don't expect from them what we can't expect from ourselves. A man of God is just that . . . a man. Divinely called, but humanly tempted.

I've come to the conclusion that the more you try to walk in the light, the more darkness lurks around every corner. From what I've seen in my *lifetime, and I'm talking up close and personal, for a minister of God that darkness looms oh so close. This is why it's so very important that we continue to pray for the women and men whom God has called. Knowing this, I wrote a prayer for my father. Not my Heavenly Father, but my earthly father. I've seen so many blessings in his life, as well as so much pressure and strife. I've seen it firsthand, from ministers across our land. It's called:*

A PRAYER FOR YOUR SERVANT

Thank you, God, for now I see. That servant of Yours . .
is just a person like me.
I'm still in awe, as he preaches Your word. Help me, Lord,
I too want to serve.
A man of the cloth has a life to behold, but it's not always
easy for him to extol,
the virtues that Jesus Christ was cloaked in.
No, a man of the cloth is still vulnerable to sin.
I used to think the one sitting up there, whooping and shouting
was a man so rare.
Indeed, He is . . but still human and frail.
There's but one thing to do,
and that's give my trust to You. For only You are the One
to set me free.
Please, Lord, teach me only to look to Thee.
Please reveal to me that which is right. Please keep me, Lord,
in Your holy light.
Not just me, Lord, but your servant there too, who lifts up Your
word, help us both to live in truth. Help me, Lord,
for I too want to serve.
Thank you, dear God, for Your everlasting word.
Amen.

CLOSE TO THEE

"IF MY PEOPLE WHO ARE CALLED BY MY NAME SHALL HUMBLE
THEMSELVES, PRAY, SEEK, CRAVE AND REQUIRE OF NECESSITY MY
FACE, AND TURN FROM THEIR WICKED WAYS, THERE WILL I FROM
HEAVEN, FORGIVE THEIR SIN AND HEAL THEIR LAND."

2 CHRONICLES 7:14 (AMPLIFIED)

What a blessing to know when we are happy or hurting, in need of a healing or a hug, we can call His name. All the way from Heaven, He hears our voice, extends His hand, and gently wipes the slate clean once again, so we can continue aiming for Paradise. We can lie in the darkness of our rooms, or look up toward the light of morning, and know that He is always there.

Prayer is our venue for asking questions. We can have a one-on-one conversation without uttering a word, or we can break down all our inhibitions knowing there are no barriers between us and the living God. We ought not be concerned about how we look when we come before the throne, or what it is we want to say, for the Bible tells us not to worry. He knows before we utter a single word. *Isaiah 65:24 (NIV)*:

"BEFORE THEY CALL, I WILL ANSWER. WHILE THEY ARE STILL
SPEAKING, I WILL HEAR."

Our ancestors had no theological education, but they knew how to pray because they didn't get caught up in using just the right words. They knew what was written. They knew the meditations of their hearts would be seen through Divine eyes, and that would be enough. Yet, there is instruction in the Bible on how to pray.

First of all, we are to humble ourselves before Him as little children, and then according to *Romans 8:26–27 (God's Word)* call on the Holy Spirit:

"AT THE SAME TIME THE SPIRIT ALSO HELPS US IN OUR WEAKNESS,
BECAUSE WE DON'T KNOW HOW TO PRAY FOR WHAT WE NEED. BUT
THE SPIRIT INTERCEDES ALONG WITH OUR GROANS THAT CANNOT BE
EXPRESSED IN WORDS. THE ONE WHO SEARCHES OUR HEARTS KNOWS
WHAT THE SPIRIT HAS IN MIND. THE SPIRIT INTERCEDES
FOR GOD'S PEOPLE THE WAY GOD WANTS HIM TO."

Many times we limit ourselves when we pray. We try to tell God
how to bless us. True, the Bible says to be specific when we pray, but
what we are also guided to do is to preface our requests by opening up
our minds and hearts to His Divine will, letting it supersede even that
which we think we want or need. It is only when we do this that we
unblock the tunnels of our lives and allow our blessings to flow forth.
So many of our prayers are ineffective. They bind God's will for us because we limit our possibilities when we use our own words.

- Instead of praying for a mansion on a hill, let's pray for safe shelter.
- Instead of praying for a Mercedes (black with gray interior, please),
  let's pray for reliable transportation.
- Instead of praying for an attractive mate who will meet our every
  need, let us pray that we might be a worthy companion.
- Instead of praying for perfect children whom we can dress up and
  parade around for others to admire, let us pray that we be deserving parents and that He bless our children with good health.
- Instead of praying for a job in which we make lots of money, let us
  pray for a career in which we can use our calling to serve Him.
- Instead of praying for recognition from others, let us pray long and
  hard that God will always know our name.

Sometimes we try to "claim" our blessing. We pick out a certain
item, such as a house or car, which we feel we deserve. We may visualize it, light a candle, or walk around it seven times. There is a difference, however, between praying for something in the name of God

and claiming a material item or station in life because you think you just have to have it. People misconstrue the passage in the Bible that says in *Psalms 84:11 (KJV)*:

"NO GOOD THING WILL BE WITHHELD FROM THEM
THAT WALK UPRIGHTLY."

The key word here is "good." We need to stop to question whether God wants us to have it.

Spirituality is such a personal and private part of our lives, and while we want to seek fellowship with others, when it comes to having our little talk with God, there is instruction giving us correct counsel. Jesus tells us how to pray in *Matthew 6:5–6 (NIV)*:

"AND WHEN YOU PRAY, DO NOT BE LIKE THE HYPOCRITES, FOR THEY
LOVE TO PRAY STANDING IN THE SYNAGOGUES AND ON THE STREET
CORNERS TO BE SEEN BY MEN. I TELL YOU THE TRUTH, THEY HAVE
RECEIVED THEIR REWARD IN FULL. BUT WHEN YOU PRAY, GO INTO
YOUR ROOM, CLOSE THE DOOR AND PRAY TO YOUR FATHER,
WHO IS UNSEEN. THEN YOUR FATHER WHO SEES WHAT IS
DONE IN SECRET, WILL REWARD YOU."

It also tells us in *Matthew 18:19 (God's Word)*: "If two of you agree on anything here on earth, My Father in Heaven will accept it."

When we do get together with others for joint prayer we feel the power. That's what group prayer is all about. We remember *James 5:16 (KJV)*, which says:

"CONFESS YOUR FAULTS ONE TO ANOTHER, AND PRAY ONE FOR
ANOTHER, THAT YE MAY BE HEALED. THE EFFECTUAL FERVENT
PRAYER OF A RIGHTEOUS MAN AVAILETH MUCH."

Joint prayer is potent. The Circle of Seven prayer organization has proved that to us. To know there are other people praying with you and for you—and, most important, giving God the glory—refreshes the soul. Each month we jointly take our problems and concerns to the Lord in prayer. And although some of us initially started out with laundry lists of wants and "gotta-haves," most of us have now grown to the point where we are just as likely to say "Lord—thy will be done."

Each circle has evolved to the point where its members spend more time counting their blessings than discussing their limitations. We have learned that when we limit our prayers to specifics it's hard for us to recognize the blessings He has in store for us.

We all are capable of serving others in a special way. We all can be blessed with a ministry that makes a difference, and offers others a way to tap into the enormous power of the Universe through our relationship with God. Scripture tells us in Acts 6:4 (KJV):

"BUT WE WILL GIVE OURSELVES CONTINUALLY TO PRAYER,
AND TO THE MINISTRY OF THE WORD."

This is what we are charged to do with the Circle of Seven. This is now part of our life's work. When we seek Him, we will find Him. When we pray, either for ourselves or one another, we extend our hands and our hearts to accept His grace and protection.

Most of us can say that at some point in time, someone has prayed for us. Maybe it was our family, our friends, our co-workers, or perhaps someone we didn't know at all but who knew of us and sent forth a petition on our behalf. We need to thank God for those people, because they knew we needed a sacred word even when we didn't realize it ourselves.

LINNIE: *I often think of when I left California en route to Albany, New York. I was young—just out of college—and I had spent my whole life in California. I still remember my family's reaction when I told them I was moving to Albany in two weeks. A city where they had no ties, and I didn't know a soul. My parents were concerned, but didn't want to dis-*

courage me from spreading my wings. My aunt Rosa and uncle Brown just thought it was a bad idea period and were against it. But there was no stopping me. I was determined to go. They began their prayer vigils immediately.

Moving to Albany seemed to me to be the adventure of a lifetime. Never mind that I had never spent any significant time in snow or cold weather. Never mind that in Southern California you go to the ski slopes for a few hours with maybe a thick sweater and you come home before it gets too cold. I discovered Albany was a little different.

I remember the first big snow storm. I called my workplace not expecting to find anyone there because I couldn't imagine anyone going out in weather like that and needless to say they were all there. They laughed at me all winter. They laughed at my "California" coat (Not heavy enough.); my "California" car (What were snow tires?); and my "California" boots (Slick leather with no traction. Didn't do too well on ice. I fell every other day.).

But God looked after me and surrounded me with good people. Like the auto mechanic from Sears who saw my California tags and took the time to teach me how to drive and maneuver my car in snow and ice (that man probably saved my life). Or, the co-workers who would help me scrape the accumulated ice and snow off my car before we left in the evening. Or, the neighbor who gave me a jump many mornings when my battery froze and showed me how to unfreeze my car locks (these just weren't skills you needed in Los Angeles). And there were so many others who crossed my path at just the right time.

I know now that God took care of me during that period because left to my own devices I would probably have ended up an icicle. I didn't think much about it then, I was just trying to survive. But looking back on it now, I can clearly see His intervention.

I am so thankful for all the prayers sent forth on my behalf during this period. As soon as I said I was leaving, people I hardly even knew started praying for me. They prayed that I would have a safe journey to

Albany and that I would find God's goodness and mercy once I got there. Their prayers were answered.

A NEW DAY

"GOD CAN STRENGTHEN YOU BY THE GOOD NEWS AND THE MESSAGE
. . . OF JESUS CHRIST. HE CAN STRENGTHEN YOU BY REVEALING THE
MYSTERY THAT WAS KEPT IN SILENCE FOR A VERY LONG TIME."

ROMANS 16:25 (GOD'S WORD)

With reverence, we reach back to the past embracing the values and traditions of those who came before us. With Christian optimism, we stretch toward the future accepting our responsibility in aiding a world that is in need of healing. As a community, we're ready to take a closer look at God's laws and find a way to incorporate them into our lives. But how do we reach back and move forward at the same time? How do we bring the good things of the past and make them relevant to a rapidly approaching and uncertain future? We can succeed only if we stay centered in Spirit.

According to God's promise, our prosperity is already here. Our joy is within our reach. Our Lord, our ancestors, our history, are all leading us down the road of illumination, and toward our destiny.

Each and every one of us is allowed to walk the path if we bring enough faith for our journey. If we want to be more fulfilled along the way, if we want to be more spiritual as we grow, if we want to live the Faith Formula and be led by the concept of Divinely Inspired Living, then *Matthew 7:13–14 (NIV)* tells us what to do:

"ENTER THROUGH THE NARROW GATE. FOR WIDE IS THE GATE AND
BROAD IS THE ROAD THAT LEADS TO DESTRUCTION, AND MANY
ENTER THROUGH IT. BUT SMALL IS THE GATE AND NARROW THE
ROAD THAT LEADS TO LIFE, AND ONLY A FEW FIND IT."

Spirit prepares us for the trip with a warning not to follow the crowd. If we want all of the blessings, all of our healing, all of the happiness that has been promised us, then we must avoid the path that most would take. We already know the road won't be easy to find or easy to travel. But we also know, the secret of how to get there is not hidden from us. It is waiting to be revealed.

It is said that perception is reality, but this is only if we fail to seek out a greater understanding of the world. A deeper lesson is waiting to be learned. When we begin to raise ourselves up and view every event in life from a spiritual perspective, we open our eyes to what's really happening around us. Our faith increases as Celestial serendipity or "coincidence" begins to occur more regularly. We need to teach ourselves, and then teach our children, how to tone our faith muscles. The more we use them, the stronger our faith becomes.

When we walk by faith and not by sight, we realize that regardless of what appears to be happening in the world, all things are possible and most situations are better than they seem. When we have faith and put our trust in the Creator, we won't worry about tomorrow. If there are two gifts we can offer you, they are the benefits of dreaming and the blessings that come with peace of mind. God *will* take care of you! He's proven it through us. We each were moved through faith to put aside the vision of what we thought we would do with our lives. Events showed us what confidence in God was all about.

Once we accept that we can see only so far, we let our faith be the measure of how we live. We have no idea of what lies before us—no possible way to fully understand. We can only search for evidence by reviewing the good fortune of our past, and the blessings of the moment. Our conclusion? God's vision is infinitely more prosperous than anything we could ever see for ourselves. When you place your trust in the One who is greater than anything imaginable, then, even when facing challenges, there is a peace that never goes away.

Psalms 29:11 (KJV) holds the promise:

"THE LORD WILL GIVE STRENGTH UNTO HIS PEOPLE;
THE LORD WILL BLESS HIS PEOPLE WITH PEACE."

It is that peace we want to give to you. For when you have peace, which is born of faith, which comes through surrender, you will be strengthened with the knowledge that *this too shall pass.* God has big plans for you if you let Him into your life.

ANDRIA: *Linnie and I are acutely aware of just how far all of us have come by faith. We've survived only because of our faith. We've thrived only because of His willingness to never leave us alone. It's a mystery to me why God, through His magnificence and majesty, moves in us, through us, and around us . . . but He does. Words could never express the joy, revelation, humility, and peace I have found in Christ. I want so much to do and be all that He has in store for me. This book was never an expected part of my journey, but, nonetheless, it was preordained from the beginning of time. Do I believe in destiny? Call it what you like. I believe in God, His miracles and His unending desire to move me toward His light. Lord, let me be blinded by Your light, so I may forever be committed to showing others how to live in the ecstasy of knowing You.*

LINNIE: *As we bring this book to a close I can't help but reflect on God's completeness. He is everything and more. He started this project, He gave us the structure and the words, and He made it possible that this book be published and read by you. To say this has been a labor of love is an understatement. But, beyond that, Andria and I have both been brought closer to God and the Word.*

As we searched for appropriate scriptures we were reminded of the universal truths found within the pages of the Bible. We developed an appreciation for Bible study and interpretation. We also developed a deeper understanding of the powerful force in our lives that set all of this in motion — God. We realized that this journey began long before we set pen to paper. Even before we met in Albany some twenty years ago.

I know some would say His ways are mysterious, but I say His ways are complete — no need for interference from man. Just let Him work it out. Take it all to Him — the little things and the big things.

I remember my feelings at the beginning of this project — when He first told us to write This Far by Faith. *I can see now it was all in His hands from the beginning. He did things according to His will at the right time in the right way. He filled the empty spaces. He has shown me all things are possible with faith. I anxiously await the birth of His blessings. As I write this I look forward to the birth of my second child.*

We have grown so much since He first spoke to us regarding this project. But we know that this is only a small part of what we must do. We will continue to spread the Word. His Word. We will continue to walk by faith. At this point we couldn't do it any other way.

Let's walk this blessed road together. Let's do so holding hands with Christian confidence in our past and assured hope for our future, for surely we've come *This Far by Faith.*

"I AM ALPHA AND OMEGA, THE BEGINNING AND THE ENDING, SAITH THE LORD, WHO IS, AND WHO WAS AND WHO IS TO COME, THE ALMIGHTY."

REVELATION 1:8 (NIV)

A PLACE WHERE MY SOUL CAN FIND REST
REMEMBER THIS

✸ **GOD IS HERE FOR YOU ALWAYS. HE IS ETERNAL.** Learn about Him and study His Word. Realize that God is not a passing fancy— Prepare to spend the rest of your life getting to know Him better.

✸ **JOIN OTHERS IN WORSHIP AND FELLOWSHIP AT THE CHURCH OF YOUR CHOICE.** Worshiping with others in the House of the Lord, the church will brighten your day, sustain you during the week ahead, and restore your faith. If these things are missing from your church experience, don't give up going to church. Instead, work at making church what it should be. Always remember *Psalms 27:4 (NIV):* "One thing I ask of the LORD, this is what I seek: that I may dwell in the house of the LORD all the days of my life, to gaze upon the beauty of the LORD and to seek him in his temple."

✸ **TAKE EVERYTHING TO GOD IN PRAYER.** Prayer is the most efficient way to talk to God. Do not worry what to say or what to ask for. Speak from your heart and don't be concerned with the words you use. Pray alone and pray with others. Start your day praying, pause at midday and pray, and end your day praying. A prayer can be as simple as "Guide me Lord" or "Thank You, Jesus."

✸ **WALK BY FAITH NOT BY SIGHT.** The world will not provide the answers you seek. The world paints the picture it wants you to see—which may or may not be based on Divine reality. God's portrait is always accurate. Trust Him with your heart—not your eyes, ears, or mind. Learn to simply lean on Spirit; it's true each and every time.

A PLACE WHERE MY SOUL CAN FIND REST

PRAY FOR THIS:
A NEW DAY

Our Lord promises us there will always be a tomorrow. A chance to start anew with His forgiveness and His love. He allows us to bring the lessons of the past to the new day. We must use this knowledge to spread the Word to others. That is our purpose on this earth: to spread the light to the coming generations.

❦

PRAYER FOR A NEW DAY

Dear Lord, here we are again, thanking You in
advance for Your blessing.
We seek Your guidance and Your wisdom as we
prepare to enter the new day.
Heavenly Father, show us what we need to
bring forth from our past,
as we prepare for our future.
Let us always remember what our eyes have seen,
so we can bear witness to the coming generations:
We will tell them of our fight, to provide grace
for our children,
We will tell them of our culture, how You painted
us with a colorful stroke,
We will tell them of our laughter, how the bad
times were made good,

We will tell them of our faith, it has brought
us to where we are.
Let us always remember what our hearts have felt,
so when we speak of You, our sincerity will be shown:
We will tell them of Your love, which surpasses
all warmth and goodness,
We will tell them of Your peace, which makes
the rough places smooth,
We will tell them of Your joy, which is the
reason for our living,
We will tell them of Your promise, that we will
never walk alone.
Let them seek us out, when the world provides no answers.
We will show them the way to You, they can
follow the well-lit path.
Together we will walk, in sunlight-laden meadows,
and meet You at the gate of everlasting life.
Please, Dear God, be with us, help us get the story right,
Thank You, Father, for this journey,
Thank You, Master, for this light,
Amen.

For more information on This Far By Faith Enterprises, Inc., or the Circle of Seven © Christian prayer ministry, visit us on the web at: www.ThisFarByFaith.com

Scriptural References

Acknowledgments   v
Matthew 17:20 (NIV)   v

Introduction   xiii
Hebrews 11:1 (KJV)   xiii

Chapter One:
The Sound of His Voice   1
James 5:16 (KJV)   7
John 16:12-14 (NIV)   9
Matthew 18:19 (God's Word)   7
Psalms 29:3-9 (NIV)   1

Chapter Two: My Soul
Looks Back and Wonders . .   13
Deuteronomy 18:13 (KJV)   28
Ephesians 1:11 (NIV)   22
Hebrews 10:35-36 (KJV)   26
Hebrews 11:1 (KJV)   16
James 4:7 (NIV)   30
Luke 12:27-28 (NIV)   15
Matthew 6:10 (KJV)   23
Matthew 12:37 (KJV)   26
Philippians 4:6-7 (God's Word)   29
Philippians 4:8 (God's Word)   27
Proverbs 14:30 (NIV)   28
Proverbs 16:3 (Amplified Bible)   18
Psalms 105:1-5 (NIV)   13
Zachariah 6:15 (NIV)   24

Chapter Three: Give Me
That Old-Time Religion   33
Deuteronomy 4:9 (NRSV)   33
Ephesians 6:4 (God's Word)   43
Isaiah 53:5 (KJV)   46
Isaiah 54:17 (CEV)   46

Mark 3:33-35 (KJV)   40
Matthew 16:23 (KJV)   46
Proverbs 22:28 (God's Word)   48
Psalms 55:17 (KJV)   38
Psalms 62:6 (KJV)   46
Psalms 63:1 (KJV)   45
Psalms 77:11 (NIV)   42

Chapter Four: Families—
The Ties That Bind   51
Deuteronomy 12:7 (NIV)   53
Ecclesiastes 3:1, 4, 5, 8 (YLT)   60
1 John 3:1 (TLB)   64
Joshua 24:15 (KJV)   67
Matthew 7:1 (NAS)   58
1 Peter 5:5 (KJV)   54
Proverbs 31:26 (Amplified)   54
Psalms 5:2-3 (NIV)   65
Psalms 18:30-32 (NIV)   66
Psalms 68:5 (KJV)   56
Psalms 121:5-8 (NIV)   66
Romans 11:18 (Amplified)   51
1 Timothy 5:8 (NIV)   56

Chapter Five: Friendship—
Real and Imagined   73
Ecclesiastes 4:9-10, 12 (NIV)   73
Ephesians 3:17-19 (NIV)   86
Job 2:11-13 (NIV)   75
Philippians 2:13 (KJV)   89
Proverbs 18:24 (RSV)   76
Proverbs 22:24-25 (NIV)   77
Proverbs 27:6 (NIV)   87
Psalms 55:12-14 (KJV)   81

Chapter Six:
Love—Always and Forever   91
Colossians 3:14 (NRSV)   91
1 Corinthians 6:18   103
1 Corinthians 13:1 (all versions)   108
1 Corinthians 13:4 (NIV)   97
1 Corinthians 13:5 (NIV)   98
1 Corinthians 13:6 (NIV)   98
1 Corinthians 13:7 (NIV)   99
1 Corinthians 13:8 (NIV)   99
Ephesians 4:27 (NIV)   105
Ephesians 4:32 (KJV)   107
Galatians 5:16, 17, 22, 23
  (God's Word)   101
Galatians 5:22, 23 (God's Word)   103
Hebrews 10:36 (NIV)   96
James 4:2-3 (NIV)   95
John 17:24 (God's Word)   100
John 17:26 (God's Word)   100
1 John 3:18 (God's Word)   101
Song of Solomon 6:1-2 (NIV)   97
Song of Solomon 8:6 (NIV)   104

Chapter Seven: Marriage—
For Better or Worse   111
1 Corinthians 4:2 (NIV)   122
1 Corinthians 7:14-15 (NIV)   127
Ephesians 5:22 (God's Word)   116
Ephesians 5:25 (God's Word)   116
Ephesians 5:28 (NIV)   124
Ephesians 5:33 (God's Word)   111
Exodus 20:14 (KJV)   123
Luke 10:27 (KJV)   122
Mark 10:8 (NIV)   130
Mark 10:9 (KJV)   125
Mark 14:38 (NAS)   123
Matthew 7:3-5 (NIV)   117
Matthew 19:5-6 (NIV)   127
Proverbs 23:12 (KJV)   128
Proverbs 31:10-11 (NIV)   114

Proverbs 5:18-19 (KJV)   119
1 Thessalonians 5:17 (KJV)   128
1 Timothy 6:10 (KJV)   129

Chapter Eight:
Children and Parenthood   135
Deuteronomy 5:6-21
  (all versions)   141
Exodus 18:20 (KJV)   141
Exodus 20:1-17 (all versions)   141
Isaiah 54:13 (KJV)   147
Job 5:25 (NIV)   150
Joel 1:2-3 (NIV)   138
Mark 10:14-16 (KJV)   135
Matthew 19:14 (NIV)   138
Philippians 4:13 (all versions)   151
Proverbs 13:24 (NIV)   144
Proverbs 19:18 (NIV)   144
Proverbs 20:11 (NIV)   143
Proverbs 22:6 (NAS)   136
Psalms 23:1 (KJV)   151

Chapter Nine:
A House Is Not a Home   155
1 Corinthians 12:31 (NRSV)   159
Ecclesiastes 5:11 (NIV)   158
Ezekiel 24:10 (NIV)   166
Hebrews 13:2 (NIV)   173
Luke 16:13 (any version)   160
1 Peter 3:9-11 (NIV)   157
Proverbs 3:33 (NIV)   171
Proverbs 17:1 (NIV)   155
Proverbs 24:3-4 (God's Word)   164
Psalms 119:133 (KJV)   161
Ruth 2:7 (NIV)   160

Chapter Ten: Jobs,
Careers, and Callings   177
1 Corinthians 4:12-13
  (God's Word)   185

Genesis 41:11 (KJV) 179
James 1:2–4 (God's Word) 188
Jeremiah 23:1–4 (God's Word) 182
John 15:20–21 (God's Word) 184
Matthew 5:15–16 (God's Word) 194
Matthew 5:16 (KJV) 194
Matthew 10:19 (all versions) 186
Matthew 11:28–30 (KJV) 177
2 Peter 1:5–7 (God's Word) 188
Philippians 4:11–14
(God's Word) 189
Proverbs 3:27 (NIV) 182
Proverbs 8:17 (KJV) 195
1 Samuel 12:11 (all versions) 185
2 Thessalonians 1:11 (NIV) 190

Chapter Eleven:
Crossing Raging Waters 199
Amos 3:7 (KJV) 203
Ephesians 2:8 (RSV) 213
Ephesians 6:18–20 (God's Word) 210
Hebrews 11:1 (KJV) 212
John 16:33 (KJV) 210
1 John 2:8 (NIV) 204
Luke 6:37–38 (NIV) 206
Luke 23:34 (KJV) 209
Mark 11:25 (NIV) 207
Matthew 6:34 (NIV) 217
Matthew 12:33 (God's Word) 212
Matthew 12:34–35
(God's Word) 212
Matthew 12:37 (God's Word) 212
Matthew 18:21–22
(God's Word) 208
Nahum 1:3–4,7 (KJV) 199
Proverbs 28:20 (NIV) 220
Psalms 9:10 (NIV) 199
Psalms 27:4 (NIV) 245
Psalms 29:11 (KJV) 217
Psalms 107:29 (KJV) 209

Romans 3:23 (NIV) 207
Romans 5:3–4 (KJV) 213
Song of Solomon 2:11–12
(Amplified) 200

Chapter Twelve: A Place
Where My Soul Can Find Rest 223
Acts 6:4 (KJV) 239
2 Chronicles 7:14 (Amplified) 236
Ecclesiastes 3:1,6 (KJV) 230
Ecclesiastes 3:14 (God's Word) 230
Ephesians 4:16 (NIV) 227
Genesis 28:16–19 (NIV) 223
Hebrews 1:9 (all versions) 232
Hebrews 2:17 (all versions) 232
Hebrews 10:24–25 (NIV) 228
Isaiah 11:5 (all versions) 232
Isaiah 65:24 (NIV) 236
James 5:16 (KJV) 238
John 1:14 (all versions) 232
John 13:1 (all versions) 232
Luke 1:35 (all versions) 232
Luke 7:1 (all versions) 232
Matthew 6:5–6 (NIV) 238
Matthew 7:13–14 (NIV) 241
Matthew 18:19 (God's Word) 238
Matthew 18:20 (NIV) 228
Matthew 19:16 (all versions) 232
Matthew 27:34 (all versions) 232
Psalms 23:1–6 (KJV) 225
Psalms 27:4 (NIV) 245
Psalms 29:11 (KJV) 243
Psalms 84:11 (KJV) 238
Psalms 95:1 (KJV) 227
Revelation 1:8 (NIV) 244
Romans 8:26–27 (God's Word) 236
Romans 16:25 (God's Word) 241
2 Samuel 22:2–3 (KJV) 225
2 Timothy 3:13–15
(God's Word) 231